"*Aging Disgracefully* blurs the lines between work and life when it comes to love, lust, and the search for self-redemption. I held my breath rooting for a winner and finished the book rooting for them all!"

—Kathleen Tighe Kurke, President Emeritus, The Pinnacle Society

"*Aging Disgracefully* made me laugh and cry. I learned some things about my own life and choices through Danny's eyes. No surprise though—Danny Cahill has been imparting wisdom, wit, and empathy to the recruiting world for decades. Bravo."

—Danny Sarch, President, Leitner Sarch Consultants

# AGING DISGRACEFULLY

*a memoir*

AGING DISGRACEFULLY

AGING DISGRACEFULLY

AGING DISGRACEFULLY

AGING DISGRACEFULLY

*Danny Cahill*

GREENLEAF
BOOK GROUP PRESS

*Aging Disgracefully* is a work of creative nonfiction. In an age where eye-witness testimony is often overturned by DNA evidence and ten people can't play the parlor game Telephone without butchering the original message, it seems worthwhile to point out that while all events are portrayed to the best of my memory, they are *my* memories. Therefore names and identifying details have been changed, and certain events have been compressed or changed for narrative purposes.

Published by Greenleaf Book Group Press
Austin, Texas
www.gbgpress.com

Distributed by Greenleaf Book Group

For ordering information or special discounts for bulk purchases, please contact Greenleaf Book Group at PO Box 91869, Austin, TX 78709, 512.891.6100.

Design and composition by Greenleaf Book Group
Cover design by Greenleaf Book Group

Cataloging-in-Publication data is available.

Print ISBN: 978-1-62634-398-6

eBook ISBN: 978-1-62634-399-3

Part of the Tree Neutral® program, which offsets the number of trees con-sumed in the production and printing of this book by taking proactive steps, such as planting trees in direct proportion to the number of trees used: www.treeneutral.com

TreeNeutral

Printed in the United States of America on acid-free paper

17 18 19 20 21 22   10 9 8 7 6 5 4 3 2

First Edition

*for Jane*

"Shame is Pride's cloak."

—William Blake


" . . . I've lived my whole life in shame!
Why should I die with dignity?"

—George Costanza, *Seinfeld*

# Contents

## CHAPTER 1

# My Free Fall Ends

My free fall, and the madness, stopped on my fiftieth birthday. Not because I had found wisdom or had realized the damage I was doing to myself and others, but because I found myself in an ambulance.

I had gone into the gym an hour before, determined to prove myself still capable of a killer leg workout, and while I didn't buy into what I had been hearing all week from my friends and coworkers, "Fifty is the new forty; who looks like you at fifty?" (Where does that delusional thinking lead? "Sixty is the new fifty?" "Fat is the new skinny?" How long before we arrive at "Dead is the new alive?"), I did think I still had the ability to move some heavy iron. So I loaded up the leg press sled with seven 45-pound plates on each side. The leg press is how old men do squats.

" . . . EMT Unit 137 en route, patient stable, vitals strong, request support on arrival, we got spinal issues, not good . . . "

"Uh, I'm still awake here, guys, let's work on the bedside manner."

A fiftieth birthday is tough for anyone. Add on the fact that I was born on Valentine's Day—a day guaranteed to elicit *awws* from clerks verifying your credit card and TSA agents checking your driver's license—and it gets even tougher. Throw in being born on Valentine's Day when you are divorced and live alone and, well, you go to the gym to stop thinking about it.

There are two hooks at the bottom of the leg press sled. When you have completed your reps, you slide the hooks under the weight, and the weight is suspended until your next set. I finished my tenth rep, my quads spent. When I went to hook the weight, the entire hooking mechanism fell off the sled poles. I probably should have yelled, but my old nemesis and guidance counselor—shame—kicked in, and I said nothing as the 630 pounds of weight, obeying gravity, began to slide down toward my face. My knees were being pressed against my chest. With no hooks to stop it, I realized, the slide wouldn't finish until it made its way down the machine's track, leaving my legs behind my face in a porn position I had previously viewed but never experienced. Near the very end of the ride, I heard a surprisingly loud crack near the base of my spine.

They tell you, in moments like this, that things seem to slow down. Flashes of your past are supposed to come back to you. I always thought this was a convenient plot device for filmmakers with a smoke machine and a paucity of imagination. But damn, I can confirm that between the time it took for some guys who heard me scream to get the weight off me, and the time I was lying in the ambulance bed with a searing, burning pain, I did seem to have forever to think about my two years of free fall. How I had lost, in order, my mother; my wife; my home; my cats; nearly all my friends; the trust and affection of nearly everyone I worked with; and now, apparently, at a time when I was utterly alone, my ability to walk.

I probably should have thought this was Karma. That would have been rational, and I could have made a case for deserving it. *But that's not me*. One of the ways I make a ridiculously great living is being a motivational speaker. And on the way to the hospital, I was already thinking I could now justify buying a Segway. I could whirr around the stage and use my free hand to click the PowerPoints that would document my amazing battle and recovery. (How I would get the Segway on and off airplanes never occurred to me. I was spitballing.)

Even better, I could finally end the drama. I had blown up my life over the past two years. Complete carnage. But this would bring it to a close. I couldn't stop the free fall through choice, so it had been stopped for me, by a free-falling weight. And then I felt so damn grateful I was almost giddy! Because now I would have time to write my book! I had done a series of successful seminars for consulting clients on aging gracefully. At fifty, I had eight percent body fat—the physique of an amateur bodybuilder. I had made a name for myself onstage for a sort of boundless and contagious energy, and I looked much younger than I was. I was a wealthy entrepreneur who owned one of the nation's largest headhunting firms, and I was in constant demand as a speaker. So my seminar on aging gracefully was always well received and always followed by email testimonials thanking me for the inspirational example: for being the "real deal" and "walking the walk." I was qualified to turn my seminar into a book, right?

*Absolutely not. As you will see, I was a complete impostor.*

But I didn't know this as I was wheeled into the ER. I only knew that whatever it was that drove me out of the poverty of my childhood, whatever force drove me to work eleven-hour days as a cold-calling salesperson until I had mastered the craft and started making huge commissions;

whatever demon insisted I buy a company I couldn't afford and build it into a multimillion-dollar success; whatever essence within me made me eschew days off, and vacations, and starting a family in order to write and sell plays that were produced off-Broadway and to start a speaking business when I was a decade younger than my youngest competitor—that part wasn't false, and it hadn't left me. I had an irrepressible sense that my story was not over and more good was coming if I would only recognize the opportunity. This injury, this free fall of madness, *it was all good!*

. . .

They asked me three times who they could contact in case of emergency. Each time I said there was no one. The exasperated woman, just trying to follow procedure, said, "There must be somebody you would want us to contact in case something happens." But there wasn't. I had seen to that.

And then someone's phone buzzed. It seemed completely normal, even in an ambulance, for all of us to check our phones, and I wouldn't have been insulted if they stopped monitoring my vitals to read a text. It was certainly how I lived. But it was my phone, and it was Kelsey. No one is networked like Kelsey.

**Oh. My. God. I heard you left the gym in an ambulance!**
**Are you OK? Where are they taking you?!**

Texting seems to have revived religion, and young women especially seem to praise Him with every communiqué. I love words and found Kelsey was a rich source of new language, and I copied her phrases, often unintentionally, in my seminars. It made me cooler; my material seemed more relevant. I wasn't going to respond. I had found that strength. We were done. And she must have sensed it.

**Danny, please don't punish me. You were there for me. You saved my life for Chrissake. Please let me take care of you now. Please.**

For the first time in two years, her pleas didn't work. My free fall of madness had ended. I had a book to write.

## CHAPTER 2

# Willpower

I go around the country and listen to salespeople say cold calls are scary. Why, I ask, what can they do to you? And I tell them about willpower, about the secret I learned when I was twelve. This was the 70s, when kids sat on street corners instead of playing video games. I was with my crew and, while few people in this audience will remember, there was a catchphrase going around the country. You would hear it on TV sitcoms and in commercials and all day long at school: "Oh, bite me." Being kids, we sharpened "Bite me" into a more sexually charged "Eat me," and in my neighborhood, some genius turned it into this: "Eat me, I'm a cookie." It became ubiquitous and, as such, annoying.

So, one night we're hanging out on the steps of North School, and as the cars slow down to make the gradual turn on Route 4 to Goshen, I decide it would be hilarious to yell, "Eat me, I'm a cookie" at the cars as they pass. It was summer, and they could hear us. That was kind of the point. It was fraught with a low-grade kind of danger. A blast. A Camaro that today would be called "tricked out" but then was deemed "souped up," with jacked-up shiny wheels and racing stripes, sped by, and I had to yell "Eat me, I'm a cookie" extra loud to be heard over the blasting FM converter box. But he must have heard me because he brought the car to a screeching halt. And out stepped a greaser. An Elvis leftover. About nineteen. Leather jacket, slicked back hair, big "shit kicker" boots. In the early 70s, there were a lot of these: tough guys who wouldn't buy into long hair and the drug culture. He walked up to us, and my friend Kenny said we should run. But there really wasn't time. I could feel my hero complex kick in. I had to save my friends. "Who yelled that?" he asked. I told him I did, and I added that in case he didn't hear me with his Roy Orbison tunes on, "I said, 'Eat me, I'm a cookie.'" Now at twelve, I was a husky, athletic kid. I had been in fights, but they were minor and consisted of pushing and taunting more than punching. So it was a shock when he grabbed me by my tee shirt, lifted me up, and punched me in the face. He told me to take it back, and I said, "Eat me, I'm a cookie." My friends gasped, and he punched me again, square in the mouth, and as my lips split, blood started running down my chin.

"Just take it back and I won't hurt you," he almost pleaded, and I repeated my clever aphorism. Now, embarrassed that he couldn't shut me up, he cocked his arm behind his head, resembling a quarterback throwing a deep route, and he punched me as hard as he could. I heard a crunching sound in my mouth, and I realized I was spitting out teeth as I repeated the phrase. By this time, my friends were scared, and they told him to leave me alone. He sat on my chest, and I was getting dizzy when he said, "Jesus, kid, just take it back."

And that's when I saw it. He was afraid. He was old enough to know that he was now in really big trouble and that this whole episode was officially not worth it. He didn't want the humiliation of not being able to shut me up, and he didn't want the cops knocking on his door. He was trapped. I had the power! I was in charge! In that moment, as ridiculous as it seems now to me, I was more than willing to die before I would relinquish that power. People without willpower are helpless before people who have it.

I spit once to clear my mouth and throat. Blood and chunks of lip and teeth flew out. "Oh, I just thought of something. What was it? Oh yes, I remember. EAT ME, I'M A COOKIE." I stared at him. I tried to smile with whatever mouth I had left.

He got up. He was shaking. "Your friend is nuts," he said, and he walked, a bit too fast, to his Camaro and took off. Word got around at school. No one ever picked a fight with me again until I left for college, where word of this legendary incident hadn't reached. In college, I got my smart ass pummeled.

If you have the willpower, folks, even though you are the one making the cold calls, you are in control. Others are afraid of you. Your bosses tell you it's a numbers game. And it is, but it is also a game of willpower.

**From Danny's "Overcoming Cold-Call Reluctance" Seminar**

. . .


"For the guy lying down, how about some layman's terms?"

" . . . I said the CT scan and the spinal X-ray show a compression fracture. That's fine; that heals, no surgery for that. But we throw in twenty years of soft-tissue issues that you never addressed; your IT band, which is like granite; maybe some arthritis; and your psoas muscles . . . uh, those are your abdominals that were doing the work for your whole back . . . they gave out. Collapsed actually."

"See, all I heard just now is that I have great abs. Fantastic."

". . . if you give me eight weeks of nothing, no going to the office, no seminars or travel, followed by a few months of physical therapy, then maybe, maybe a year from now, you'll recover some or even most of your functionality. Screw with it, and this could become intractable."

"Meaning what?"

"Meaning this is your life. From now on."

A nurse came in to ask for permission to give the agitated guy two rooms down some drug that would give us all a little peace and quiet, and I looked at my phone. Kelsey has no impulse control. She sends first and asks for forgiveness later.

**Fine. Fuck you. I never loved you and neither did Sydney.**
**Whatever happened to you, I hope it fucking hurts for a long time.**

The doctor sat down on my bed and folded his hands. Here comes his big close.

"Look, I spend all day every day trying to get people to summon the willpower to move. To fight the atrophy, I need you to find the willpower to do nothing. And I'm getting the sense that doing that is going to be really hard for you."

*Oh, Doc, please,* I thought, *you have no idea who you're dealing with.* But, people-pleaser to the end, I gave him the solemn nod he needed.

*Yeah, Doc, I know a little about willpower.* The green light pulsed on my phone. Kelsey was the most talented employee I'd ever had. But the willpower piece? Not so much.

**I'm sorry, I didn't mean that. You know that.**
**I love you and Dez loves you. But OMG, you are the**
**most stubborn and willful man in the world.**

## CHAPTER 3

# Recognizing Patterns

. . . Look at this resume. This guy has been a quality control engineer for Associated Spring in Bristol for twenty-two years. He is responding to your posting for a quality manager in San Fran. Is he qualified? Sure! Did he say in his cover email he has no problem relocating? You bet! Would I send him? No freaking way! Let's look at his patterns. He was born in Bristol. He lives there now. With his wife, who he met in high school. Their whole family is there. His daughter is sixteen, a cheerleader no less! His wife works part-time. In Bristol. He is in the Rotary Club, referees basketball, and is on the town zoning commission. I'm sure he went to San Fran for a convention years ago and thought "Crooked Street" was cool and cable cars were quaint, but I promise you one true thing about this candidate that even he doesn't realize: He will die in Bristol . . .

Harsh, right? Judgmental? That's your job. My job is to keep you from taking years to learn this about people. They don't change. They establish patterns, and they keep to them. Oh, sure they consider change, they talk to therapists about how healthy change would be, they buy self-help books and watch TED talks that tout the benefits of change, and they go out on interviews for new jobs and flirt with change. But then the offer comes; and they get petrified; and they make an excuse to not change; and they turn down the offer, waste your time, and stay right where they are. And next year they'll get sick of themselves and call you again and say they're ready. This time they mean it. But they're not, and they don't.

Now, thank God some do change jobs, or headhunters like us would starve. Some are brave, but most—let's be real—don't change jobs until they are about to lose the one they have. Amateurs waste time trying to change patterns. Pros know that when it is all said and done, odds are people will revert to their already established patterns.

**From Danny's "Headhunting Rookie Retreat" 2-Day Workshop**

. . .

One of the chief hypocrisies of my life is that I became wealthy by placing people in jobs, at being an expert in what people fear and desire when they change jobs, but I've never changed jobs—not even once. I started at the headhunting firm, Hobson Associates, right after college and never left. I never even needed or had a resume. I have no idea what people really feel when they look for a job. When Sydney and I first met and fell in love, she found this story charming and inspiring. Less than a decade later, she would be banishing me from our house with the stinging words, " . . . You are nothing but biceps, a Benz, and an acute sense of irony."

And so, when the car service dropped me off at my condo with my crutches, ice bags, and bottles of Vicodin and Flexeril, it was, of course, ironic that there were only two positions that relieved the pressure and pain in my back: lying flat on a hard surface, and kneeling down. Prayer position. With my master's in literature and all my theatre experience, it never occurred to me that things that were trite were only trite because they kept happening to people.

So, if I have to kneel on my ottoman while writing or eating for the next few weeks, I can deal with both the irony and the ignominy. If—as I found—it was easier to crawl to the fridge and eat whatever was on the lowest shelf than it was to try to stand, then fine. I got this. If sleeping on the hardwood floor was the only position that didn't induce spasms, I was cool with that. I had come to associate short-term pain and sacrifice with success. Being in pain made me hopeful that a worthwhile prize awaited me. It was how I had lived; it was a pattern I had come to rely on and trust. Patterns were safe. I made a lot of money recognizing and respecting patterns in others.

. . .

"You didn't tell me she was beautiful."

We were at Kelsey's coming-out party. She had smashed all the rookie production records, many set by me fifteen years earlier, and she and her husband, Jay, had recklessly bought a house using her first commission checks as a down payment. A young salesperson going into debt is usually a sales manager's dream. But when it came to Kelsey, I was protective, cautious. I tried to talk her out of it. I assured Sydney I must have mentioned her looks.

"No, no, I would have remembered that. You mentioned, ad nauseam, the energy, the chutzpah on the phone with the clients, how fast she learns, her surprising vocabulary given she didn't go to college, but you never mentioned the exotic looks. Or the banging body."

I was about to tell Sydney, condescendingly, that I don't notice such things with twenty-two-year-old girls; that I saw her strictly as a potential moneymaker and senior member of my team, a high-impact protégée; that when I saw that kind of potential, I considered it my mission to develop it to its maximum. All of which was true, but it was also true that I took in her beauty every time she visited my office. Syd spared both of us this silly soliloquy by walking over to Kelsey, whispering in her ear, and disappearing with her into the first-floor bedroom where people had piled their coats. She was going to get her own intel, with no filters from me.

On one hand, I was angry. I was crazy about Sydney. I loved her ferociously and talked about her so often and with such romantic effusiveness that she was dubbed "Saint Sydney" at work. We had only been married a few years, and we were a match on every conceivable level. She taught composition at a community college. I had my MA in English and my periodic forays into professional theatre. We were both athletes and competitive as hell. We went for runs together, lifted weights together, played tennis and golf. A onetime Olympic-style weightlifting competitor, she could squat more weight than I could, and she could drive a golf ball farther. (When we joined our country club, and the Cahills were called to the tee over the loudspeaker, men would leave the terrace and putting green to see Sydney unleash her long and furious swing. A guy's swing.) And Sydney was extraordinarily beautiful: a redhead with long, thick tresses, an aquiline nose, and wide-set eyes. Her look was arresting. I once told her when we first met and were still just friends, "No one in the world looks like you."

But as I made small talk with the other guests and kept an eye on the closed bedroom door, I realized I had no right to be angry with Sydney, not if I meant what I preached about people and their patterns.

Five years earlier, Sydney was not yet a college teacher. She was taking graduate classes at night, but her day job was in my world. She was a headhunter. It wasn't her calling, but she had just enough extroversion and charm and just enough need for the attention, praise, and money that came from succeeding in commission sales, to be pretty good. I had broken so many production records that word was getting out that "this kid in Connecticut" was doing things differently.

In the world of professional search and placement, the business model was entirely client-centric. The company paid you a fee to find a candidate, generally from a competitor, who could do the job effectively with minimum training or ramp-up time. In this paradigm, the candidates were essentially treated as product. They didn't pay you a dime for the service, so logic said the candidate's perspective was simply secondary. I didn't see it that way. I told all my companies I had two clients: them and the candidate. I would look out for both of their interests. Even though only the company paid me a fee, I reasoned that if the candidates were treated with respect and trust, they would be better employees; they would stay longer, increasing my value; and they would refer their friends to me. Eventually, when they became managers, they would use only me out of loyalty.

As simple as this seems now, in the phone-jockey, Wild Wild West, straight-commission, executive-search world of the 80s, it seemed idealistic and naïve. Until it started working. Big time. By my third year, I was the top producer in my company's history; by my fourth, the top producer in the state. In my fifth year, I bought my company from its original owner, and by my seventh year, I started getting calls from program chairpeople putting together their annual recruiting conferences. Would I come talk about my methods? I didn't know there was such a thing as recruiting conferences. I didn't know how I would describe my "methodology." But I was starting to hire people at my firm, and I thought having to put together a speech would force me to give some structure to any training I'd have to give new employees. And I thought I might be able to recruit some people to work for me if the speech went well. But even if those practical reasons didn't exist, I would have done it anyway. I wanted the rush of being in front of the audience.

Sydney was at the first conference speech I ever gave, a local gig in New Haven. We later conveniently compressed our history when people asked us how we met. And parts of the story were absolutely true. I couldn't take my eyes off her. The signature crimson locks, then curly, the impossibly wide smile and mischievous eyes, the athletic legs wrapped in a tight skirt. She sat up front, unafraid to be called on. And she laughed. Loudly and freely. And she took notes at the right places. Cocked her head to the side if she disagreed with the point I was making. And when it came time to role-play, I made a beeline for her, and when I asked her to pretend that the candidates we sent out on interviews were infants, she rocked her arms and made cooing sounds to the imaginary infant, and my heart enlarged so fast and furiously that it was all I could do to remember there was an audience of three hundred people watching our every move.

In the compressed version, she came up to me after the speech, and we chatted—mostly about graduate school because I had gone to Wesleyan while working and she was going to archrival Trinity College while working, and there was instant chemistry, but sigh, she was married, and so it was not meant to be. And then . . . well . . . what do you know, we met again a few years later, and she was divorced and living alone and working as a waitress at night while she finished school and looked for teaching jobs. We started dating and . . . well, it was just fate. One of those things.

In the less convenient, truthful version of how we met, she was married, and I was in a long-term relationship. Her husband Pete was a hilarious and genuine guy, two years younger than her, and my girlfriend Mariah was soulful and sweet and spontaneous and devoted to me. She was deeply suspicious that my newfound speaker celebrity would change our dynamic. When women like Sydney came up to me after speeches (and the speeches now came nearly every week as word got out that I not only had a new approach to the business but also presented the material in an entertaining way), it made Mariah crazy. She said it would change me, and I bristled even as I felt it happening.

Sydney and Pete and Mariah and I would hang out together at bars, go to the beach, and have dinner parties at our respective condos. I tried to convince myself that this was not a front and that if I couldn't be with Sydney, having her as a friend was a worthwhile consolation prize. But I would find myself making excuses to call her at work and wouldn't tell Mariah. We were exchanging notes that never mentioned either my significant other or her spouse. The more Mariah asked me what was wrong, the more I felt suffocated. Before I could decide what I really felt or wanted, I stopped by Mariah's house on my way home one day and she told me she had talked to Sydney—Pete had been transferred to the Boston office of the insurance company for which he worked. Sydney would transfer her credits to a Boston university, and, while it sucked that they were moving, at least they would be only two hours away.

I saw it as a sign. I felt relief. Mariah and I made love that night with a vigor we had started to lose, and since it was always stifling in her bedroom, we went out on her porch (wrapped in a bedsheet in case her kids woke up) and looked at the diamond-studded sky. I remember thinking, *I should marry this woman. I love her, her kids are fun and beyond the endless infant stage, she is good and kind, and we see the world the same way.* Sydney was a fantasy. I slept more soundly than I had in months.

Two nights later, Sydney showed up at my condo at 10:30 p.m. We had never been alone before. She stood in the foyer. She had a speech prepared. She wanted me to know she had strong feelings for me. She didn't want to go to Boston. She hadn't loved Pete for a long time. She didn't know how I felt about Mariah, but she was moving soon, and she felt it was now or never and was it possible that I felt . . . I never let her finish the sentence. We made love on the landing of my stairs without her even taking her bomber jacket off. Later we sat wrapped in a blanket she described as "nubby" and wondered if we were up for what came next: The heartbreak of good people who trusted us. Losing the respect of coworkers who thought us incapable of such choices. Could we live with ourselves knowing we were willing to be so flagrantly selfish? And what of the patterns I was becoming so well known for identifying and evaluating?

Just recalling the mind-set with which I so cheerfully and eagerly gave up my integrity made my back spasm, and I had to roll off the ottoman and shimmy on the hardwood floor until I found a position that offered some relief.

I thought we were doing what had to be done for the greater good. We were meant to be together. Period. The end. Destiny doesn't come without collateral damage. The only thing we could do was promise we would make causing this level of pain to Pete and Mariah worthwhile by having the greatest life together ever. We had to be bold enough to believe in ourselves. We couldn't feel what we felt if we weren't meant to be. Right? Mariah, archly, coldly, called bullshit on this when I told her my decision. "You think she's not going to do this to you someday? You think this isn't going to happen all over again? You just wait, my dear, you just wait."

. . .

The bedroom door opened and Sydney and Kelsey came out, joined at the hip. Sisters united. This was to be expected. Sydney was a puppy reincarnated as a human. When she first met you, even if you were an utter stranger, she would wrap you in a huge, warm bear hug, fighting her innate urge to lick your face. I was genetically uncomfortable touching people I didn't know (as a speaker this was a big problem since people wanted to shake hands and hug after the sessions), and I marveled at her ability, hoping it would rub off on me.

"Okay, I love her," Sydney said, "in fact I am going to touch her boob as an omen, and because I touch boobs." Touching other women's boobs was a sign Sydney was two drinks and ninety minutes from having to be poured into the car for a sleepy ride home. Kelsey, equally drunk, stuck her chest out, and someone from across the room snapped their picture.

I am looking at it now. They both seem absurdly young; God, how we were soon to age each other.

Kelsey moved off, and Sydney looked at me crossly and practically started hissing.

"Did you or did you not know she is a compulsive adulteress? That girl needs a therapist! How is her behavior all right with you?"

"I don't condone it, but I'm not her keeper, and I'm not responsible for what she does outside of work."

"So you did know and never told me? Nice. How about the fact that she was raped repeatedly as a child? Does that remind you of anyone you know? How could you not think that is relevant? What am I supposed to do with that, Danny?"

"Sydney, I didn't know. I knew about the cheating. I didn't know about the molestation. That is horrible."

But I did know.

Sydney had been molested by her stepfather, a man she rightfully detested until the day he died. Not until we lived together did I begin to understand the ramifications. She flirted with men harmlessly but often, which made me crazy, and said it wasn't because she wasn't happy with me. It was because she could only feel safe if she was getting a man's approval. Getting attention was a preemptive act; it kept her in control. And she never got enough. She never felt filled up. There was a void. One man could only fill it for so long. She explained these things to me, and I understood them intellectually, but especially when she drank, which she had started to do more and more, it was hard to feel sorry for her. Instead, I felt sorry for me.

Kelsey's story was equally horrific. Kelsey's natural mom was a prostitute who gave up Kelsey and her sister. After foster parents adopted them, a friend in the family's good graces had raped both girls, still under ten years old, on a repeated basis. Kelsey offered herself to him if he would spare her younger sister.

Kelsey had told me about her history when I took her to task after hearing that she'd ended up in a random man's room at a conference where I had sent her to represent my company. I thought I was going to give a straight-up morality lecture to a twentysomething who was experimenting with her lifestyle. When she told me that she had never had sex as an adult while sober, and detailed her abusive past, it broke my heart. I wanted Sydney's stepfather to die all over again for good measure, and I wanted to track down the bastard who had hurt Kelsey and kill him.

I didn't tell Sydney this, because it felt like we were always talking about this central element in her life and its aftereffects, and it was her unimpeachable justification for any behavior she wasn't proud of. I wanted us to move past it, not let it define our lives. I also knew she would then feel in competition with Kelsey. I thought she might break out the sister act, so I never gave her the chance. So I told Sydney I didn't know. And Sydney said she believed that I didn't know. She had asked Kelsey whether she had told me, and Kelsey had said there were some things you just don't tell the boss. Kelsey had anticipated my lie and lied to cover for me, and as crazy as this would later prove to be, I took it as a sign of love. She understood me.

. . .

It is almost funny now to recall how embarrassing it was to be at a party with my wife grilling me over the extent of my relationship with my twenty-two-year-old budding superstar. I was too old for this crap. And it was preposterous. Sydney was my world. I was tested weekly on the speaking circuit. After my sessions, there was always a cocktail happy hour. And once they were fortified by alcohol, women approached me. The conferences were their one week a year when they were away from their families for the weekend, and I quickly found out the married ones were the most aggressive. And because—as Sydney often reminded me—we only met because she approached me at just such a conference while she was married, she would never believe how I told her I handled these situations. I made the obligatory appearance at the parties, never drank ("I can't, have to speak in the morning"), and left within an hour. I never said good-bye. I went to the restroom and never came back. They would often call my room and taunt me about running off. What was I afraid of? I knew their ardor had little to do with my personal appeal or me. The "speaker conquest women" were well known on the circuit. A few times a woman spurned and full of herself would press me. I had a simple answer—"I love my wife"—that Sydney would never hear because to tell her I had to admit the advances happened in the first place.

My only slip occurred because I was played so well. I had a reservation at a Chicago hotel, and there were a hundred people camped out in the lobby. Apparently half the hotel had no power, and these poor folks had been waiting for their rooms for hours. I checked in, assuming I'd have the same issue. But I was lucky, and the clubroom reserved for the conference VIPs was available. Two hours later, I headed out to have dinner with a client. On the way out, I ran into a woman I had known for years. She ran a big agency in New Hampshire and had never been anything but nice, and never sent out a vibe. She stopped me in the lobby. She still had no room and was losing her mind. Could she please, please, please use my room to shower while I was out and she would return the key to the front desk and I could pick it up when I returned? I knew how grubby plane travel made you feel. Your breath, your skin. I wasn't going to be in the room, so it wouldn't feel awkward. So I said yes.

When I returned a few hours later, she had left my key at the front desk, and I thought I had been a Good Samaritan. Until I opened the door and she was sitting cross-legged and naked on the bed. She was beyond drunk and began some rant about what she wanted me to do to her, but I barely heard a word she said. This was before cell phones, and all I could think was that if Sydney had called to see how my day went then my life was over. She would never believe me, and I wouldn't blame her. I kept shaking the woman. "Did you answer the phone?!! Did the goddamn phone ring?" But she passed out within minutes. I covered her with the bedsheets and slept in the armchair.

When Syd called in the morning and apologized for falling asleep before she called to say good night, I fell back on the bed and felt my blood pressure begin to level off. I hear people in long-term marriages talk so reasonably about being attracted to other people. "Of course," they say. "That's just biology. We just choose not to act on it because we have a deeper commitment." Okay. In those early years, I stood weekly at a podium in front of an audience of hundreds of often amazingly attractive women who were staying at the veritable dorm that is a conference hotel. Their availability was heightened by alcohol and opportunity. But not only was I not tempted, I was barely aware. The only downside to the acclaim and money and emotional rush I got as my speaking career grew was that it kept me away from Sydney. I missed her viscerally at night. Being away from her made my stomach hurt.

. . .

Yet here we were. Kelsey smiled at her new friend from across the room. Syd raised her wineglass, then turned away and whispered that she wanted to go home. We were both saved from the scene becoming ugly because someone asked her to sing. This happened at almost all parties where there was a piano or a guitar. Sydney has, along with all the other gifts God gave her, perfect pitch and the voice of an angel. She ran through her routine, "Oh, I have been fighting such a cold." "You guys aren't drunk enough to listen to me." Followed always by, "Oh, okay, maybe one song." There was always someone at the party who hadn't heard her sing. And I loved isolating my gaze on that person once Sydney began. Their eyes got wide open. Then their mouths. You could read their minds: "Are you telling me she is beautiful and witty and fun and a professor, and she can sing too?! That just isn't right."

Kelsey tugged on my shirtsleeve mid-chorus. I was so in love that I was actually irritated. "I hope one day someone looks at me like you look at her."

CHAPTER 4

# The First (or Last) to Know

What are you going to do when they find out who you really are?

**#2 in Danny's "12 Killer Interview Questions" Seminar**

. . .

Shame is lame but guilt is actionable. Guilt makes things happen.

**From *Endgame*, Danny's Best-Selling Series on Closing on Job Offers**

. . .

It had been ten days since I got home from the hospital, and I still hadn't told anyone at work that I had severely damaged my back. I still hadn't told Jolene (who scheduled all my seminars and who accompanied me on many of the trips to run all the A/V and cue the video segments that I use for dramatic and comic purposes) that I would have to cancel my near-term calendar, and perhaps close my speaking business altogether. Leah, the general manger and heir apparent of my search firm, and from whom I had no business secrets, called me after a few days and asked, "Are you on vacation?" I told her I felt inspired to do some writing, and I knew there were no pressing training sessions on my calendar, so if she didn't need me, I'd like to stay home—but if she did, I'd be there in an hour. I said this lying flat on my back on my hardwood floor with a rolled-up towel under my knees to relieve pressure. I hadn't showered since I'd been home. I couldn't figure out how to pull it off spasm-free. I had never taken a week off without giving Leah plenty of advance notice. So to be out ten days and say I was taking more indefinite time was crazy talk, and she knew it. "Uh, sure . . . no, we're good. Take all the time you need. Boss, are you okay?"

I had a personal chef, Paul, who came to my house once a month, spent the day cooking my high-protein, low glycemic carbohydrate, moderate "good fats" meals. He would measure the precise amounts for each meal to the gram, store them in Tupperware, and mark them "Day One, Meal Two," etc. Five meals a day plus breakfast. I ate precisely 3,100 calories a day, with precisely 300 carbs and exactly 1.5 grams of protein for every pound of body weight, and I drank ninety ounces of water a day and two cups of black coffee. Every day. Zero variation.

"What do you do when you travel?" I was often asked.

"I pack food or ship it."

"Okay, so what do you do when you have a cheat meal?"

"Your question intrigues me. It implies I have a cheat meal. That would imply I cheat. I don't."

At 5'11" I weighed between 188 and 190 pounds, with eight to ten percent body fat. The only variance was the insidious effect of travel on water retention. I called Paul and canceled his delivery, figuring I had enough meals stored in the freezer to last three to four weeks. Then he wouldn't get to ask me why I was in the middle of the floor or appearing to have intercourse with the ottoman. Worse, what if he offered to help? The thought of the potential humiliation made me shudder. The toilet became an odyssey for me: once I crawled to the bathroom, I would hoist myself up and do essentially a gym parallel bar dip movement, suspending myself over the bowl because I could not bend over or lean back. When I was done, I would lie sideways on the bathroom floor to wipe myself, and it never felt clean or complete. The whole process was so enervating that I began to eat less and less. I don't know how long I would have gone on with this whole charade. I don't recall having any rational plan. At some point, I would have to tell someone. Every day I would plan to call my older sister Hanna and explain that I might need some help, or at least tell my office there had been a fundamental and potentially permanent change in my ability to function, but then I would let the day pass. I was helped by my bottle of narcotics and muscle relaxants. I would check my email in the morning, tend to any urgent business situation, and then, faced with the option of staring at my ceiling (the slightest shift sending a river of spasms up and down my back, glutes, and hamstrings), read until the weight of the book or iPad, held directly out in front of me, would tire my arms, or sleep the day away, drug-addled but pain free. I would weaken by late morning, choke down the pills without crawling to the kitchen to get water, and wake up in the middle of the evening, when I would repeat the process.

By week two I had gotten sloppy. On Mondays, I would crawl upstairs, put a handwritten "Do Not Disturb" sign on my bedroom door, and hide out while my housekeepers of many years, the mother-daughter team of Brenda and Trudy, cleaned my condo. They would assume I was sick, and I figured by next week I would come up with some other excuse or perhaps be well enough to hide in my garage. But in my hazy, trancelike anomie, the days got away from me. I found myself being shaken awake, lying in my gym shorts in the middle of the floor of my living room. Apparently, I had lost more weight than I realized, and they had never seen me looking this rough. Hell, I hadn't ever seen myself like this—unwashed and with the makings of a Unabomber beard. I had to beg Trudy, who assumed a mental breakdown on my part, not to call 911. I explained about my injury, my limited mobility, and my loss of appetite related to my difficulties in the bathroom. I spoke quietly and carefully, trying to slow their darting glances at each other, glances that transparently read, "What should we do?" Brenda grabbed her car keys and said she was going to the grocery store and pharmacy this minute. She instructed her daughter to run a bath and said they would carry me in if necessary, but they were not leaving until I was clean, fed, and situated properly. When she left, Trudy kept staring at me. Her face was blank. Finally, when I gave her nothing, she said, "But you're rich. Why would you choose not to get help? Why didn't you call anyone? Why didn't you call us? Why would you live this way?" As I averted my gaze from Trudy's understandable mix of disgust and wonder, I was suddenly back at my mother's house on that final Sunday afternoon.

. . .

"If you do this, you are not my son any longer. Do you understand? I will disown you the second you sign those papers."

"Ma, you can't take care of yourself anymore. The place smells like shit, and that's because you no longer can get to the bathroom."

"That's not true." But she looked away.

"And do you know what you weigh? What? A hundred pounds? Less? You don't eat. I come to visit you, and the fridge is empty. Why don't you call me if you need food? Or anything, for that matter? Why would you let yourself suffer? I'm an hour away, Hanna is ten minutes, Tony is the next town over, for Christ's sake."

"You're very busy, I know that. And Hanna and Tony don't care about me." When they stopped by, she told them she knew they were busy and that I didn't care about her. We all knew the game.

"Ma, when Dad died, I promised to take care of you. I can't let you stay here. This is why I have the power of attorney. To make these calls."

"You listen to me, young man. I worked in a rest home for thirty years. That's how we got the money to keep us alive. I know what those places are like. I will die here in my home, thank you very much."

"Ma, it's not safe. You won't pick up the phone to get help. Why?!"

Her eyes flashed, narrowed, got hard. The way they had when I came home drunk for the first time at fifteen and she told me she would not allow me to waste my gifts.

"I want you to want to see me. I'm not a plant that you water. I'm not an item on a checklist of things you have to do. I'm your goddamn mother."

My mother always cried quietly, like there was someone in the next room that she couldn't let hear her for fear they would come in and punish her for being weak. It was far more effective than hysterical wailing. I waited her out. She was right. I hated coming to visit. The stench of the house—not just from her incontinence but also the four packs of cigarettes she smoked every day, the piled-up garbage, and worse—the memories. She had been cruel to my dad my whole life, and I had taken her side because she had the power and he was ineffectual. But like an ex-president, in the decade since his death, his stock had risen with me. I realized how kind and gentle he had been, how authentic and even wise. Things he'd told me in passing would find their way into my seminars without my conscious thought. I took it out on her. And she sensed it.

She had never learned to drive, which was common for Italian women of her generation, so her daily needs became frustrating over time. When my dad first died, we were all very attentive, but slowly we all went back to our lives, and visiting my mother was a duty we all hated, especially because her temper got shorter, her depression deepened, and her situation grew sadder. She needed me more than ever, and I ignored her because I knew she would let me off the hook. She would never reach out to me; she would never admit weakness. Sydney would urge me to visit Mom more often, but I would give her the look that said, "You weren't there, you don't know what that house was like."

"Ma, in the home you'll be looked after. You'll have people your own age to talk to. You won't be lonely."

"Can't I come live with you? You and Sydney have that big house. I won't bother you."

I couldn't tell her the truth. Because the truth was shameful and selfish. I was done with that life. I had worked very hard for my fairy tale. Syd and I had careers, sports we competed in, friends we entertained, the money to go where we wanted on a whim. I didn't want to deal with my mom's overarching sadness. I didn't want to fight her over meals or carry her to the bathroom and wash her every day like I did when I visited. Seeing her in this diminished and bitter state made me so profoundly sad that I was unable to grant her a simple and fair request. When I was a child and could not take care of myself, she didn't shirk her duty. But now that the tables were turned and she needed me to take her in, I never even took it seriously. Instead, I rolled Sydney under the bus.

"Ma, I can't do that. You know how much I travel. Thirty weeks a year. That's not fair to Sydney; that's not what she signed up for."

I blamed Sydney. Sydney, who would have embraced me wildly if I told her we had a new roommate and treated my mother like gold 'til the day she died. I allowed Sydney, the most nurturing human I ever knew, to be the bad guy. My mom could see she wasn't going to win, so she turned cold. This had always been her way. When I misbehaved as a little kid, she would tell me to get away from her. This would terrify me, and I would grab her legs and wrap myself around her. She would pry me off her and push me away. She could go days without talking to me. There is such a fine line between strength and sickness, between free will and free won't.

"Sign the papers, and I will never talk to you again. Make up your mind."

She held the papers out to me, daring me to sever our bond. She almost looked smug. But she hadn't realized how far I had come, how much I had learned from her. I took the papers and signed my name with a flourish.

"You're going to miss the hell out of me, Ma."

"Don't count on it. That's why I had two sons, so if I lost one, no big deal. And those are the last words I will ever say to you."

Was she lying? I hoped so, but I didn't know. She was that good.

. . .

Kelsey had taken to stopping by my office and having offline conversations. Sometimes about business, but usually not. Conversations about oral sex—"no woman likes to do it, I don't care what they say"; about how Tommy Bahama shirts make guys in their thirties look older; about how she wished she had gone to college but now that she had a child and was making 200K a year at twenty-three years old, she probably would never go. I had a hard time throwing her out of my office because she was quickly becoming our most gifted and productive recruiter. She was outworking everyone, she was hilarious, and the conversations with her were always much more interesting than whatever work I was doing.

She asked me if I told lies, and I told her I did, that most people who grew up as poor as I had told lies out of shame. I would tell my friends someone in my house had measles so they wouldn't ask to come in and see our squalor. I would say I wasn't hungry or had just eaten when I first started working so my coworkers wouldn't feel sorry for me when I didn't have the money to go to lunch with them. She asked me when the last time I lied was, and I admitted it was that very morning. Sydney had called down from upstairs where she was playing her beloved Tetris on our computer and asked what I was doing. I was doing absolutely nothing, simply zoning out before my day started, but I told her I was shaving. A simple, harmless lie. This is what happens when you grow up in a house where you hear your mother on the phone making up stories to buy time with collections agents or to get our landlord, Mr. Zappula, to let us have more time to pay the rent. Lies become the norm. Everyone is on a need-to-know basis when it comes to the truth. The great thing about Kelsey was that she understood this immediately and didn't judge me.

"I get it. You want Sydney to think you are doing something positive, even if it's as lame as shaving; you don't want to puncture the image of the type A, perfectly-evolved husband."

Yep. As long as the essence is true. I would, after all, soon shave. "You see, Kay (I had given her a nickname of affection, and people in the office would later say this was when they knew), I think you have to be absolutely honest in life, but I'm not sure you need to be completely honest."

"Yeah, I saw that DVD where you said that." She seemed offended.

"Well, Kay, I try to say things in my seminars that I believe."

"I want you to say things to me you don't tell people on DVDs or in seminars."

"So what are you lying about?"

"I don't want you to think any less of me if I detail my frequent forays outside my marriage vows. Look, I either need to tell Jay what I've done and start over, or I have to borrow 10K from you and get an apartment for me and Desiree and start over alone."

"I'm not sure those are your only two choices. You can stop cheating, starting now, and never say a word about the affairs, and hope he never finds out. You want to tell him for selfish reasons, to absolve your guilt, but you'll only hurt him and destroy any trust he'll ever have in you."

"Ever cheated on Sydney? Come on, you never tapped one of your groupies?"

"Never. Why do you look like you feel sorry for me?"

"So if I asked you for 10K what would you say?"

"I'd say, 'Check or cash?' Now go back to work."

"So you're telling me to keep lying," she mused, stopping at my door.

"Uh, I believe I said to stop lying."

"I don't know if I can do that. I'm not that evolved. But I'll never lie to you. Promise."

. . .

The day my mom died started with me invoking her name when I made a mortgage payment online. Some poor people who become wealthy are frugal their whole lives, but my odd variation was to pay all my bills months ahead of time. This often confused the bank, and they would apply the extra money to the principal, and when I called them on it, they told me their systems weren't set up to handle someone paying that far ahead, and then they would often delicately suggest I discuss the basics of compound interest with an accountant. When I got to the end of the transaction, they asked for my PIN, which was my mother's maiden name. I had no sooner punched it in than my cell rang. My older sister. She and I had met with my mother's oncologist the night before. Her four-pack-a-day cigarette habit, starting at age eleven and lasting a staggering sixty-five years, had finally taken its toll. She had liver cancer, and it had spread, and there was absolutely nothing they could do. By this time, she had been at the rest home for three years, had made friends, regained weight, gone off her antidepressants, and had completely forgiven me. All's well that ends well.

My sister and brother had taken to refusing to buy her cigarettes, but after banishing her to the rest home, I cut a deal with her. I was done telling her how she had to live. She loved cigarettes, would easily prefer to die than go without them, and the smoking of them and the anticipation of smoking them, she told me, took up some of her useless, long days. So I bought them for her by the carton. And that got me back in. She was the cheerful Mom I knew as a young child. The one who told me I was special. The one, long after my bedtime, I heard hissing at my dad at the kitchen table after I had explained a political reference made on the show *Laugh-In*. My father was saying that, yes, it was remarkable I got the joke at my age, but it wasn't fair how my mother ignored her other kids and so clearly favored me. "He's different, for Christ's sake," she said, "anyone can see that. I have a responsibility." The oncologist had a responsibility as well; to tell us that we could either attempt chemo, which would be arduous and would only buy four to six months, or we could cease treatment, make her comfortable, and let her go. We had agreed to discuss it with my mother after he gave her the news.

"Where are you?" my sister asked.

I was over two hours away from my hometown, in the lobby of an office where I was waiting, along with my promising young recruiter, Will, to pitch a retainer at a client. We had arrived early, so I was paying bills and looking at my portfolio.

"Mom's going to die today."

Once the doctor told my mother the options, control freak to the end, she willed her body to shut down and took an immediate turn for the worse. I couldn't help but admire it. She was out of here. I told my sister I had to drop Will off and then head back; it would be easily three hours. She said she understood and would tell my mother good-bye for me. I told her to put her on the phone. At first my sister balked. My mother had an oxygen mask on and was weak, but she knew I was not about to relent.

"Put her on the phone, please."

"Hi honey," she said, and I could picture her holding the mask away from her nose, trying to sound cool. "How's everything?"

"Ma, I'm going to ask you something, and before you answer, try to remember when the last time was that I ever asked you for anything, and how—whenever that was—you probably said no."

"Such a wiseass."

"I need you to be alive in three hours. Can you do that?"

And I hung up. I told Will what the situation was, and he offered to get a cab home. Will was not only a great addition to our staff, he was also the only male in the office who had a completely platonic and authentic relationship with Kelsey. When I broached the subject on the ride down, he said, "I need a girlfriend I can leave in a room with a bunch of drunk guys and know nothing would ever happen. I love Kelsey, but that's not her." I told Will I appreciated his offer, but I would drop him off at our office. I knew my mother. She would wait for me.

*Today I will become an orphan* was my first thought as I took the elevator to my mother's room. Then I thought of the many times as a young child I had watched my mom, napping on the couch before her long shift at the nursing home, and leaned close to make sure she was breathing. She would often sense my presence, open her eyes to tiny slits, and whisper, "Mommy's okay, Honey, she just needs to rest." If you had told that five-year-old he could have his mother until he was in his mid-forties, he would have made that deal in a second.

My mother, doused in morphine, seemed like the most rested person in the room. My younger sister, Doreen, was only two years away from being forced into a rest home herself, from the advanced multiple sclerosis she had been fighting since her teen years. Hanna, pregnant at forty-eight with twins after one final last-ditch fertility treatment, was clearly crushed that our mom would never know her grandkids. My older brother, Tony, a leftover hippie with my dad's overt sentimentality, was a mess. They were all exhausted. The doctor had told them a nonstop vigil was crazy. The process could take an hour, or it could take days. I told them all they had had their time and now it was my turn. Go home, and I'll call you. Everybody out. They did the obligatory protesting, but they were glad to go. And when they left, and I turned back to my mom, she had fallen asleep. Or had she? I grabbed the room's lone chair, pulled it close to her, and leaned in to make sure she was breathing. Forty years were washed away when she opened her eyes to those same tiny slits and told me she was okay, she was just resting her eyes. She told me to go home and be with Sydney. But I wasn't leaving until she was gone. I had let her down so often. I knew it wasn't much, but I would pass this test of being a good son.

"Do you know what's happening today?"

"Yes."

"Scared?"

"Nah."

"Let's start there. Lying. You've done it my whole life. Sometimes I could see why, what it got you, but so many other times, it seemed like a waste. There was no benefit. Why did you do it?"

"At first, to cover things. You know very well the kind of things. So people wouldn't judge, so I could buy time if I didn't have the money." She shrugged. " . . . But later, I don't know, sometimes you lie so often you don't know you're lying. Sometimes it's just habit, but mostly . . . "

"Mostly?"

"To keep people out."

"I find myself struggling with it now, Ma. I hide things that don't matter. I decide what people have a right to know. What they can handle."

"Good! Glad to hear it. Keep it up. Keep the bastards out. It's the only way they can't get to you. What's true anyway? There are all these levels. You're old enough to know that by now."

The nurse came in to take her vitals, which made my mother roll her eyes. Is it "true" to have someone on a morphine drip so she can die in peace but monitor and record her blood pressure and pulse? So much

had changed in the ten years since my mother called me to tell me my
dad had died. Back then her lying would make me crazy.


My mom: Hi, Honey.

Danny: Hey, Ma. How are you?

My mom: Honey, your dad is gone. I wanted you to be the
first to know.

Danny: Okay. Are you alone? I'm on my way.

My mom: Don't drive like a maniac, Honey. Hanna is on her
way.

Danny: So you called her?

My mom: Yes, she's very upset.

Danny: So, I'm not the first to know.

My mom: Uh . . . no, you are. I didn't tell her what it was about,
just to come over.

Danny: You wanted to surprise her, did you? Add some excite-
ment to her grim, grey day?

My mom: Uh . . . kind of . . .

Danny: So if you didn't tell her, why is she 'very upset?'

My mom: Oh fine, I told her! This is no way to treat a widow,
young man.

Danny: I'm sorry, you're right. You and Hanna relax. I'll call
Tony and Doreen for you, okay?

My mom: Well . . .

Danny: Seriously? Just tell me, is there anyone you didn't tell
besides me? Am I, in fact, the last to know? Are there leaflets in
the neighborhood? Has the obituary already appeared?

My mom: Oh, you and your drama . . .

My mom saw the truth as a boring straight road. Lies were curves. You had to react to them, lean into them, and then you could accelerate out of their turns. You ended up at the same destination, so why the fuss? She knew both Hanna and I would want to believe we were the first children called when my dad died, and it was within her power to grant us that request. The fact that it was not true was not relevant to her. The lie enabled her to make two people happy instead of disappointing one. She saw this as proof she was a superior person.

By early evening, she was starting to fail. She seemed to be shrinking. She said no to the Jell-O they offered her, and she could tell she was scaring me because I kept squeezing her hand tighter and tighter.

"If you tell me, 'It's okay to let go, Mom,' I'm going to die disappointed in you."

I laughed. *But wait. Was that a signal? Was there something she wanted to say?* I asked her if I had been a disappointment. I asked her for forgiveness for being a high testosterone brat in high school, for being ashamed of the way we lived when my friends were around, for not being there as often as I should have been the past few years. She waved her hand dismissively. She now had to talk with the mask on, so there was a whistle-like effect when she spoke.

"You? How could I be disappointed? Look at all you've done, and you've worked so hard, and you took care of me and Daddy and now poor Doreen. Everyone is so dependent on you. I'm just sorry . . ."

She stopped. Me and *my* drama? I knew this was for effect, but it's hard to tell a dying woman to pick up the pacing and lose the drawn-out pauses.

" . . . I'm sorry you and Sydney don't have kids."

She mercifully went on a coughing jag that seemed to last ten minutes and that I thought might end things. Once she calmed down, she flashed an evil smile and told me to go in the closet and get her purse. I knew what that meant. I brought it to her, and she told me to lock the door while she unzipped a compartment and pulled out her Marlboros and a box of matches. I held her oxygen mask off the bridge of her nose while she puffed, replaced it so she could gather her strength for the next puff, and we repeated this until she was done.

"Did you ever love Daddy? You sure didn't seem to."

"Oh God. Hanna asked me that this morning."

"And what did you say?"

" . . . that he was the love of my life and things weren't always what they seemed."

"She buy that?"

"Hook, line, and sinker—is that why you aren't having kids? Because of us? You're smarter than that."

"Okay, I didn't want to say anything with Hanna being pregnant. It's not a competition, but Syd and I are trying, Ma; we're going to have a kid."

"Are you just saying that because you know I'll never know either way?"

I was fully capable of such a lie, and would have probably said it had I thought of it, but a month earlier, on a gorgeous morning, the kind the weathermen put on their list of Top Ten Days, I came back from the gym to find Sydney lounging on our expansive deck that overlooked a nature preserve protected by state law. We would always have this view of Broadbrook Mountain. She had made coffee, and as I kissed her, she reflexively handed me *The New York Times Book Review*. It was the kind of serene moment I never had as a child, the reason I had worked so hard. It was perfect. And when I lowered the paper to tell her how happy I was, I saw she was crying. Not bawling, but quietly crying. Slow, bitter tears. At first she said nothing was wrong, but I was having none of that. She shrugged her shoulders, saying, "Nothing is growing here."

"For real, Ma. You think you want to stick around and see the little rug rat?"

"Sorry, honey. It hurts too much."

I was trying not to cry. I didn't want to waste one moment we had left. But she had me against the ropes and decided it was time to put me on the mat. So she delivered the haymaker.

"I hope someday you get to say to your child what I am about to say to you. And I hope you mean it as much. You were everything to me."

Then she had another coughing jag. And then she fell asleep. I sat by her bed for the next nine hours. She never woke again. She had delivered her exit line, and there was nothing left to say.

Strange thoughts came to me during the night. It struck me for the first time, although it was perfectly obvious had I bothered to think about it, that my mother very probably never had sex again after we moved to the tiny row house on Newfield Road in 1963. She slept on the couch in the living room, and my father slept in my bedroom. My sisters occupied the other sliver of a bedroom. My mother worked nights and my father days. My father suffered from heart disease from his midforties until his death at sixty-six and clearly was incapable. No sex for the past four decades of her life! Or was I wrong? Did they find a few moments on those rare days when they had the house to themselves? No, I wasn't wrong. I could feel it. But it shouldn't have surprised me. This was a woman who could make dinner with whatever was left in the house, claim she wasn't hungry, and sit in the corner and turn up the volume on the TV when we could clearly hear her stomach grumble.

When they came in to wash her late in the evening and then decided to leave us be, I remembered the day I came home from the first day of high school and captivated her with my description of what it was like to take a shower in Phys Ed. I had never taken a shower before. We had a bathtub and problems with our artesian well, so we rationed who could bathe on what nights. We often just used a washcloth and soap in the kitchen sink to prepare for school. My mother had never been in a home with a shower either, and she was curious what it felt like. When my dad died and I offered to buy her a smaller, newer house, she wouldn't budge, but I remember her being tempted by the idea of having a shower. The more successful I became and the more I was able to do for her, the more insular she became. She didn't want a new house, although she was grateful for not having to worry about rent anymore; she didn't want to go away on a vacation or see the sights in New York City. By the end she wouldn't even leave the house to have lunch. A life of deprivation had become habit, and rather than embrace the abundance I could now give her, she wanted less than ever. It made me crazy. I would not let her make me feel ashamed for no longer needing to be ashamed! So I showed up less and less. I went out to the nurse's station and asked if they had allowed my mom to shower in the four days she had been hospitalized, but they told me they only washed patients at their bedsides and assured me she was kept clean. They didn't know I just wanted to know if this extraordinary record was intact. My mother had never experienced a shower in her life.

It is hard to believe in God after you have seen your mother take her last breath. It happened right after the morning sun had lit up the room, and it was loud and final. When I saw her face go slack, and her body release all muscular tension and her breathing stop, it was hard to believe some spirit was hovering over her former, restrictive unit and was now unleashed in some happy, eternal way. It seemed obvious that there was nothing. Nothing.

I sat there with her for a few moments. I didn't need more time to get used to the idea she was gone. I needed to gather myself so I could make the proper presentation to anyone I had to tell. How would I shape and control this moment? How would I mask what I was feeling? My mother had been a registered nurse in her early twenties, but once she married my dad, a simple factory worker, she had stopped working and her four children came at the predictable intervals for a postwar couple. But then my dad's factory, which had been laying off people for years, called his number. Within a few years, his poor diet and early drinking and smoking abuse caused hypertension and heart issues. He couldn't work enough to support the growing brood, so my mother had to go back to work. She found she had been out of the game too long for Charlotte Hungerford, the lone hospital in town, so she had to go to the minor leagues. There was a convalescent hospital (aka elderly housing/ rest home) in town, and she began working the midnight to 8:00 a.m. shift for wages essentially half of those of a staff nurse.

Much later, as I muddled through marriage counseling, I was shocked when the doctor labeled this decision of my mom's—one I saw as heroic since it kept my family alive—as abandonment. I thought of abandonment in the obvious ways: divorce, running away, even death of a parent. I still had my mom, but I went from seeing her every day, having access to her at will, to finding her already sleeping when I got back from school and not yet home when I left for school in the morning.

"Uh," my therapist assured me, "abandonment while still present is often the most powerful and painful kind." Later, Sydney and Kelsey would leave no doubt about that.

I opted for the sympathy that comes from expressing gratitude while grieving. I broke the news to the nurses and thanked them for the way they did their impossible job. Then I went to the visitor's lounge and called, in order: Leah, to tell her I would not be in today, mentioning casually my mom had passed, and to ask her to cover two interviews and to intercede in a deal I was managing; my sister Hanna, who said she would call the funeral home and get that whole end started; and then Sydney. The phone rang four times before she picked up. I was hoping for voice mail.

"Hi. She's gone."

"Oh, Danny, I'm so sorry. She loved you so much. What can I do for you? Do you want me to call school and come there?"

"No. No. You go to your classes. It is what it is. I just . . . "

"What, honey?"

"I wanted you to be the first to know."

## CHAPTER 5

# Fake It Til You Make It

All successful people fake it until they make it. Learn and master your craft, of course, but as you are doing so, fake it! I did! I was an English major placing engineers at twenty-two years old, and I could barely steer my car—let alone tell you what an engineer did. Did I embarrass myself sometimes by asking idiotic questions? Sure! But by the end of the first year and a few thousand questions, I was an expert. I placed more engineers than anyone in my firm ever had.

The same year I graduated, a friend of mine, who wanted to be an actor, moved to New York City and started auditioning. He knew I had writing aspirations, was fooling around with playwriting, and he asked me for a funny monologue so he could stand out. So I wrote one about a college nerd's first moments meeting a pothead roommate. Simple. Hell, I had lived that!

I later got a call from a guy who was at the audition and heard the monologue. He was trying to find a one-act play to enter into the prestigious Ensemble Studio Theatre's Marathon of One Act Plays. He asked me whether the monologue was out of a one-act play, because if it was, then he'd love to read it. I said, "Yes sir, but it's Friday, and I'm going away for the weekend. Can I send it to you Monday?" He said sure, and that night I went home and wrote my first play. I never left the house. A few months later that play was being performed off-Broadway.

So it shouldn't shock you that years later, when I was one of the country's top recruiters and someone asked, "Do you ever speak at conferences?" I said, "Sure I do, what do you need?" even though up until then I didn't even know they had conferences! You fake it 'til you make it!! I see nothing inauthentic about this. I *knew* I was destined to be a speaker, I knew I had a way with words, and I knew I understood how and why people make decisions. I wasn't about to not succeed just because it hadn't happened yet. Once you make it, guess what? You're not faking it anymore. You are that person! You've become what you always were. Only now the world has vetted you. You will be surrounded your whole life by people telling you that you have to pay your dues. No you don't! Dues are paid by the untalented and the ones without the guts to fake it 'til they make it.

**From Danny's "Keynote to Rookie Salespeople"**

. . .

"I can give you a narcotic that will allow you to sit on the plane, but you can't take the narcotic and give a speech. You'll be so loopy you won't be able to put two sentences together—what then?"

"I'll fake it."

"I can't support this. You are starting to respond to the physical therapy and the deep tissue work. The lidocaine is giving you enough relief to lie flat on the floor and walk a little. Why mess with the recovery? It's one speech."

It was a big speech. The national staffing association's annual conference. We routinely generated three to five times my speaking fee in DVD sales and membership subscriptions to my online training and mentoring business. But that aside, I was by this time a huge draw for the conference. Hundreds of people booked their flights and registered for the conference because I was headlining the event. I had to be there. I made my case. Dr. Boylan heaved the same heavy sigh I had seen my whole life in this sort of dynamic. The sigh meant they knew I had won.

"I'll give you four pills. What I'm going to give you is just short of morphine, and I will never give you more. So forget about coming back to me for next week's speech. You take one while in the car to the airport. You take a second one when you get to the hotel and need to sleep. You're on your own for the speech, and I'm telling you do *not* take one in the morning before you speak. I don't care how much it hurts, because you will not be functional. You will be humiliated. Take one on the plane home. Take one when you get home. Rest for two days, and I mean complete rest, and then come in for your lidocaine shot."

When he handed me a small bottle with no scrip on the front a few minutes later, he looked like the underling in the action movies who has to actually fire the torpedo or unlock the nuke or fire the kill shot. His look said, "This is the wrong thing to do. But it's my duty."

By this time, I could walk short distances but still had to kneel at all other times—otherwise the searing pain would return to my right hip and lower back. Mainly, I was petrified of two things: going into spasm during the speech, being unable to continue, and being helped off the stage like an old feeble man; and the two-hour flight. Until the Fasten

Seat Belt sign goes off, the FAA mandates you stay in your seat. There was no way I could sit for the required half hour. Once I sat down, the longest I had lasted since my injury was thirty seconds. Then I would have to kneel or stand or the spasms would start, followed by unbearably intense pain.

I took the first pill as I knelt in the backseat of the car service I hired several times a week to get to the doctor's or to get groceries. Once I got through security, I decided to conserve energy, swallow some pride, and request a cart to take me to my gate. I had always resented two things about these carts even as I understood their value. First, why do they get the right of way? I get it that these folks can't walk, but why do they have to get there before the rest of us? Why do we all have to scatter like pigeons? Second, why is the horn fallout-shelter loud? It was amazing how much less annoying these carts were once I was actually the passenger! Scatter losers—I got a narcotic kicking in here!

"Sir, sir! You have to wake up now. Sir!?"

I forgot what a big baby I was when it came to drugs. I have a high tolerance for pain and no tolerance for drugs, recreational or otherwise. In college when my friends would pass a bong around the room before going out, I would take two hits, wish them well, and crawl up in my bunk. When Sydney was prescribed Xanax for her fear of flying and offered one to help me sleep after a caffeine binge, I slept for eleven hours straight and would have been stuck for an answer if asked my name or address. Dr. Boylan was right. This stuff was crazy. I felt no pain in my back or hip, and once the captain and his distressed flight attendants woke me up, I was not only able to walk; I jogged to baggage claim.

At the hotel I took half a pill and slept in bed for the first time since the accident. As I showered and suited up before going downstairs to do my keynote, I felt the familiar tightening of the IT band, the deep burn in my right hip. I was very close to taking another half, but I made a judgment call. I had been a professional speaker long enough to know the power of adrenaline. I had done seminars while flu-stricken, without sleep after canceled flights, and I knew that as soon as I felt the energy of the crowd and I was introduced, my body would get me through the speech. It had been so long since I had performed, I knew once I got the first laugh, saw the senior salespeople nodding at the wisdom of what I had just proposed, saw people scurrying to reproduce my PowerPoint slides before I whisked them away, I would be fine. ("There are two kinds of theatre," Edward Albee said, "the quick and the dead." He would have liked my speeches.) I actually forgot about my plight. It was only at the very end, when I thanked the audience for their time and hit them with my killer, closing anecdote, that my body decided: enough; time to pay. I held the podium and waved as they rose to their feet. No speaker ever wants a standing ovation to end, but that day I wanted them to get the hell out of the ballroom. I waited until every last person was gone and waved over the program chairperson assigned to me. I filled him in quickly, and he got a friend, and they carried me out the back, through the sales offices, and up a service elevator, to my room. I knelt down and took the pill.

I thought the hard part of the trip was over. I found mixing coffee with the pill enabled me to stay coherent and yet get the benefits of the narcotic. I was all but pain free as I walked to the baggage claim area to meet my car service. She knew me so well by this point that she didn't even have the cardboard sign with my name printed in black Sharpie. But standing next to her I noticed a little girl, no more than five or six.

She looked through me, and her eyes narrowed into crow's feet that would disappear the second she found her target. No movie's jump cut could match the metamorphosis I was about to witness. Her face widened; it was as if someone was tickling her eyes, and her hands reached for the sky as she jumped up and down. She had no vertical jump to speak of, but she did have Daddy in view. I had seen it a thousand times, in various forms. Parents greeting sons and daughters home from Iraq or Afghanistan. Girlfriends, dressed fetchingly in boots and tight jeans, holding balloons that might as well have been tied to their necks. I remembered well the early days, when Sydney would rent a bunny costume and jump around as she saw me coming around the corner. (Later she would greet me sans costumes, and then she would ask if I minded driving myself to the airport, and in the end, she would tell me to wake her when I got home. And I would pass.) So I knew the thrill and joy of a loved one greeting you after a sojourn. But somehow this was different. Now that I knew I had thrown away any chance of ever being a father, I knew that I would never experience what it might feel like to be some little girl's or boy's whole world. Climbing into a limo so that I could go home, take a drug, and sleep through another day, all in the hopes of someday being able to return to doing this same old gig without pain, seemed simply to be a waste of life. My heroic journey to find a way to speak was nothing but a joke. We got the bags and got in the limo.

"Mr. Cahill, do you need to stop? Are you all right? Is the hip really bad?"

Fake it 'til you make it. I told her I was good. It was all good.

## CHAPTER 6

# The Drift Begins

Thank you very much—what?! What? Are you heckling me already? Ah, yes . . . boy what an idiot I was for going public with that nugget last year. So for the uninformed in the audience, the question was "Is my wife pregnant?" Uh, no. So far I have been unable to slip one past the goalie. To catch you up, my wife and I were this power couple. I had my career, she had hers, second marriages, lots of aspirations, places we wanted to see, all kinds of plans! No kids. We had Maine Coon cats. Then she hit thirty-five and lost her mind. Really. She would stop kids in the mall and start talking to them in this weird language. "*Izza such a face, look at that little izza face*!!" "Syd, leave the kids alone, you're scaring them."

We would go to our friend's houses for dinner parties, and she'd go right to the bedroom to play with the babies, even after their mom had gotten them to sleep. So she sits me down and says we need to have a kid. I remind her I don't need kids, I have employees who act like kids, and she should have told me about this potential turnabout before I signed the ultimate Non Compete. But she worked me over. She got to me. I was getting older, how many vacations can you go on, how many pools can you sit by, how many golf courses can you play? Were we really that selfish? She said we'd be fantastic parents and, for evidence, cited how great I was with our cats, mere hours after complaining that I never changed the litter box. I weakened when she said it was the ultimate expression of our love for each other, but I folded when she said, "Look, with your employees you can only screw up their work lives—with a kid, you could screw up their entire life."

So off we went. More sex than ever. What a deal, right? Oh, but everyone who has had fertility issues in this audience is going, "Uh, it's not that kind of sex." It's not On-Demand sex. It's sex on demand. "I don't recall asking if you were in the mood, Mister, now shower up, and I'll see you upstairs. Stat!" And I thought it would be easy! Especially when she educated me and said it was only possible a few days a month. I thought, *I'm a senior executive. I'm only effective a few days a month! I got this!* But you know what I found out this year? Fertility is not a game for senior salespeople—it's for rookies! It's a numbers game! Throw enough against the wall and something will stick, if you'll forgive the disgusting imagery. But anyway, thanks for asking, and now you have a heads-up, cause if she starts to ovulate during my speech, I am out of here.

**From Danny's "Intro to Most Keynotes for Months"**

. . .

# The Drift 1

The Drift, as I think of it now, started in the office of our assigned specialist at UConn's Center for Reproductive Services. Sydney had done her homework. On the drive over, she told me the physician was board certified in reproductive endocrinology, that UConn was a member of SART, and that it has some of the highest success rates in the nation. On the short drive over to Farmington, she described the IVF process she had already determined we were going to try if we had failed all the tests. When she got to the part where she informed me I would have to inject her with a syringe on a daily basis, I cringed. Sydney was not only deathly afraid of needles, but her entire relationship with pain was low on tolerance and high on histrionics. I had seen her stub her toe and drop to her knees and writhe in pain; a dollop of hot grease rebounding off a pan onto her wrist would elicit a string of "motherfuckers" that would make Samuel L. Jackson proud. In this area, we were alien to each other. I felt embarrassed for her when she would overreact like this. She thought my way—silence and denial—was insane.

I could never bring myself to tell her how I had learned to be proud of my pain tolerance. I was ten, running in the yard, and tripped. Breaking my fall with my hands, I came down directly on a broken bottle, and it went clear through my hand. My sister screamed and ran for my mother. She saw the bottle sticking through my hand, and after taking half a second to gather herself, said, "You know what would be interesting? If you could go to the hospital to get this taken care of without crying. Only an amazing little boy could do that. I bet you could, though. Let's see." I remember my neighbor, Mr. Rossetti, who gave us a ride to the hospital, turning white when he saw my hand; the intake nurse at the emergency room thinking I was in shock because I wasn't crying; and the doctor telling me it was okay to cry as he looked over at my mother. She shook her head, so I smiled at the doctor. Like an insane person.

Sydney, steeped in years of therapy where all roads led back to her mother, would have had a field day with the story. She patted me on the thigh and said she wanted to prepare me for what she was sure the doctor would say.

"Don't be upset if he tells us anything uncomfortably personal."

"Why would I get upset?"

"Honey, infertility is often about aging. A man's sperm count and quality drops as he ages. Plus there is the reality—you never got a woman pregnant."

"Because I was raised in the 70s. All the girls were on the pill. Then, when I was young and single, AIDS broke out! I'm only forty-four for Christ's sake; my guys are gold-medal freestylers!"

"Well, we'll see. It's been almost two years. Something is wrong."

The incriminations had mounted over time. When Syd didn't get pregnant in the first few months, she wanted me to curtail my speaking engagements so that I was available the moment she ovulated. Since the sessions were often booked a year in advance, that wasn't possible. So I would get a call halfway across the country saying I had to get an early flight because she calculated that we had sixteen and a half peak hours left. She had read somewhere about the miraculous effect gravity had on fertilization, so after we finished making love, she would roll her legs over her head in a reverse somersault and stay in that position for ninety seconds, staring at the bedside clock.

Since I was an ardent cyclist, she would often imply that my hours on the rock-hard seat had damaged my testicles. She would hint that perhaps I was being less than forthcoming about my not only moderate but also flat-out babyish use of the recreational drugs so prevalent in my youth, and how that might now play a role in our failure to conceive. Underlying her smug façade was her competitive advantage. She had been pregnant, briefly, in college. The fact that it didn't take at the time was not a crisis but a relief. There would be time for kids later.

Now it was later, and since it wasn't happening, and we knew empirically that she could get pregnant and that I had never gotten a girl pregnant, the problem was mine. She had hitched her star to the wrong guy. I was letting her down, and that killed me. The idea of being a dad had become like being a porn star to me: I didn't necessarily want the lifestyle, but I wanted to be considered qualified. So bring on the IVF, the surrogate. Hell, let's adopt! I wasn't hung up on the child being "my blood" or carrying on my genes. I was, in fact, pretty sure it would be better for the world at large if my genes were stopped in their tracks when I was done with them. But Syd was adamant. No adoption. She could only envision a child with a blend of all our good traits, with none of our flaws, and she thought the true satisfaction of parenting came with hearing your parent's voice in theirs, the involuntary mimicry of mannerisms, comparing baby pictures thirty-five years apart and seeing the same facial expressions and smile. To her, that was the whole point! I would shrug and admonish her by saying that the whole point was to have someone in our lives to love. This was true, but I couldn't tell her why I knew it to be true.

. . .

Three years earlier, on the day Kelsey had Desiree, I went to the hospital. She called me at the gym at six in the morning to say she was heading to the hospital and to ask me if I would mind following up on an offer interview she had going on that day. I told her to stop being crazy and get off the phone. She reminded me for the hundredth time not to label her. She was still going to be the same driving, hyperproductive salesperson; she was not going to be "that girl," who calls after the maternity leave to say she can't bear to be away from the kid and wasn't coming back. She had the baby at noon and left me a VM that it would be lovely if I came to see Desiree. I had planned to go with Leah and the rest of the women in the office the next morning, but that night, I jumped on 91 South and went to Yale New Haven Hospital. At the valet parking stand, a man was selling giant balloons, and I thought it would be a much better gift than whatever conventional fare was in the gift shop. But it was a blustery and rainy day, the balloon got away from me, and I had to chase it down the circular driveway. I got soaked and felt foolish, but I was grateful to have a story to tell Kelsey, in case it was uncomfortable or weird that I had come alone and so soon.

When I walked in, she looked exhausted. I had never seen dark circles under her twenty-three-year-old eyes, even with all her late nights and hangovers. She looked incredibly beautiful. She smiled when she saw me—not just not surprised, but almost like she was wondering what took me so long. Then they brought in Desiree. And they laid her on Kelsey's chest. And suddenly her questions from so many months ago— "Should I have it? How can I have it? How can I be a mother when I have no clue who I am?"—all seemed senseless and wrongheaded. Desiree's hair was jet black like her dad's, and yet her eyes, her face. It was Kelsey.

"Desiree," Kelsey said, "This is the boss. His name is Dan. He's the first person from Mommy's world to see you! Isn't that cool? I can't believe I'm letting you see me this way."

"You look perfect. So does she."

"I know, right? I don't know what I was thinking; I'm going to love the crap out of this kid."

"You've always been precocious. You had prepartum depression."

Sydney was dead right about kids. They were magic. But she was dead wrong about them having to be yours. Kelsey raised Desiree's tiny hand and made her wave at me, and while I had no rights, and no place there, I didn't feel that way. I could love this kid.

. . .

Dr. Geisler would have made a horrible headhunter. The best head-hunters practice disruptive honesty and cut to the chase. They have to. Eighty-five percent of the time you are leaving voice mails for people who have no idea who they are or what they want, and you get five seconds before someone elects either to press the delete key or to listen to your message. I made my mark practicing and then preaching the transfer of enthusiasm. If you don't have an enthusiasm that is contagious, whatever you *do* have is contagious nevertheless. Dr. Geisler made us crazy. He danced with us.

He told us we were not alone. Six million couples struggle to conceive every year. (Great start—we were commoners.) He told us that he was glad to see we were nonsmokers since smoking was often the culprit, and I could see Syd smile like he had given her a gold star. There were no issues he could see with PCOS or endometriosis or chlamydia, so we had that in our favor. Syd was cloying and over-the-top chipper with him, as if winning the affection of this doctor would somehow factor into our chances of having a baby. But I outearned doctors by being able to read people instantly. And this guy was playing us. He was working his way up to delivering the bad news. I felt sorry for him. I saw it every day. Headhunters have to tell the candidates who didn't get the job the bad news, and I always delivered the news immediately. "Hi, it's Danny, you didn't get the job. I'm sorry." And I'd let them recover and then try to reassure them there'd be other jobs.

"So," he practically sighed, "while, of course, on the grand continuum, you both are young people. Forty-four and thirty-nine . . . "

Syd interrupted him to remind him she was not quite thirty-nine yet. She had three more months. He labored to smile. Then he hit us with the facts. In people thirty to thirty-five, the fertility rate was fifteen percent. It dropped to five percent at forty. Ninety percent of a woman's eggs are abnormal over the age of forty. Even if we used IVF, our chances were around twenty percent and would drop precipitously when Sydney hit forty. He said he wasn't trying to discourage us, but he didn't want us to think IVF was a sure thing. Trying to be cool, he said it wasn't a "slamming dunk." I probably would have been compelled to correct him on the slang usage, but Sydney wanted answers, and she took over. What was our problem? She asked him flat out if my sperm count was too low.

"Uh . . . no," he said, scanning the test results in front of him, "pretty average actually. No, it's all in order; sometimes we just don't . . . some significant blockage and scarring. You had fibroids removed, yes?"

Syd didn't move. The air went out of the room. He reviewed the surgery she'd had a few years earlier, but she didn't hear him. It was *her*? It somehow had never registered with her as a possibility. He went to great lengths to assure her this was not atypical and in no way meant the IVF was going to be the wrong solution or wouldn't work. But she didn't hear him. Then he made the classic pivot to business and had to qualify his customer. He told us each IVF treatment would cost $17,000 and would not be covered by insurance and asked us if that would that be a problem. When I said no, he brightened and suggested we get started as soon as possible.

In the car, I asked her if she was hungry, and she didn't respond. The doctor had recommended we practice the injections on oranges, and I suggested we stop and buy some, but she didn't seem to hear me. I pulled over.

"Listen to me. We're going to be fine. We're going to make this happen. We're going to have a goddamn brood before it's all said and done. We're not even going to be able to keep track of them all."

"Maybe we weren't meant to do this. Maybe it's me. Maybe it's all been a mistake."

"What? Syd, do not go there. He never said that. He never said it was any one factor or either one of us."

At the time, I thought she was saying God was handing down a punishing judgment. But now I wonder if she was saying that if she hadn't met me, and had stayed with her first husband (who was eager to have children and wasn't so self-absorbed in building a business and having his ego stroked on the lecture circuit), she would have small children already. I had kept her from having a family.

I don't know what she was thinking, of course, and maybe she was thinking all of these things at once. But as she listlessly slid her car seat back, I knew something had changed between us. Something fundamental. With all the events that ensued, and all the terrible reasons we gave each other to let go, I know The Drift started that day.

CHAPTER 7

# A Few Good Days

Question: Uh, Mr. Cahill, I've been a recruiter for about seven years, and I'm a big fan, follow you online, have your book, the whole nine. So here's my question: I keep getting offers for candidates that get turned down! They tell me when I first get their resume they are miserable, they "have to get out" of their job. I get them exactly what they said they wanted, and then they turn it down. What's going on?

Answer: The truth is these candidates who say they are miserable are in fact not miserable enough. They have bad days, and on those days they respond to you, but they have a few good days too. Then the fear of change kicks in. And another year goes by.

Question: So how do I know who has the courage to leverage and who is fooling themselves?

Answer: You look for an interceding event. We all have our limits of misery, and then we have to act or we can't live with ourselves anymore. You're looking for an event that makes them have to act, despite the fear of change.

**From "A Live Webchat with Danny"**

. . .

So far I have seen two surgeons, an osteopath, a chiropractor, and someone who simply has the word "healer" on his door. They all make me
feel guilty about seeing them without my doctor's knowledge, but I
want faster results even though I'm improving. The surgeons want to
cut me. I tell them the therapists say surgery should be a last resort. And
they both smugly say, "When the pain returns, you'll be back."

. . .

Good days and bad days. I often think if we hadn't been wealthy, Sydney
and I would have found a way to stop The Drift. We would have been
forced to confront our gradual distancing from each other. But we could
afford our routine. We would fight, and we both had a profound need to
win when we fought. Then we would isolate ourselves for a day or two.
I'd work late. Suddenly her school called a meeting. A friend called, and
she was meeting her for dinner. We wouldn't continue the argument;
we'd just freeze each other out. We'd still have breakfast together, and
we'd play with Gatsby and Hadley, our two Maine Coons, but we'd
channel our affection to them. She would hug me before I went to work,
but it was brittle and brief. By the third day, I was off to the week's
speaking engagement. Most businesses hold conferences on Friday and
Saturday, so I wouldn't return until Sunday. By then, we'd be over our
bruised feelings. We would realize how immature we were being, and
we would both involuntarily brighten when we saw each other, and the
process would start over.

Then again, if we hadn't had money, maybe we would have ended
much sooner. Maybe without the escape of our many long weekends
to New York City or my weekly business excursions away from home,

we would have realized much sooner how serious our issues were. Maybe only wealthy people get to indulge themselves during The Drift. I know divorced people tend to look back and see that their problems had existed for a long time before some "interceding event" caused the break. There's no question that the very things that originally impressed Sydney about me began to annoy her, and vice versa, but I still think it wasn't just that the money allowed us not to notice our problems. I still believe the hardest breakups occur because you still have good days, even as you realize most of the time you are having bad days.

# In the Same Week during The Drift

### One

I stood before our huge bedroom closet, completely lost. I had over fifty suits that were custom-made for me staring me in the face, but their time had come. We had decided at the office to go business casual, and I often had no idea what that meant or what I should wear. I was glazing over when I heard Sydney take the Lord's name in vain in the most disgusting manner she could conjure up. I knew what that meant: I had not closed the shower curtain. This made her crazy. She told me over and over that closing it would reduce mildew and mold, it takes like half a goddamn second, and it is disrespectful to her and a hostile gesture to keep forgetting. Usually I apologized. But today, because I said nothing and she therefore thought I hadn't heard her, she repeated the blasphemous phrase louder, and I went into the bathroom with my own enumerated rationale: "If it takes half a goddamn second, do it your goddamn self. What is hostile and disrespectful is that you can't let go of such a tiny thing. These are problems worth getting upset about? Are you joking?" And then the day and night were lost. We had long ago made a pact that we would never go to bed angry, but if we stuck to that now, we'd be zombies.

By midweek, we were still not talking, so I stayed in the den upstairs. One night I was reading David Sedaris's *Naked* on our futon couch. By the time I had finished, around eleven, there was no choice. This was one of life's moments, and I had to get over my petty self and experience it. I walked into the bedroom, and she tried to avert her eyes. I told her I had a gift for her, handed her the bookmarked copy, and got in under the covers beside her.

Sedaris had a short piece about a man who goes into a bathroom at a party and finds a gigantic turd in the bowl that he can't dispose of. Part of Sydney's charm was the combination of her sophistication and her appreciation of earthy humor. She once told me that I could try as hard as I wanted in my seminars to make people laugh, but "nothing is funnier than farts."

She said she wasn't in the mood, but I said, "Shut up and read. You'll see." I put my hand on her bare belly when she started to laugh because Sydney's most genuine laughs started in her belly and rolled like ocean waves. Sedaris's story is so brilliant and so funny that it didn't take long for the tide to start going out and then rush back in. Soon, she was in tears. I asked her to read the final story, "Naked," out loud to me, and she did, and it was twice as funny. Soon we were both exhausted from laughing—as much from seeing each other laugh as from the story's gamboling compassion. We turned off the lights and held each other. It was not a sexual embrace. It was deeper. Better. And she would repeat a Sedaris phrase, and we would both start laughing again. I loved her so much in that moment, as much as David loved Hugh, as much as anyone has ever loved anyone. And The Drift had to bide its time.

## Two

The only cinema "art house" left in Hartford was showing a documentary on Stephen Hawking, based on his mainstream success with *A Brief History of Time* years before. This was the kind of thing Sydney would say yes to enthusiastically when I would suggest it and then mope about when it was time to go. She saw us as an intellectual couple, but it was usually up to me to drive cultural choices; she preferred a bottle of wine, sweatpants, and a Bridget Jones movie. As usual, she fell asleep in the opening few moments, and I had to wake her to go home. Refreshed from her nap, she asked me about the flick on the way home, and I went off on the kind of tangent that used to make her giggle at my sheer capacity for wonder but now largely irritated her.

"Syd, this dude is nearly paralyzed, he has to use this machine to talk, his life is horrible by any objective measure, but does he hate the world like I would if I were him? No. He is charming and vital and even though I could barely follow just the physics *talk*, he, like, figured out the *fucking cosmos* . . . like the origin of the universe, like how black holes emit radiation . . . and he found a way to combine Einstein's relativity theory with quantum mechanics . . . and he is able to relate this insanely abstract stuff to images and analogies that people can actually understand. Not me of course, but a lot of people!"

"You are such a freak." She yawned and turned on the seat warmer on her side of the Benz.

"No, you want to hear the freaky part? Married twice and three children. Can't move or talk. How, you ask? They never went into that little piece of quantum mechanics. But that said, you can't watch this guy suffer and produce and then feel good about yourself because you remembered to floss in the morning, which by the way, I forgot to do."

"Oh God. You're not talking to me anymore, you're writing a seminar."

The next weekend we were at a party at the house of one of her faculty colleagues. At this point in The Drift, we wandered away from each other at parties. She told the same stories over and over, and the speaker in me—forced to find new material—found this hard to take. I would try to track where she was with her alcohol intake, so I knew when to suggest leaving, but it was getting harder. She could drink more and more without appearing drunk. She could also get much meaner on less alcohol than previously. At one point as she was holding court, I wandered over.

" . . . I was amazed by this film. Nearly paralyzed, and yet what other physicist, besides Einstein, has had his impact? And the way this really abstract stuff was made accessible—astonishing! I'm telling you people, you have to see it. It's riveting, although (sotto voce), if you can figure out how the guy ended up with two wives and three kids, let me know!"

On the way home, after she asked me whether I was okay to drive, and fell asleep with her head against the window, I told myself that if I pretended we were still dating, I would find her shameless pilfering of the Hawking story hilarious. There was a mischievous charm to it, and a reassuring, loving quality to her need to lean on me for party material. But The Drift was under way, and I was seething. Suddenly I realized she was sound asleep, and I didn't have to hold it in.

"You know what Syd, what if I wasn't okay to drive? Then what? How do we get home from anywhere we ever go?

"You know, if you choose to be bad company and sleep when we go to the movies, it's totally not cool to lecture at a party based on getting the CliffsNotes from me. And kill with a story you yawned at. Just saying.

"Funny, isn't it? Even Hawking found a way to have kids. Maybe his wives didn't drink."

Suddenly her eyes opened, and my heart stopped. Had she heard me? That would be nuclear.

"You awake, honey? Thanks for getting us home safe. Love you."

An hour later she was in her alcohol-induced coma, and I was wide awake. You are never as lonely as when you are in a marriage that is failing. I flew through the channels on the remote twice without stopping, picked up a self-help book that insisted it would only take thirty days for me to regain control of my life, put it down, and emailed Kelsey. This was a couple of years before smartphones became ubiquitous, but Kelsey was born in the age of constant connectivity. It was mildly thrilling, but not surprising, when she replied a few moments later. It was after midnight.

> "How's Dez?"
>
> "Phenom. Kind of annoying she's not reading yet, but she is only one. I should probably get her tested."
>
> "Does she sleep through the night?"
>
> "Apparently more than you do! What's up, Boss? You okay?"
>
> I summarized the night. The party. Hawking. In the recounting, it seemed stupid, and I said so. I told Kelsey I was sorry to bother her and to have a good night.

"You clearly need casual and meaningless sex. Where do you want to meet?"

"Settle down."

"Just trying to take one for the team, Boss. So let me tell you what you tell me when I come into your office blathering about a deal: 'Crystalize it for me. One sentence. Go.'"

"Sometimes I think Sydney was made for me and me alone. Other times, more often lately, I think that if I traveled the world and met all four billion women, I couldn't find one more ill-suited for me. I don't believe in sweating the small stuff, and she believes in only sweating the small stuff."

"Whoa."

Soon, when The Drift ended, before the world imploded, Sydney would find this email and others. She admitted she sat at the computer one day and put together likely passwords before she found the correct combination of my birthday and my first dog's name. (How thrilling it must have been for her to see the Welcome on the screen as she was allowed in.) She accused me of emotional infidelity, and she was right, but by then we had crossed over to a point of no return. Emotional infidelities would soon seem an innocent and quaint notion. If we both had known what was to come, I'm sure she'd have granted me those emails and I'd have told her I didn't need to write them. But there was no stopping The Drift now.

## CHAPTER 8

# *Acceleration*

We don't want candidates getting off the phone with their headhunter and thinking, *That was a nice, pleasant conversation!* I want them getting off the phone with me and be unable to think straight for the rest of the day. I want their heads spinning. How do I do that? After they tell me they aren't moving because they have a good job, I say, "So what? Are you doing what you really want to do, or are you doing what someone else wants you to do? Or worse, are you doing what you wish you wanted to do because life would be so much simpler if you really wanted what you have?"

**From a Recruiting Seminar during The Drift**

. . .

# The Drift 2

A year into The Drift, I could never sleep on Thursday nights. If I was in a hotel room, I could at least focus on the next morning's keynote performance, but if I was home, it was horrible. I would wander the house, grab the laser pointer, and run it up and down the wall, making Gatsby stir-crazy. I would read, fast-forward my way through a yoga DVD, and take a golf club and practice the inside-to-out swing path I could never replicate when playing. Eventually I would give up and go to bed. Even though I was exhausted, my heart would pound, a low-grade panic attack would rise in my chest, my eyes would sting. I would look over at the clock. Midnight. One in the morning. When will Syd be home? Thursday nights were coed soccer nights, and they had begun to haunt me. I had predictable stages I would go through during the night.

### 9:00 p.m. to 9:59 p.m.

Okay. The game was at seven. You have your drink with the team and rant about how some idiot kicked you and there should have been a red card, blah, blah, blah. Then you get on the road. You should be home any minute.

### 10:00 p.m. to 11:59 p.m.

Jesus, I hope she's okay. She could easily fall asleep at the wheel after running around for two hours and having a couple of drinks. Please, God, don't let her get into an accident. Her safety is all that matters.

### 12:00 a.m. to 2:00 a.m.

Does she think I am a fucking idiot? What good has ever befallen a married person out after midnight? Which "soccer boy" is it? Gerry? Mike? Jamie? How dare she bring these guys around at picnics and house parties and let me make them drinks and chat them up? Well, I'll tell you one thing. No one is sleeping in this house tonight until I get some goddamn answers.

But when her car headlights lit up our bedroom's bay window at 2:00 a.m. and the garage door opened, I felt nothing but pathetic relief. She was still mine. She came home. I would pretend to be asleep as she leaned over to kiss me, her smell a mixture of alcohol and perfume. Even had she reeked of sex, I'm sure I would have been able to deny it to myself. As she turned and headed to the bathroom, I opened my eyes. The woman who left the house at 6:00 p.m. in a nylon sweat suit and Puma sneakers was in a sundress and pumps. I watched her wash her face. Was it splotchy as it often was from cardio, as it often was from alcohol, or from the aftereffects of sex? All I could think of was how she had announced there would be no sex if I didn't get up and shave, since my beard "tore up her face." I instantly conjured up Jamie's face and his constant two-day stubble.

Within a couple of minutes, her alcohol-enhanced snoring would begin, and I would sit up and simultaneously be grateful my world was intact and loathe myself for not having the fortitude to confront her. I had made my mark in the recruiting industry by asking the tough questions. I would make live calls out of phone directories on a speakerphone in front of thousands of people with no fear. I led my firm through deep recessions and never faltered. But on Thursday nights, I was an abject coward and the worst kind of hypocrite. I advocated finding the truth by day and then hid from it by night.

. . .

My only respite during The Drift was the office. My sweet spot for hiring and training headhunters was entry-level college grads. Everyone told me to stay away from that profile. "They have no business experience so they make fundamental mistakes." "They will exhaust you." But I didn't see it that way. They had energy, had just come from a culture of learning for four years, were computer savvy, and were hungry. I knew from my own experience as a twenty-two-year-old in the business that your first job and first boss were profound experiences and that, if you did make it, leaving them would be like leaving your mom on the first day of kindergarten. Young people who made it would stay loyal. And some of them, like me, were naturals at reading and influencing people. Emerson said, "Wisdom is a function, not of age, but of soul." Teaching someone new how to close a deal, and later seeing them buy their first nice car, an engagement ring, a house, was immensely satisfying, and in my childless world, I enjoyed being not just "the boss" but also a paternal figure, someone they could come to for advice. Someone who believed in them.

While I was in The Drift, my company was in the middle of a five-year run when nearly everyone we hired was twentysomething, and because they had so much in common, they bonded in a big way. They all went at it happy and hard. Hobson Associates became known as not only a super successful search firm, but also a fun place to work where the recruiters were young and a little crazy. I fed off their energy and pushed them hard. They had come aboard just as job boards like Monster and social media tools like LinkedIn rocked the industry. On the road, I heard about these innovations in their infancy, and I forced the staff to implement and adapt. They did, and the company revenues and our zeitgeist of coolness increased. We had, though not consciously, wrought and developed a culture. There were inside jokes and narratives you wouldn't share with a spouse—not because you were hiding something, but because they wouldn't get it. You had to know the backstory.

We couldn't wait to get to the office to talk to each other about what we were really thinking. We acted like a high school clique, insular and arrogant, hard to penetrate.

Sydney hated the change. She stopped wanting to go out to our company happy hours. "The girls are so mean-spirited." She warned me constantly of being held legally liable for the rampant drinking and pot smoking. I would bristle since I wasn't partaking. I sanctimoniously reminded her that, one, I wasn't going to judge their personal lives, and two, someone who drank as much as Sydney was on precarious moral ground. Then Sydney stopped socializing with the company altogether. There was no announcement. She and I didn't operate that way. She would simply say she was busy, tired, or not feeling well. She encouraged me to go, which I would later realize freed her up to be where she really wanted to be. Often, I would come home after making an appearance at a company event to find that while she was too tired to attend our function, she had managed to find the energy to go out.

I'm sure I would have confronted Sydney sooner about it if it weren't for the fact that I got such a shot of adrenaline at work. Every day I got to escape to a place where I felt valued and where I received genuine affection. I was sure Sydney still loved me, but I wasn't sure we liked each other anymore. And some Thursday nights, as I watched the clock or stared out at the stars from our spacious deck, I blamed myself. I was "on" all day, entertaining clients on the phone, doing webcasts for training clients, meeting with staff in "the situation room" (that's how they referred to my office when a deal was going down), and creating content and PowerPoints for the week's trip. Recruiters make hundreds of calls a day, and every one of us knows the feeling of walking in the door at night and having nothing left to give your family. Many were the

Thursdays I would pose the questions to Gatsby and Hadley as they lay warming themselves near the fireplace: "Did I create this? Did I drive her to this?"

The Drift gathered speed. The accelerators were in place, and they had momentum they would not easily relinquish. I told audiences that every candidate would say, "Sure, I'm always looking," but this was just reflex without accelerators that created a desire for change. Accelerators were usually unexpected and always disruptive to the structures of homeostasis to which the candidate had become accustomed. An accelerator could be a new boss, a redefined territory, a demotion or transfer to a different location that disrupted day care. Rumors of a layoff or buyout. Accelerators scared you into the action you knew full well you should already have taken.

. . .

### Accelerator #1

Soccer season had ended. Now it was almost summer. In a triumph of fear over reality, I thought without the "soccer boys" we would find our way back to each other. I had convinced myself Sydney had crossed no lines, was simply bored, and was trying to send me a message that I had ignored her and she needed more attention. I had convinced myself this was to be expected as a reaction to the fertility issues that had rocked us. So when I called home and asked her if she wanted to see a movie and get some dinner now that Thursdays were freed up, I had planned to broach revisiting in vitro or adoption. But I knew from the way she sighed I would never get the chance.

It was a sigh chastising herself for not having the sense to lay this out earlier. "I thought I'd start mountain biking. There's a club Maura told me about. I'd have to buy a bike, of course, . . . well actually, I did buy a bike. I hope that's okay. It was eleven hundred dollars." She knew me. I would instantly assure her that eleven hundred dollars was no problem rather than ask her why she suddenly wanted to mountain bike—when I biked nearly every weekend and had bought her a road bike to join me that sat idle in the garage for years. She would be biking, she explained, twice a week. Thursdays and Sundays. I told her I hadn't heard her mention Maura. Was she a new faculty colleague? No, she was a friend of Gerry's. Soccer Gerry. It turned out—and now she decided to pull the Band-Aid off the wound—her whole soccer team was in the mountain-biking club. The soccer boys were not only not going away, but they had added an additional day.

"But honey, you go to the movie, you know I fall asleep anyway. I won't be late, I don't think. I don't really know how the whole mountain-biking etiquette goes. I'm sure we'll eat something."

. . .

**Accelerator #2**

The girls in my office ate lunch together. I never joined them, but I could hear their laughter. Free-spirited and raucous, and as The Drift deepened, the sound was a siren call. One day I walked by and saw Leah, who had been with me over fifteen years at that point, showing the younger girls a stack of photos. I stood behind them and had to smile. The photo was from a volleyball game at our annual company summer bash. As with all things where a score was kept, I had to win. Were you tall? Could you serve properly? Were you willing to throw your body with reckless abandon to the ground to make a dig? Yes, fine, you're on my team. Kelsey stopped Leah in her tracks when she saw a photo of me, shot from behind, where I was leaping to spike a ball. My back was ripped with sinewy muscles; my legs were tree trunks; and my arm, outstretched to make contact, revealed a washboard of serratus anterior and intercostals. I felt a surge of pride. Kelsey had never seen me dressed in anything but a business suit.

"Wait, sister, wait just a goddamn minute! Who is that and why did you guys ever let him go?"

I stepped back. I was confused. Had Kelsey seen me and was busting my ass? Leah laughed and shook her head.

"I know, right? Guess what. That's Danny!"

"No way. Really!?"

*Oh, come on. Enough now.*

Leah proved her case by finding another photo, a face-on one of me just after the game. My hair was thick and jet black. I was completely jacked, the sweat pouring down my face, my free hand incongruously holding a beer. I still remember my measurements: 195 pounds; 6.5 percent body fat.

"Back in the day, huh?" said Karen, a tad wistfully.

Kelsey nodded her head slowly and sadly. And what she said next, almost to herself, sent me backing out of the room before I was discovered, and right to the men's room.

"I got him too late."

I secured the deadbolt in the men's room and stripped down to my underwear, putting the toilet seat cover down and piling my suit on top of it. I looked in the mirror. They were not teasing me. I was not the guy in the volleyball picture. This was at once perfectly obvious and completely shocking to me. I still worked out; I watched what I ate. I was the Spartan who wouldn't have more than one drink and never ate fried foods or dessert. I tried to sell myself that I was in far better shape at forty-five than others, but it didn't take. Why didn't someone tell me this had happened to me? Why wasn't I warned? A few nights later, as Sydney was on all fours rubbing her face into Hadley's splayed belly, I noticed how luxurious her hair looked, how lean she was, how her butt seemed higher and rounder, and told her so.

"Down fourteen pounds so far. Ten to go!"

Instead of calling her out on this classic and obvious indication of her foray into adultery, I silently declared an end to détente and to the beginning of the arms race. It was time to get an appointment with Harley.

. . .

## Accelerator #3

Smoking pot hadn't been part of my life for two decades. Every quarter, Hobson Associates had a sacred day—the Associates Dinner. David Mamet said, "Coffee is for closers," and in our world, "Dinner was for top-producing recruiters." The top producer of the quarter picked a swanky restaurant. All expenses were on the company, which meant a lot in our culture. Everyone dressed to the nines, designated drivers were assigned, drugs were purchased, and plans were made for going out after the dinner. My attendance was mandatory to pay for the dinner, heap well-earned praise on the contributors who'd qualified, and signal the beginning of the real night. When I said congrats and good night, the fun started. Strip clubs, dance clubs — I really didn't want to know. The stories — cleaned up to avoid me freaking out — were always retold the next day, when people would come in late, often sick, occasionally still drunk, and always exhausted. Late in the day of one such planned evening, I ran headlong into one of our rookies as I came out of the cafeteria. Hot coffee exploded all over both of us, and the resulting stains to my just-dry-cleaned white shirt meant I had to stop home to change before heading to the dinner. People were just beginning to text at the time, but Syd didn't even have a smartphone yet, and I wouldn't have called her anyway since she was coming home later and later with weaker and weaker excuses almost every night and I was in full denial. I saw a car I didn't recognize in the driveway, and even though I thought I had memorized all the soccer boy's cars, I didn't know for sure. I looked in as I passed by and saw an ashtray balanced in the center console between the stick shift and a coffee cup. In the ashtray was a joint held by a clip. I opened the door to the house and the smell of pot was overwhelming. I rushed inside and up the stairs. I could hear faint voices in the den. I stood outside the door and recognized the laughter.

Pot-smoking laughter. Leftover laughter from moments before. I opened the door and all but yelled, "Gotcha!" There was Sydney and a girl who was probably twenty. Since turning forty, I had lost my "age gauge," and everyone under thirty looked twelve. Between them sat a laptop and a pile of printouts. The girl introduced herself. She was the daughter of one of Syd's friends, getting some help writing a college admittance essay. When I changed shirts and headed out, Syd walked me to my car. She said the look on my face when I opened the door was pretty obvious, and she owed me an apology. I had no idea what she was talking about.

"She's not *my* student. She's *a* student. But that doesn't make it okay that I was drinking wine during the day, even at my own home. As soon as I saw you looking at that wineglass, I felt horrible. I'm sorry, I should know better. School is school, work is work."

"Right. Right. That's all I'm saying. You have to separate. People get the wrong idea."

. . .

The seating chart was critical at the Associates Dinners. You wanted to sit next to the funny people. Sandy was a good choice because he always told stories of his early dating disasters. Mike was also a can't-miss because he always mispronounced basic things on the menu, and when he was asked if he wanted tap water or bottled, he would shake his head and order a shot of whiskey. If you qualified for the Associates

Dinner, you had been paid anywhere from $10,000 to $50,000 in com-missions. You came to dinner flush. Arthur Ashe once wrote about his early days on the tennis pro circuit, "We were young, and making great money, and playing a game for a living, and the world is none of those things." My recruiters were characters who weren't in touch with the concept of "later." They were going to eat and drink and ingest recre-ational drugs tonight and deal with the headaches and clenched jaws and stomach issues in the morning. Being incapable of such behavior, I admired it.

Kelsey always sat next to me. She didn't even have to jostle for position—everyone assumed it was her place. I found myself loosen-ing up, as I nursed my obligatory one glass of wine. Loosening up didn't mean that I told stories about myself. It was more that, as those evenings became more informal as the night wore on, I asked ques-tions I couldn't ask in a business environment. How did young moms know when a child's cry meant they were hungry versus they were hurt? What did it feel like as a parent to hear your son's voice change with puberty? How much sex do young people have? Why do I not get hip-hop? These evenings were illuminating, edifying, raucous, and funny. I wondered if this was the release Sydney sought when the soc-cer/mountain biking was over and everyone sat around drinking and ordering appetizers. Did she speak of me as I often did of her? Did I have a nickname like she did? At most Associates Dinners, after I rolled out an anecdote, someone would make a toast, in absentia, to Saint Sydney. At one point, someone asked if we were still trying to conceive, and as I reflexively deflected the question and changed the subject, Kelsey, for the first time ever, put her hand on my thigh. She leaned over and whispered, "You okay?"

An hour later, I wished everyone a good night, told them to behave, and for God's sake don't drive drunk. I headed out. Kelsey, out of nowhere, said she was tired and could I give her a ride to her car back at the office? This stunned the table. Kelsey was their go-to party girl. The night had been planned for months, and it was only 10:00 p.m.! Then I felt it: their looks of judgment. There had always been rumors about Kelsey and me. We had an undeniable chemistry, and I spent a lot of time with her at the office because she had the most sales activity and was the most ambitious and successful recruiter I had. She was a prodigy; no one could deny that. The people who had been with me for over a decade would dismiss the gossip and assure the rumormongers that the boss would never do such a thing. But for those who believed there was more to it, the idea of us leaving an Associates Dinner together lent credence to the existence of a potential scandal.

In the car on the ride to the office, Kelsey took the empty Diet Dr Pepper can in my center console and announced proudly, "I have two great skills. One is oral sex, but you are my boss and, more to the point, driving at eighty miles an hour; the other is that I can make a pipe out of anything. May I? Don't worry about Syd smelling it, we'll roll down the windows."

I thought about the scene I had left a few hours earlier in my den and told Kelsey she could do as she liked, as long as she could drive home. After punching a hole in the can and trying out some other improv moves that were clearly annoying her, she threw the can out the window and began to dig her way through her seemingly bottomless Coach purse. She exclaimed, "Yes!" and I found the strength to refrain from telling her she sounded like Marv Albert because I hated it when she didn't get my cultural references. She pulled out the Zig-Zag papers she had found and began rolling the joint.

"It's tragic there's no money in doing this. I am fantastic at it."

"I'm pretty sure there not only is money in it, but that the cartel's hiring standards are less than stringent."

She took a hit and handed it to me, but nothing had changed since my hapless high school days. I was trying to watch the road and reach for the joint, and I at first touched the lit end and recoiled. Then, I managed to hold on but took a hit that was so weak and ineffective that when I exhaled nothing came out of my mouth. Kelsey laughed, then somberly put her hands in prayer position and imitated a Zen master's voice.

"And the student becomes the teacher! Don't worry, Boss, I got you."

She took a massive hit, her chest expanding. Then she tapped me on the shoulder, and I turned to her. She leaned in and kissed me, pushing my mouth open with her tongue, and then blew the smoke into my mouth.

"That's called a shotgun."

"I can think of another word."

"Did it work?"

"Define 'work.'"

We laughed. We were nearly at the office, and we didn't repeat it. It was a one-off. Nothing to report. Nothing to see here, folks. Everyone go home. I felt the buzz of the pot and the taste of her mouth. I quickly did the math. Cheeks aside, I hadn't kissed anyone but Sydney in a dozen years. But this wasn't a kiss. Was it?

I once asked Kelsey, during one of our many chats in my office, how her husband could be so gullible. How did she get away with the number of nights she got home late or didn't come home at all? I knew she had her "wingmen" on my staff. People who would cover for her and say she was with them. I knew that having a cell phone as her only phone kept her husband from calling the house or hotel or bar she was claiming to be at. But still, after a while, wasn't it obvious?

"His need to believe helps, but I'm that good. No one lies like me!"

Back then, her candor about her lack of integrity and shame seemed oddly brave and part of her charm. But just before she got out of my car, she showed me that, like all master criminals, even she could get sloppy. Her eyes darted to the rearview mirror, and I thought I saw a flash of headlights. An on-then-off sort of flash from among the rows of cars in the parking lot. She seemed eager to leave after that. She leaned over and gave me an appropriately detached "boss hug," made a joke about how her husband was probably going to be busted with porn when she came home this early, and walked to her car. She pulled away and some instinct told me to circle around past the area where I had seen the lights flash. Among my recruiters cars I recognized Evan's Jeep, but he was still with the gang at the restaurant. His car seemed to be the one where the light was coming from, but I was clearly wrong. I got on the highway and was about ten minutes up the road when I turned around. My instinct—perhaps fueled by the paranoia pot always enhanced in me from the time I was a young devotee—had kicked in, and I drove back to the office. I stayed far enough back as I pulled into the driveway so I could see the office foyer but still be blocked from view by the side of the building.

Evan's car had been moved to the front spot near the door, and Kelsey's was beside it. The lights inside the office were turned on. A planned rendezvous? I told myself this was nothing of note; Evan was a known scoundrel in our office. He was a handsome young man I loved like a little brother. We often worked out together, and he was completely open about the steroid cycles that he did every summer that took him in no time from a guy in decent shape to an Adonis. He said he would stop when he got married and wanted kids. They were young, experimenting, and making bad choices. It had nothing to do with me. Who was I to judge? So why did I feel flashes of rage? Was it because they were having an inappropriate interoffice affair and using my building? Nice try, but no. I could see why it was convenient and useful. We had couches and a shower. The largest couch was in my private office. I had absolutely no desire to interrupt them. I wiped my mouth, thinking of the makeshift kiss, and drove home. What kind of person would find a creative way to kiss me all the while having a preplanned hookup? Why doesn't anybody tell me what they really want? Sydney was sound asleep in our overstuffed chair in the den, with a blanket around her and Gatsby in a coma on her lap. An emptied package of hot dogs, the crumbs from a sleeve of Oreos, and the omnipresent bottle of Chardonnay were on the kitchen counter.

The next morning, I sat out on our deck with my coffee. It wasn't a beautiful morning. It was my way of signaling to Sydney to leave me alone. When she opened the sliders, careful not to let our Maine Coons outside, came over, and sat on the chaise lounge, I could tell she didn't want to fight either.

"Honey, I'm going through something. I know you know that. I'm going to see Selma about a change in the dosage on my Lexapro and to talk through some stuff. I need you to bear with me, okay?"

I hugged her. Hard. Maybe that way she wouldn't sense my flagrant hypocrisy.

"Can you put, 'Don't stop loving Sydney' in your Franklin Covey planner, please?"

. . .

Kelsey had told me she was good. I was about to find out how good. Maybe she could feel something was amiss when she saw me at the morning staff meeting, or she made a guess, or I hadn't been as clandestine as I'd thought and they had seen my car. She stopped in my office during prime phone-calling time. This was a no-no in my office. Talk later. Make cold calls now.

"Got a minute, DC?"

"Kelsey, if it's about a deal, I have all day. Because that is what I'm here for, what you're here for—what, in fact, this very building is here for, closing deals. So we can all pay our bills . . . "

"Uh, and in other breaking news, women can now vote."

"But if you want to have another heartfelt discussion about how you don't love your husband, or how awful you feel about another meaningless sexual liaison, I kinda think you need some new material, or at least someone new to tell it to."

"Okay, whoa! Oh, I get it. I freaked you out in the car last night. Look, it's completely cool."

"The car? No, that was nothing. Anyway, do we have a business reason why you're in here during prime calling time?"

"Absolutely not. I'll get back to work. This was strictly personal and kind of massive to me, but never mind. I thought we had some level of bond that we obviously do not."

"No dramatic exit, please. I swear to God I don't know why they call it management when it's really just babysitting. I'm sorry. If you have a personal issue that is really bothering you, of course I'd like to help you. Sit! Thanks. Now give."

"I took seriously your lecture about not fraternizing with clients, about how complicated it could make the business relationships. So I have now branched out to people in our office."

"I'm not sure you quite understood the gist of my reasoning behind that particular monologue."

"Evan and I had planned to hook up last night after the dinner. We've sort of been moving in that direction, and so last night we decided to meet here. I drove back after you let me off."

"So you want me to know you and Evan are now seeing each other? Is that what this is?"

"Oh God, no, it was a hookup. Or would have been. I wanted you to know I bailed on it. I couldn't go through with it. He was pretty pissed. I don't blame him. He could have stayed out with the crew."

"I don't get it. You couldn't go through with it because you realized someone you worked with was too close for comfort?"

"No. I could have gotten past that, sad to say. No. I bailed because of you. Because of the moment in the car. The way it felt. The way you looked at me. I don't know. It's not about you. I'm not trying to bring you into it. I just needed you to know. I'm not looking for a response. I'm going back to my desk."

I gave myself some time after she left my office. And I thought, as she wanted me to, of how much she must care for me to have denied her own drunken impulses and Evan's unpleasant insistence. Evan! She preferred me over Evan! A young man in his prime! But none of it rang true. The same gift that enabled me to work an audience or close a recalcitrant candidate was often a curse when I wanted to believe someone's utter crap. I waited until lunch and hung back while others used the microwave and fetched their lunches from the fridge. Evan walked in and started adding his whey protein to the muscle-building shake he had like clockwork every day. I told him to step into my office and closed the door behind him. Now he was concerned. I had an open-door policy. I was known as a good decision maker. That didn't mean I always made good decisions, but I was good at making them. Everyone who came into my office with a problem left with a solution.

So this was a novel experience for me. "The owner of our cleaning service called me this morning. He's not happy."

"I don't get it."

"You know, I didn't even know they cleaned at night. I should have—my basket is always empty in the morning. But last night he had a woman on duty, cleaning very late. She heard some noises, kind of unmistakable . . . "

"Oh shit."

"I know, right? She was disturbed and wanted me to know she thought it was creating a hostile work environment for her to have to see what she saw. So, yeah."

"Fuck, I'm sorry. For the record, I told Kelsey I was totally cool with driving to my place. But you know, it just made sense at the time to stay here."

Hearing her name made my stomach sink. I told him I would smooth it over with the owner of the cleaning service but to kindly refrain from a repeat performance. He nodded. Then, pathetic though it was, I tried one last time to give Kelsey the benefit of the doubt, to attribute his acknowledgment to immature bragging to the boss. I laughed and smacked him playfully on the cheek, dying to hit him harder.

"Buddy, you are so easy to mess with. There was no cleaning lady. I made it up. I was playing a hunch. You two have been so obvious lately. You are so busted. So if it didn't happen, you can spare me the swagger act."

"What? Wow, Boss. See, that is why you run the place. That sixth sense. No, I totally fucked her. It's not a challenge to tap that when she's drunk. Word to the wise, Chief."

I had created the moment and had to stay in character, but I wanted to tell him to stay away from her. She had a family, a child. She was not his.

. . .

**Accelerator #4**

With about fifteen minutes left in my keynote, in full command of the audience and building toward my showy ending story that always brought the house down, I felt the urge to urinate. No worries, right? I routinely made the drive from my house to New York City and never needed a rest stop. I was a camel. I could play three hours of tennis without going to the bathroom. Up until now. I started to feel the buildup I only associated with my college days of drinking beer. A powerful urgency. I was working so hard to quell the need to relieve myself that I started to sweat. Then it became clear my worst fear was about to be realized. I would wet myself in front of three hundred people. I briefly thought of standing behind the podium and trying to urinate into one of the many water bottles I kept out of view. This was absurd, of course. I had no choice. I announced I was sorry, but I was having a stomach issue and needed a brief moment. I ran off the stage, barely making it to the bathroom. When I finished, I looked down and saw a urine stain on my trousers. I stood on the trash can so that my groin was high enough to blast the hands-free dryer on the spot and returned to the stage. I had always taken solace in the fact that, at least on stage, I had outrun shame and it would never factor in that part of my life.

But I was wrong. I saw a urologist two days later. He asked me some questions, gave me a prostate exam, and then asked me if I had noticed that I was waking with rigid erections less and less frequently. It was the first time I had thought of it, and yes—they had dropped off considerably. He looked at my recent physical's blood tests and told me my PSA level was fine. "So what's the deal?"

"The deal is welcome to middle age. Stop drinking a lot of water before you speak and absolutely no caffeine, especially diet soda."

"Can't I reverse it? Aren't there drugs?"

"Yep, good ones. And they have side effects. Right now you don't get an erection in the morning—on the drugs you won't get one, period. Look. Relax. This is good news. You don't have any disease. You're just aging. There are worse things."

Are there? I loved caffeine. And erections. Was this what was in store for me? The gradual taking away of the things that you took for granted, the things that made you who you were?

. . .

### Accelerator #5

Sydney had just walked in from her weekly therapy session with Selma. Gatsby and Hadley always ran to her when she came in, and she always, without fail, would exclaim, "Mommy's home!" and pick them both up. Tonight she ignored them, stood in front of me, and murmured, "Selma says you have to get rid of the gun."

The gun was a running joke with our friends and us. We got it because I traveled so much and I wanted Syd to feel safe and be able to protect herself. Our house was literally in the middle of a nature preserve, at the end of a cul-de-sac. My most senior employee, Victor, was the president of the local gun club, and he was an outlier in the ultrablue state of Connecticut. He was always packing. When I asked him for help, he sold me a .38-caliber Smith & Wesson snub-nosed revolver and refused to hand it over until I promised to go to a Saturday morning class for training. (I never went—decided I had seen enough movies.) I brought it home, and it scared the hell out of both Sydney and me. We opted to keep the unloaded gun in our bedside table but to keep the ammunition in the hall closet. I pointed out to Sydney that this may not be optimal, that I doubted an assailant would allow us to call time-out and go get our ammunition. But she was adamant. She had read too much about people who owned guns ending up being killed.

By now I had forgotten we even had the gun. But I was stuck. The rule about her sessions with Selma was simple: I had no right to ask what they talked about. Therapy was personal. I understood this intellectually, but often, since her behavior directly affected my life, it was hard not to inquire. Since Selma had put Syd on antidepressants, things were so much better. I had a lot of faith in Selma. But as The Drift deepened, I began to question what kind of advice she was giving Sydney.

"Get rid of the gun. Sure. Are you okay?"

"I'm not trying to scare you—I'm not going to hurt myself. But you need to get rid of the gun. Tomorrow."

The next day I brought the ammunition and the revolver into the office. I gave Victor a flimsy excuse about seeing Charlton Heston on TV ranting about the NRA and I just couldn't be a hypocrite anymore.

That night it hit me. Sydney was emphatic that she wasn't going to hurt herself. So why did we need to get rid of the gun? Perhaps she was not the one in danger. Maybe she was afraid the person she was going to shoot was me.

. . .

### Accelerator #6

Kelsey emailed me that she needed me to clear the Situation Room. This meant a deal was hanging in the balance, and she needed my help. She often got companies to give her their executive searches because she charmed them. She had no qualms about flirting with the company reps or the candidates if they were male (and they usually were). With candidates, she'd get too close. Too buddy-buddy. I had told her this works on the front end but can cause problems later in the placement process when it's time to close the deal. When Kelsey tried to get tough at closing time, the candidates or clients often felt betrayed or manipulated. This would make Kelsey feel guilty, and she would back off just when she needed to hang tough, often losing the deal. In these cases, I would take over. These closing calls were how I made a name for myself as a young recruiter. I tried to teach my people to detach from their clientele. Friendly and warm and enthusiastic and empathic to be sure, but friends? Nope. Get a dog.

Kelsey brought me up to speed on the situation. The candidate was unemployed, had previously been making $200,000, but our offer was only $180,000. It irked him tremendously that he would be taking a step back, said he had another offer for $225,000, and told Kelsey she had to get the new company to match his other offer or he would turn it down. Kelsey called our client, and they declined to change the offer. I dialed the number and punched the speakerphone, signaling Kelsey to stay quiet and slip me notes if necessary. It was Go Time. Our fee was $60,000 dollars; fifty percent of that was Kelsey's commission. Enough to pay her mortgage for a year. Just as the candidate picked up, Kelsey slipped a note to me saying she might puke. I pushed my wastebasket toward her with my foot. I loved these calls.

"Jeff, Danny Cahill, Kelsey's boss at Hobson. I'm meddling, to be blunt. I've seen this scenario a hundred times, and I called to tell you this dog won't hunt."

"Excuse me? What's that supposed to imply?"

"You're going to blow this, Jeff. You're playing with fire. You don't have another offer. I know it and you know it."

"What?! Are you calling me a liar?"

"Not at all. I'd call it a calculated risk. More like a bluff, only not as clever. Did you know we have a backup candidate and the company was torn between which one to choose; that they were concerned you might have lost your edge since you've been unemployed for seven months?"

"There's no other candidate. Kelsey would have told me. That's bullshit. I'm calling Kelsey."

"I took this over for Kelsey, and this is the fun part of being the owner. I make the rules."

"How do you know I don't have any other offer?"

"Because if you did, you would have taken it, and been a coward, and emailed Kelsey that you turned down our job. Look, I get it. You worked hard to get to the 200K level. It's a psychological threshold. But if you turn this down, you'll be unemployed even longer. Say three months . . . three more months of you living off savings. Stepping over dollars to get to dimes."

"Look . . . you don't have the right to call me in the middle of this . . . who the hell do you think . . . "

"It is now 9:00 a.m. At 9:30, I'll have Kelsey call the company and tell them to hire the backup candidate and withdraw their offer to you. Thirty minutes. You have a nice day. Jeff, for what it's worth, I completely respect what you were trying to do. Bye now."

I hung up and looked over at Kelsey. She was as white as a sheet.

"Uh, Boss Man, you know if I caught you in a bad mood this morning, or you don't feel well, maybe you should have told me and we could have put this off."

"Relax, Kay."

"Not for nothing . . . but I have a daughter to feed, some credit card craziness to do with shoes . . . I mean, I know 60K isn't much to you . . . maybe I should call him . . . "

My phone rang. I put it on speaker. Kay saw the name on the caller ID and gasped. I love this business.

"Fine. Tell them yes. I'll take it at $180,000. I don't appreciate how you did this, but I get your point. It's not personal you know. I wasn't trying to play them. That's not who I am."

"Jeff, I get it. And you will make 200K, and soon. By getting in there and being as awesome as Kelsey and the client say you are. You're doing the right thing. I've heard nothing but good things about you. Sign the offer letter and send it back and let's put this behind you."

"Thanks for your help, Danny."

"Congrats, Kelsey."

"I don't get it. You bitch-slapped him and he said thanks!"

"It's called the Take It Away close. Learn it and use it. Now go celebrate. I've got things to do."

"Can I just say I'm not sure I've ever seen a man do anything hotter than that? I'm soaked. Is that too much information? Thanks, DC."

. . .

**Accelerator #7**

Sydney left a message on my corporate voice mail during lunch that she thought it would be nice to meet at Chili's after work. She knew she wouldn't get me live. She knew my schedule and that I lifted weights before work and did cardio at lunch. Maybe it was because I had several enervating interviews that day; maybe it was the overtly cheerful tone in her voice; or the casual choice of restaurant. What happens of import in a Chili's? For whatever reason, my guard was down.

"I know it is supposed to be uberconvenient, but it annoys me that the menus stay at the table here. You know why? Because out of habit, after I'm done ordering I try to hand them back to the waitress, who doesn't want to take them, because they stay at the table, and there is this weird, strained moment . . . "

"You don't need the menu. You always order off the Guiltless Grill. Always."

"Well it's a great concept, tying some defective emotion to food. Bring on the Jealousy-Free Jambalaya. In fact, I might open the All-You-Can-Eat Shameless Sushi Bar."

"I'm not sure I want to be married anymore."

Luckily for me, I knew what a panic attack felt like so I knew I wasn't having a heart attack. I smiled at Sydney as if I were expecting this. You can leave me. You can hurt me. You will not shock me.

"This about one of the soccer boys? If it is, I'd recommend the Guilt-less Grill."

"Absolutely not, and I'd appreciate you not going there again. They are friends. Period. I'm talking conceptually here. We used to be able to do that. Marriage was created to promulgate the family structure. That's its purpose. We don't have that purpose in common."

"Well, there is that pesky idea of loving each other forever. I seem to recall some vows to that effect."

"Children allow you to reprioritize, and you express love through them. With no children, you put this absurd pressure on each other. No one person fulfills all of another person's needs indefinitely."

"So what are you, 'conceptually,' suggesting? You spend your whole life in a series of relationships that are all front-loaded? You stay with the person until the intoxication wears off and then move on?"

"Exactly! Why not?"

"Because you get old."

"Well. I'm not old yet."

She turned away. She suddenly brightened and waved to a woman she recognized who was putting her name in with the hostess. And something about her phony smile, masking her suffering, took me back. I was nine years old. My mother ushered us all into our tiny living room and said she and my father needed to speak to us. My father signaled for her to speak, but she stared at him, and then he smiled Syd's sad, phony smile. He was on his own.

"The important thing we both want to say, is that even though your mother and I will always love each other very much . . ."

He couldn't continue. She wouldn't bail him out. So I did.

"You're getting divorced."

My two sisters started crying immediately. This started my mother crying. My father shrugged his shoulders haplessly. This has always been my problem as a salesperson. It is hard to stay patient and let the other person finish when I already know what they are going to say and how I am going to respond to overcome their objection.

"We decided it would be better if I moved out. Yes."

My older sister said that made no sense. "Families don't live apart. You just said you love each other."

"She doesn't get it, Dad."

"But you do." He almost seemed amused.

"I have some questions. How will we pay the bills?"

"I'll still pay the bills. I'm going to try to get a second job part-time. Nothing will change."

"Uh-huh. And where will you be?"

"An apartment on Oak Avenue. Right in town. You could walk there."

"I don't think I'll be doing that."

"Okay."

My little sister ran wailing out of the room. My older sister glared at my mom, who she clearly decided to blame, and ran after my little sister. I walked up to my father and proffered a formal handshake.

"You have to do what will make you happy. I'll take care of them. Don't worry. I wish you all the best."

My father ignored my hand and lifted me up to hug me. His body shook, and I could feel his warm, wet tears running down my neck. (You can leave me. You can hurt me. You will not shock me.)

Time passed. Nothing happened. It was weeks before my teeth didn't clench every time one of them cleared their throats. Most of me was glad our abject little world stayed intact. But part of me lost respect for them. They gave up on their happiness.

. . .

We left Chili's in separate cars. I had to go home and pack for a morning flight to Houston. Sydney said it might be best if she gave me some space and met her friend Aggie for a drink. Two hours later she called me.

"I'm sorry. I rolled that out all wrong. I don't want to lose you."

"What *do* you want? And perhaps more importantly, what is all this brown wrapping in our freezer?"

"Oh. It's venison. Jamie went hunting and came back with more than he could eat so he wanted us to have it. I couldn't say no. That would be offensive to a hunter."

"I thought hunting was offensive to us, but okay. So honestly I don't know if I'm packing for a two-day business trip or forever. It's a tad disconcerting and really will affect the amount of laundry I do."

"I think we need to see someone. I think we're in trouble. I could get a referral from Selma. Would you at least think about it? Please?"

I assured her I would. I didn't know what else to say. There was a pause, and I could hear people laughing in the background. She said she and Aggie were getting a bite to eat, but some big game was on and people were acting up. I almost asked her to put Aggie on the phone. But I didn't want to be that guy. So instead I hung up, folded some shirts and socks, and texted Kelsey. Just to say hi.

I *was* that guy.

## CHAPTER 9

# The Rush

If you really want to be a great recruiter, stop agreeing with things that you know are not true! If a client wants someone with ten years' experience, but wants to pay entry-level money, you don't say, "I'll see what I can do"; you say, "It's not happening." Great recruiters are not pacifists! Stop agreeing with things that aren't true just to make people happy or to avoid conflict. Because it accomplishes neither.

**From Danny's "Dealing with Difficult People" Workshop**

. . .

"Good Lord," Harley Derringer said to me when I took my coat off.

I considered this a personal triumph. Harley was a bit of a Jesus freak.

My doctors had cleared me to work half days, and if I took half a Vicodin and drank enough caffeine to offset the narcotic, I could even drive to work and stay awake the entire morning. I couldn't sit in a chair, but I could pile up the cushions from my office sofa and kneel on them to keep the pressure off my back. I refused to use the walker my doctor recommended, so I moved slowly and listed dramatically to my right side. I would stand for staff meetings, and without warning, if I moved the wrong way, a spasm would shoot through my lower back and hips. I'd involuntarily expel air and shudder in a way that scared people. My staff would look away. Leah came in one day, sat opposite me, and stared. I shrugged, "What?"

"I know you think you're inspiring people. I know the message you mean to send is you are committed and tough. But that's not the message we get. We're sad for you. Please go home."

She was right that I was feeling tremendous guilt about not being in the office every day. What I didn't tell her was that I didn't know what else to do with my time. I had worked for years to get to a place of which every entrepreneur dreams—my business ran at a high level without me. Now work was abandoning me too.

Harley Derringer was a character. Two decades removed from his days as an amateur bodybuilding champion, he parlayed his knowledge of nutrition and the science of fat loss into "Lean for Life." Older than I was by several years, he was still outrageously muscular, though his skin reminded me of wax melting off candles in that odd way of middle-aged bodybuilders. Despite a bout with skin cancer, he tanned every day, and on the days he overdid it, he was Cheetos orange. All bodybuilders shave their bodies, but Harley shaved his head too, and when he crossed his arms for the picture on his business cards and website, he could have been auditioning for a Mr. Clean commercial. Harley was so obsessed with being muscular and lean that his dysmorphia made me seem normal and ambivalent by comparison.

He pulled no punches. He was infamous for telling women that they were not big boned but fat. I hadn't seen him since my accident at the gym, and when I started to explain my situation and diagnosis, he pointed dismissively to the scale. He was disgusted with me. Then he broke out the calipers and measured my body fat with the same procedure we had now used every three weeks for four years: my triceps, my upper back, my obliques, and my stomach. He pinched hard, hit the button that calculated the number, and wrote it down on my chart. He rubbed his eyes in a world-weary way that seemed out of proportion to the matter at hand. I would have laughed if it had been someone else's body.

"The last time we met you measured at 189 pounds and 8.9 percent body fat. Now you are 167 pounds and 11.8 percent body fat. You have lost twenty pounds of muscle! You are smaller, and you are fatter. What a disaster!"

You might think I had the right to get upset. I had a fractured spine! The narcotics ruin your appetite. And I couldn't work out. I often went into spasm holding the coffeepot up or stepping out of the shower—how could I lift weights?

But I wasn't upset. It's why I was here. Harley was singled-minded. He never asked me about work or love or life. He told me he had one thing to offer me: He knew how to remove fat from my body while maintaining muscle mass. He was a Christian minister of some sort, and with others he often tried to use his faith as a means of motivating people to change their eating habits. He tried it once early on with me.

"Jesus wants you to be lean."

"I must have missed that commandment. I really doubt he is that much of a micromanager, Harley. What say we stick to macronutrients and leave Jesus out of this?!"

And that was that. He never brought it up again. But as he sat there wondering what to do with my puny, pallid self, I realized I was here as a matter of faith. I did need to believe there was a way back, and not just from the accident. Harley sighed.

"I'm going to pray for you."

And this time I didn't scoff. I wasn't offended. I would take all the help I could get. I simply thanked him.

"It'll be like starting over. Like that day we first met, and you showed me the pictures."

. . .

Previously, before I had even made my very first appointment with Harley, I took a very unscientific survey. Meniscus tears had taken Steve off the bike; rotary cuff soreness kept Lennie from renewing his gym membership; and the pecs he once displayed in deep V-neck tee shirts were now man boobs. The increasing demands of growing families meant Mark and Jeb hadn't restrung their tennis racquets in years. They had all gotten softer, and I should have remembered my Oscar Wilde when I called them and told them I was considering committing to a hardcore nutritional and training regimen that would return me to my old level of fitness. ("It is not enough for me to succeed; others must fail, others must die.")

"Why would you do that? You're in the upper . . . like fifth percentile now!"

"Can't be done, dude, hormones and gravity. That ship has sailed."

"We were in shape to get women, Danny, we have our women. What is the point?"

Since I wasn't getting the answer I wanted, I discounted their opinions and asked others. I don't know if I asked Sydney because I was trying to send her a message—"Don't leave me for a younger man, I'll get in better shape than him"—or if I just wanted her to tell me, "Stop, let's both stop. This is crazy." I'm still not sure, but her answer was succinct, and her sigh was piercing, almost a whistle.

"You have always had body issues."

Ah, but then there was Kelsey, who didn't sigh, who was not exasperated, and who didn't shake her head and tell me the midlife crisis coming my way was transparent and tragic. She listened carefully, even folded her hands to mark the seriousness of her concentration. I took a copy of the latest *Men's Health* magazine, handed it over to her, and said I wanted to look like the cover model, a man who couldn't have been more than twenty-five. She looked at it as if reading a mortgage commitment letter, then decisively put it down on my desk.

"Feel free. The sooner the better."

So I went to see Harley, and after he weighed and calipered me for the first time, he said the words I hated more than any others. Words that I had constructed my life to avoid and that I thought I would never have to hear.

"You're an average guy."

At 5'11" and forty-two years old I was 190 pounds and 18 percent body fat. I had more muscle than most men because of my gym routine, but I had grown soft, especially around the belly. And while years before, with my cycling and heavy squatting and tennis, I would often have people look at my legs and ask me if I was a professional dancer — a question I never got after actually dancing — my butt had flattened and creased. Harley asked me what my goals were. Although I was afraid I'd get laughed out of his office, I produced the volleyball pictures Leah had shown the staff and handed them to him.

"I want to be that guy again."

Harley reviewed the photos as if he were a judge and they had been entered into state's evidence. Then he looked me in the eyes. Obsessive nut to obsessive nut, man to man.

"We can absolutely do that."

And I felt it. The Rush. It had been a long time. The Rush can be dormant from time to time, but it never leaves you if you have true drive. You feel it when you know you are about to embark on something so difficult that it will require every ounce of energy you have. People with ambition get glimpses of it, but it fades on them. It never leaves the driven. I was in my first year of recruiting, in a straight-commission job, when I could barely scrape together the gas money to get to the office, and my father questioned if taking on student loans and going to college to get a degree so that I could take a job that didn't technically pay anything was a smart choice. I felt The Rush every day. My first call each morning was to a CEO of a large company. If you called before eight, their secretaries were often not in, and in the pre–voice mail era, they would pick up. Connecticut is a state dominated by the aircraft titan United Technologies, and one day I got the CEO of one of their divisions to pick up on a cold call. I motioned to my boss, John Hobson, and he sat next to my desk and listened in. After I fumbled through my intro, the CEO cut to the chase and said my timing was good; they needed a VP of Engineering. Could I handle the search for them? I told him I absolutely could, and I wrote a note to John and passed it to him. He blanched. The fee would easily be the biggest we had ever landed. Then the CEO asked me if I could send him references of other searches I had done that were similar. I was busted. But I could feel The Rush coursing through me.

"I can't do that. You know why? I've been here all of five minutes. A complete rookie. I not only have not done a similar search, I've never done anything like one. And that, if I may say, sir, is exactly why you should give it to me."

"Sorry son, you don't lack for chutzpah, I'll give you that. But I know several headhunters who have specialized in this for years, so why would I give a mission-critical position to a rookie?"

"For two reasons, sir. One, because you can give it to them and get five percent of the time of someone who is no doubt more experienced than I am, but not necessarily better, or you could get one hundred percent of my time, since you will be my only client. What I lack in polish, I will make up for in passion."

"What's the second reason?"

"Because you never forget your first. If you give this search to me, I'll be telling this story years from now."

He laughed and told me to be at his office the next morning at ten. After I got off the phone, John said he wanted to see me in private. Once in his office, he told me that it wouldn't be easy and wouldn't matter at all if I didn't work hard because talent was cheap, but that I had something he had never seen before and he hoped to nurture it. Then he told me not to get a big head and to get out of his office.

. . .

"It won't be easy," said Harley, "and you'll have to work harder than most, because of your genetics."

If you want to have a great physique, it helps tremendously if you have the right body type. Harley showed me a chart with three distinct types: mesomorph, endomorph, and ectomorph.

Mesomorph is the one you want. Rectangular-shaped body, small joints, with naturally well-developed muscles, metabolizes food effi-ciently, can tolerate carbs better than most, responds to weight training quickly, adds muscle and loses fat easily. These are those annoying guys who can eat anything, go to the gym, work out half as long and hard as you, and look way better. Unfair.

Endomorph guys are so predisposed to fat they end up pear shaped. Soft bodies, round, trouble gaining muscle, but fat comes on with no problem. This is the guy who, past a certain age, get folds over his geni-talia and whose stomach is so distended that when you see him in the gym heading to the shower you obsess over the visual of how he has sex. Is his penis as small as it looks, or is it a proportional issue because it's buried in so much adipose tissue? Then you realize you've been staring for way too long at another man's penis.

Ectomorphs are stick men. Meth-addict thin their whole lives. Flat chest, delicate build, stoop-shouldered, and when you see them from behind, you wonder if they actually left their ass at home.

I knew what was coming when Harley exited out to his screensaver— a twenty-year-old picture of him all oiled up on a bodybuilding stage holding a trophy. But I couldn't help picturing my dad's bulging belly and my brother's narrow shoulders and knobby knees.

"You are a rare and unfortunate combination of ecto and endo. Your body wants to be thin, but you are also 'skinny fat' due to your diet. So it is very, very hard for your body type to make muscle."

"But I had that body once, and for a long time."

"You were a lot younger then. The hormones drop, the metabolism slows. I'm not saying it can't be done. I'm saying it's a real challenge, and you have to be sure it makes sense for you."

The Rush doesn't have to make sense.

After my first play closed in New York City, I started to get offers to write for other theatres. There was no money to be made in professional theatre at that level, but you hoped someone would "discover" you and your play, or Mel Gussow or Frank Rich of the *New York Times* would write such a wonderful review that you would get asked to write for film or TV, or your play would be done at a big Broadway house. Actors did off- and off-off- Broadway for next to nothing hoping they would get parts in bigger, more lucrative gigs. Meanwhile, we rehearsed at night, worked our day jobs, and all for a four-week run—or shorter if we were part of a festival. But my day job was two hours away. I didn't want to give up the chance to write for the theatre, and I didn't want to halt the headhunting trajectory of stardom I was enjoying. So I did both and kept each life secret from the other. At one point, I was asked to write sketches for a CBS comedy revue show meant to challenge *Saturday Night Live*. I'd leave the office at five, drive or take the train into New York City, rehearse or write sketches until midnight, then drive home, sleep for three hours, and do it all again. At one point, I was simultaneously rehearsing a play downtown and going to the TV studio uptown. Soon I was in the city every night and realized it made more sense to go to the office instead of driving all the way home. I'd sleep on the floor and go to the YMCA in the morning to shower before people came in for the workday. I pulled this off for months. I let the theatre people think I was just another young starving playwright, and I never told the people in my office where I went every night at five for fear of being considered less than serious about the business. John Hobson had made it clear he was looking for an heir apparent, and I didn't want my artistic aspirations to ruin my chances.

I wanted it all, and The Rush assured me every day it was my right. It never occurred to me that (once again) I was ashamed of people knowing who I really was and how I really lived. One morning, after getting in later than normal due to a temperamental director and an accident on the Merritt Parkway, I awoke to John Hobson shaking me as I lay on the floor in our conference room. When I confessed to him what I had been doing, he shook his head more in admiration than anger. He asked how long I thought I could keep up such a pace. He said I had to choose. This was no way to live. It made no sense.

The Rush and I both felt sorry for him.

. . .

### Lean For Life . . . Harley's One True Way

Harley laughed when I told him I felt pretty educated about dieting, and I thought he would be impressed with me when I told him I very rarely drank any alcohol, never had any sort of dessert, stayed away from fat, and didn't eat red meat.

"No wonder you are fat."

Excuse me? He asked me what I had for breakfast that morning and I told him I had a bowl of shredded wheat with skim milk, a plain bagel with nothing on it, and a large glass of orange juice.

"Poison."

Then we moved on to my training regimen, and if my nutritional knowledge was apparently suspect to the guru, he had to be impressed with how hard I trained at forty-two years old. I not only played 4.0-level tennis at 6:00 a.m. two days a week, I supplemented running with jumping rope, often for forty-five minutes. And if I wasn't biking outside on the weekends or walking eighteen holes of golf, I loved spin classes. Along with my six days of cardio, I did a traditional push/pull bodybuilding split.

"No wonder your muscles are so small."

Harley rubbed his eyes. I could tell he felt his lecture was going to be a waste of time.

"Cut back on the workouts. Your body is never getting a chance to recover from the previous workouts. Muscles grow when you are resting; not when you are preening in the gym looking at your pump. You get bigger muscles when you take in more clean calories than you expend, and the tissue gets to recover and use the food for growth. Work out harder, but less often. Get in. Crush it. Get out." This seemed crazy to me.

"No more cardio. You don't lose body fat by burning calories via cardio, but by controlling and cycling carbohydrates." When I told Harley I would follow up a session of squats and lunges with a bike ride, he nearly slammed his head on his desk. "Cardio is hurting more people trying to get lean than it is helping," was his radical assertion.

"Eat more food."

This one was so counterintuitive that I fought back. "I'm going to get less fat by increasing my calories by a thousand per day?! And no cardio?! I'll be a whale! I'll be that guy on the plane who hits the attendant call button and asks for the extender belt, the guy who sits at the gate and everyone stares at and prays that they are not his seatmate. But this was at the very heart of Harley's program. Most fat people, he believes, do not eat enough food.

"Your way isn't working. You don't look how you want to look. Keep doing it, and you'll get the same results."

This was indisputable. I stared at the volleyball pics on his desk and saw me staring back at myself from the far reaches of another time. I nodded.

"I'm in. So how does this work?"

He handed me his Lean for Life brochure.

## *The 10 Keys to Being Lean*

*You Can Read This and Ignore All Fads and Gimmicks and Drugs. For Life.*

### Key #1—Eat a meal every three hours. Five meals a day.

Each meal must have the correct amount of protein, carbohydrates, and fats. Your body stores fat when you go hours without eating, because it thinks it is starving, and it will protect itself. By eating every three hours, you make your body a furnace. It never feels it has to store fat.

### Key #2—Sugar is the enemy.

You will only eat carbohydrates that are low on the glycemic index (GI). (The index is a ranking of carbohydrates on a scale from 0 to 100 according to the extent to which they raise blood sugar levels after eating them.) The lower the GI of food, the slower it is digested and absorbed, which means the rise in blood sugars and insulin is more gradual. This is critical for people with diabetes but also important for weight control. If you eat high-glycemic carbs, the increased insulin production sends your body into fat storage mode.

Harley said that by controlling my GI index carbs and the number of carbs I ate, I could train my body to never store fat. He asked me if I was willing to give up alcohol, and I thought of Sydney; how brittle things got late at night after the bottle of wine she drank while grading papers, how silly and boring it was to argue with a drunk person. Most people came to Harley and said they would eat whatever he told them, but they didn't want to give up their drinking. "You have to live a little, right?" they would ask him. And Harley would glower. A life lived without being lean, to Harley, was not worth living. He didn't realize how insane this sounded to people, or how much I loved hearing it.

Harley, I would soon learn, liked to steal quotes. He didn't know I was a speaker on the professional circuit and had heard it all before. He no doubt got away with it with most of his clientele. But he channeled Covey and told me that, in order to know how much to eat, I had to begin with the end in mind.

### Key #3—Eat the right number of calories.

» To maintain your current weight, take 15 calories per pound per day. (So if you weigh 200 pounds, multiply 200 by 15.) 200 × 15 = 3,000 calories a day.

» To gain muscle, you need to add 18 calories per pound per day.

» To lose fat, you need to add 12 calories per pound per day. Unless you are trying to gain muscle and lose fat. Then you cycle. (See Key #7)

Take the total calories for a day, divide by five meals, and then eat those meals three hours apart. (So our 200-pound person trying to maintain would eat 600 calories per meal [3,000 divided by 5 = 600].)

Harley wanted me eating 3,000 calories a day!

### Key #4—Maintain the all-important ratio of carbs, protein, and fats to total calories.

» 50% of daily calories in the form of clean carbs

» 30% of daily calories in the form of protein

» 20% of daily calories from "good fats" (almond oil, coconut oil, olive oil, nuts, even natural peanut butter, avocado; nothing fried or saturated)

You need carbs for energy, you need protein for muscle, and you need fat for metabolism. This had me shaking my head.

"No," Harley said, "fat doesn't make you fat."

### Key #5—Drink only water.

No liquid calories. Water, paradoxically, will keep you from bloating. Water is what the muscles you want to see are mostly made of. Water will keep your hunger pangs down. How much? Consume at least half your body weight in ounces every day.

### Key #6—No carbs after 7:00 p.m.

You're not active after 7:00 p.m., so you don't need the energy, and your body doesn't need the energy it gets from carbs to sleep. And if you think your sexual prowess requires extra carbs, settle down; you burn more calories going for a walk around your block than you do during the average-length sex session.

I know, I know, not your average session.

Bodybuilders have carb cycled for decades, but Harley had the good sense to modify the practice for a mass audience. Most people who see bodybuilders on stage or in magazines or on the beach don't realize they only look that way a couple of weeks a year.

### Key #7—Carb cycling is magic.

Carb cycling for the non-freaks who just want to be lean for life uses a three-day eating plan that rotates the amount of carbs. Day one and two you eat 80% of the carbs your body requires. This encourages the body to use stored body fat. On day three you "re-feed" and eat 100% of the carbs you require to both replenish the glycogen storage in the muscles and boost your metabolic rate.

As Harley said to me that fateful first day, "Most people are sugar burners and fat storers, but if you do what I tell you, we will condition your body to store sugar and burn fat."

**Key #8—Work out on "high-carb" days when you need the extra calories and energy, and rest on "low-carb" days when you don't require as much energy.**

**Key #9—Don't skip meals.**

Harley was reading my mind. Sometimes I'm giving a seminar for hours, and all I have is a five-minute bathroom break. Sometimes I am in meetings or on airplanes with no access to any food—let alone the kind of clean food he was advocating. Harley folded his arms. "Bring a sandwich into the bathroom stall. Get a travel container that allows you to store multiple meals and is lined so they don't spoil. Demand the hotel give you a refrigerator; pay for it if you have to. This isn't going to work if you are already planning excuses."

**Key #10—Ignore the enemy.**

Harley said, "There will be people in your life, often those closest to you, who will question your motives. They will try to talk you out of what you are doing. They will say you look fine. You don't. These same people will say, 'Have a drink, a taste, live a little.' And if you give in, that is exactly what you will be doing—living a little."

. . .

Sydney scanned the Lean for Life brochure while I recounted my meeting with Harley, and how excited I was to take on the challenge of bringing back my old body.

"He sounds like a complete psycho. How in the world did you manage to find someone more obsessive and rigid than you?"

I didn't have to say anything. Like most married couples, we were selectively telepathic. Sydney had gotten down to her lowest weight since we dated. She had announced she was going to train for her first marathon, without asking me if I wanted to train with her. So it was practically impossible for her to draw a line in the sand when it came to me dedicating myself to a new training and eating regimen. She was a foodie, and we both knew I was being fundamentally unfair. She truly believed food was one of life's joys, and being married to me robbed her of an intimacy that came with sharing food with your mate.

She was a fabulous and passionate cook, and she loved to throw dinner parties. A morning spent shopping, selecting, and touching and smelling each ingredient (often asking to speak to a manager for ideas on how to best prepare a dish), an entire afternoon spent timing a marinade, pounding down a piece of meat to render it tender, taste testing the pasta so that it was al dente—this was all time joyously spent for her. She would stack CDs in the player and sing along while she piled pot after saucepan after mixing bowl on the granite counter. When she took something out of the oven, and it was just the right shade of brown or had magically risen just the right amount, she would pump her fist like a quarterback completing a fourth and five, and she was—there was no other way to put it—sublimely happy in the chaotic kitchen she created.

My job, since I was fundamentally useless, was to get out the good crystal and china, set the table, and to go to the package store and buy the wines that went with each meal—all carefully considered and researched by Syd days earlier. We were famous among our friends for our parties, and I did my part by making fires and filling glasses and being what I hoped was a compelling host conversation-wise, but this was Sydney's gig, and she was magnificent. Ebullient by nature, she didn't need an elaborate feast to draw people to her, but her passion's ground zero was food. There was always an obligatory point in the party where her foodie friends would ask her how she made one or more of the dishes, and Syd would promise them the recipe—and then walk them through it anyway. She was being completely genuine and not the least bit pretentious when she would open wine, feel the cork, let it breathe, and then swirl it around in her glass before taking a sip. She would close her eyes and truly experience the taste, and if she liked it, a guttural sound would accompany her childlike, appreciative smile.

And here, in the late stages of The Drift, a woman who feels life is worth living in no small measure because of how wonderful it tastes, finds herself married to a man raised in a house where there was so little food my mother often changed the subject if my sister asked what was for dinner; a man who, as an adult, committed himself to the notion that the sole purpose of food is to sustain life. And now I was upping the ante again.

As a couple, we had always had a dessert ritual. Syd loved dessert and would order whatever she liked, but first we had to deceive the waiter into thinking that she really didn't want dessert. (The fact the waiter couldn't care less and in fact was told to push the dessert tray away was lost on Sydney.)

**Waiter:** Save any room for dessert? We have a Chocolate
Decadence Mousse that is orgasmic.

**Sydney:** I don't know.

**Danny:** Let's get it. Bring two spoons.

**Sydney:** Oh, all right.

Then the dessert would come, and I would have two small bites, and she would have the rest. When rituals go, there is unrest in the kingdom, and revolt is at hand. Now the waiters would bring the dessert, and, being more concerned with fidelity to Harley than to Sydney, I wouldn't touch it. She would glare.

"You're ridiculous. I take it back. You have always been ridiculous; now you have a problem."

A problem? How could I possibly admit to that when I was getting results? Within eight weeks of starting the program, I had lost five percent body fat. I was now twelve percent, in the athletic range. With less fat came more vascularity, and my arms, always naturally big, seemed perpetually pumped. My love handles were gone, and my pants wouldn't stay on my hips. I got a personal trainer and met him at 6:00 a.m. five days a week. I increased my bench from 205 to 245 pounds almost overnight. I did heavy squat and dead lifts, and my thighs got the "teardrop" look I'd had a decade earlier. The walking lunges I did until I was dizzy made my butt rounder and higher.

At the five-month mark, Harley looked at the caliper reading, closed his eyes, and nodded his head.

"At your age, less than one in 500,000 guys are under ten percent body fat. You are at 9.8 percent, and you have gained ten pounds of muscle. Welcome to the club."

Two months later, Sydney caught me shaving my chest and stomach in the bedroom mirror. It had been at least fifteen years since I'd had chiseled abs, and—more exciting to me—I had gotten back what girls call the "money-maker." The money-maker is the V-shaped cut in the lower abdominal region that angles down from both sides of the obliques and sort of points to your groin. But Syd was oblivious to anything sexy about it. All she saw was the shaving cream layered on my chest.

"Seriously?"

"Harley says I should shave so you can see the striations in the pecs and the abs."

"And have you been in a *tanning* booth?"

"Harley says it gets rid of extra water and tightens the skin."

"You know what else will lean you out? Melanomas."

With the advent of business-casual attire everywhere and after a decade on the speaking circuit, I was getting noticed all over again as the "hot guy." And it matched my whole speaker zeitgeist. I had always been known as a "no-nonsense, keep it real" hands-on speaker. Now my lean and mean physique matched my entreaties about working hard. My physical presentation seemed to prove I practiced what I preached in a different way from my company's success or my program content. All this was happening while Sydney was in the best shape of her adult life. It didn't matter that I was not the object of her affection or the reason she was suddenly so health-conscious; it infuriated her that I would compete with her in this area and deflect the attention she should have had. But it was all I knew. I could feel I was losing her, and it scared me so much that I did everything in my power to make it worse. My inner control freak was okay with going down with the ship, but I had to be the one firing the fatal torpedo.

The one safe thing we seemed to have left as a couple was going to the movies. We would go to the 7:00 p.m. show, and I would sneak in a ziplock bag of turkey and a low glycemic "muffin" that Harley sold that tasted exactly like cardboard. But it was either that or miss a meal, and that couldn't happen. But what did happen was that we could no longer eat at the bistro across from the Cineplex after the movie, which was our routine. Sydney found this absurd and told me I was imprisoning myself, and she would wonder out loud why I couldn't see it.

We had both heard good things about the movie *Love Actually*, and Sydney called me at work to ask if I wanted to see it. I told her we'd have to go to the 9:00 p.m. show so I wouldn't miss the 7:00 p.m. meal. She asked me why I couldn't take a turkey sandwich, and I told her Harley and I agreed that I needed a full serving of a grain like oatmeal or rice for that critical last meal of the day. She sighed and said she had to teach an 8:00 a.m. class and was not going to a goddamn 9:00 p.m. show! I suggested we do it on the weekend, and she said she was going to go with me or without me, and I told her I understood. She hung up and called me back a minute later.

"Danny, listen to me. We're in trouble. You know that, right?"

## CHAPTER 10

# *Hope*

Time kills deals. Your candidate has had the offer for four days and you haven't heard back? It's a turndown. They say they are 99.9 percent sure they are going to take the job but just want to think about it? There is a 100 percent chance they are telling you what you want to hear.

Why do we hold on to a deal when we know it is already over? Hope. The despair we can handle, but the hope is killing us!

**From Danny's "The Case for Pessimism" Seminar**

. . .

The Drift ended with a whimper—brought on, I can see now—by a whimper. I had finished my speech and hustled to the airport. I made it to the gate on time, was thankful it all seemed to be going to plan, and of course the precise moment I allowed myself that thought, they announced the flight was canceled due to mechanical problems. Everyone groaned. The guy next to me rubbed his eyes and pulled out his cell phone to deliver the news to his wife. I gathered there was some event—a graduation, an anniversary—that he was now going to miss. Not having kids, I never felt worthy of the anger and frustration others felt when flights were delayed or canceled. I would like to get home, but I didn't *have* to get home, and anyway, now that I was deep into The Drift, did it really matter? The guy was pleasant and apologetic to his wife; although, I could feel him stiffen when she subtly blamed him for the airline's miscue. But then she put his daughter on the phone, and she had to be young, because his voice lifted and softened. He called her "Angel Doll," and I looked away. Since our epic fertility failures, I found myself fascinated by the conversations parents had with their kids, and I became that guy on the airplane who would catch the eye of your toddler and make funny faces and entertain them for you while you dug out the video game or snack. You're welcome! When he got off the phone with his Angel Doll, he shook his head, caught me looking, and gestured to his phone.

"She puts my kid on the phone so I can hear her all sad. You want to tell me how hearing my kid whimper is going to change Continental Airline's strategy to get me home?"

I gave him what he wanted—the universal male nod that said, "Women, right?" and that meant I knew what he was feeling, though, of course, I had no idea.

I looked around me, and everyone was on their cell phones telling whoever was picking them up or expecting them home that they would not be there. And whether it was because I felt ostracized by this collective need to connect with loved ones, or because I felt compelled to prove that I in fact had a loved one, or because it just seemed wrong to be the only one sitting there whose life was not significantly impacted by not getting home at any particular time, I called Sydney at home. She picked up and with a brightness that seemed out of proportion to the moment, to say nothing of The Drift, said, "Finally!"

"Finally, what?"

"Oh. Hi. Where are you?"

"Dallas. Flight's canceled. Who did you think I was?"

"Julie. We're doing a thing at the school. So when will you be home?"

"This was the only direct flight. It's either take the early morning flight tomorrow or fly into JFK and take a limo, but that takes three hours, and I still have my car at the Hartford airport. I'd get home around midnight."

"That's insane. Fly home in the morning. For sure."

"Right. So what are you going to do tonight?"

"Who knows? I have tons of papers to grade."

I hung up and knew what I should do next. Go to the information counter; see if there were any decent hotels within a shuttle ride of the airport. But I didn't move. I thought, *If I get home tomorrow, sneak in the garage, and find the Hefty bag of wine bottles she puts at the bottom of the garbage can and covers with normal trash, I will know she stayed home and graded papers. Sure, go with that. Buy yourself some hope.*

Instead, I dialed the home phone number. The line was busy. I tried seven more times in the next forty-five minutes. Busy signal. Plans were being hurriedly made. Or perhaps they already had plans for the day, but now that I was not going to be home at all, a sleepover was in order. I could appreciate the rush of adrenaline Sydney had to be feeling, the sense that she was no longer just waiting for something to change—she was creating change. My feelings for her were an odd mix of fury and pride.

Then came the surprise announcement that instantly changed the mood in our sorry little gate for everyone but me. They had found another plane. We would have to change gates and find another crew, and that would take ninety minutes, but we were then heading to Hartford. These were the days of flip phones, and another wave of wrist-snapping and dialing broke out. My guy told Angel Doll he was coming home and then told her that he didn't need to speak to Mommy and hung up. I was forced into the kind of choice The Drift created: Do I fly home without telling her? What if she comes home super late or not at all? Would I have the courage, finally, to act? And what if I don't call and find her in our home, in our bed, with one of her soccer boys? Would I freak out? Would I grab the fireplace poker? And who would I stab or beat? Him for sleeping with my wife? Or her for wanting him? Or both? In what order? Or would I play it all Edward Albee, calmly pour a glass of wine for myself, sit on the edge of the bed, and tell them to carry on and don't mind me.

Maybe I should just stay in a hotel and fly back in the morning. After all, I didn't really know who she was on the phone with, and I could very well be letting my imagination run amok. Sydney would never do to me what she did to her ex-husband. Hope. Right. I chastised my audiences not to be led by it, and it owned me.

Fuck it. I made two decisions. I was going to fly home. What I find, I find. Enough. The second decision was to call Kelsey. By this time, Kelsey and I had become each other's marriage counselors. As much as I hated to admit it, her skills in deceiving her husband about her extra-marital encounters gave her a level of credibility when I would tell her about Sydney's patterns during The Drift.

"She's cheating on you, Dan," was her trenchant assessment when she heard the story of my call home.

My parents called me "Danny," as did all my friends, and when it came time to brand myself as a playwright and speaker, I went strictly by Danny. Kelsey refused to go along. She told me she wanted a name for me all to herself. At the office she called me DC or Boss Man.

"You don't know that, Kel."

"Yeah, I do. And on some level, you do too."

I said nothing for so long that Kelsey asked me if I was still there. When I acknowledged I was, she surprised me with her recommendation not to ambush Sydney. "Let her know you're coming home." No doubt Kelsey's biggest fear was Jay walking in on her and one of her hookups, and she wanted to spare Sydney the pain she had so far been spared. Then she told me that if I got home and things went south, she was having a party at her house, and I should stop by. She said there was a mystery guest she thought I would appreciate, but I told her I couldn't imagine being in a mood to go to a party if things escalated at home.

Back then, the cool kids were already starting to text, but Syd and I still spoke on the phone, and failing that, left voice mails for each other. There was zero cellular service on Broadbrook Mountain, so I left a voice mail message on both the home phone and her cell, struggling to not sound scolding or upset when I said that I had been trying for an hour to get through and update her on my situation because I had caught a break and would be home just a couple of hours later than planned.

As we waited to depart, I overheard the woman across the aisle from me telling the man next to her that she had never flown before and that she hoped his wife would understand if she clung to him during takeoff and landing, and him reassuring her it was the safest way to travel. And as we all ignored the safety demonstration while the plane taxied out to the runway, I remembered the "safety weekend."

. . .

Sydney was an adjunct professor at a school sixty-five miles away from our home for two years, getting exploited by a system designed to avoid giving full-time pay and benefits to teachers. In those days, they were paid $1,200 per class, and they might teach two or three classes a semester, hoping some full-time opening would come up. It often took years, and Sydney had the luxury of being able to both afford the transportation costs and having the time to wait to get an opportunity for a tenure-track job. Finally, one came up at a college not five miles from our house. It would be perfect for her, and she was extremely anxious. Anything could set her off, and I made the mistake of trying to get her to calm down the night before she was meeting the dean by reminding her that she had been a headhunter and had mastered the performance art of interviewing; she was at her best in social situations, and no dean—man or woman—would be able to resist her charms; and she had two years of outstanding evaluations from the school she had been working for!

"This will be a piece of cake!" I assured her.

"A piece of cake. Do you know how insulting that is to me? I *have* to get this job. It may be my only chance. And what if I don't? A piece of cake?!"

"But you don't have to. Don't put that kind of pressure on yourself. It will show up in the interview. Don't give it that kind of power. I'm just, clearly unartfully, trying to show you I have faith in you."

She later told me this was the worst possible thing I could say to her, and it was proof I didn't understand her, and that she was not "safe" with me. This confused me. Safe? My whole life, it seemed to me, was designed to keep her safe. I not only tried to make sure she had everything she needed or wanted, but also in order to protect her personal safety, I wouldn't have hesitated to give up my life. But when I asked for clarification, she groaned, wouldn't elaborate, and went straight to bed.

When I came home the next night, she told me the interview had been horrible and that she was sure she didn't get the job. When she told me she was in with the dean for two hours, I pointed out that it made no sense that the dean would spend so much time with someone she wasn't interested in, but her downward spiral had started. Syd was weepy and listless. She said she was exhausted and went to bed. I turned on the television and the evening news had just started. It was 6:35 p.m. At 10:00 p.m. I heard her go upstairs.

I thought she was going into the study to work, but a few minutes later I heard a crash and ran upstairs. She was standing on the bed in the guest bedroom, and the huge picture that hung over the bed was on the floor, the frame shattered. I kept asking her what the fuck she was doing, but she didn't seem to know where she was. Her arms were flailing, and she was yelling something unintelligible while she was crying. Just as she appeared to be about to jump off the bed and onto the broken glass in her bare feet, I tackled her and held her arms down as she whipped her head back and forth and tried to kick me to get away. Then, like an earthquake's tremor, what was so primevally scary stopped almost instantly. She fell asleep, her arms went limp, and I carried her to the master bedroom, placed her on the bed, checked her for cuts that might need attention, and cleaned up the guest bedroom.

An hour later she came into the living room. Calm, sad, she sat down next to me.

"I know something happened. But I don't remember what."

When I recounted the scene, she wept quietly.

"That's what happens when I don't feel safe."

She didn't apologize. She said she was going to talk to Selma about dosage. I asked her whether these episodes had happened in the past, and she nodded slowly and shamefully. When I see shame revealed in someone, it makes me love them even more. I told her she could break everything in the house. I was never going to leave.

A few days later she got the job. And everything got so much better. It was only now, as the plane landed, that I realized I finally knew what she was feeling. It didn't feel safe to go home.

. . .

The last mile up Broadbrook Mountain to our house is straight uphill, and though I loathed it when I was riding my bike home and couldn't catch my breath, seeing the house completely dark as I approached it made the climb seem even worse. She knew I was coming home and didn't alter her plans. I didn't even go inside to verify she wasn't home. I turned the car around in our driveway and drove to Kelsey's house.

The whole idea seemed like a very bad one when the first thing I saw was a woman being held upside down by her ankles doing a keg stand in Kelsey's garage. Gravity had turned her blouse into a bib, exposing her black bra and tramp stamp. This concerned no one but me. I would have turned around and left had Kelsey not spotted me. Her face lit up. She gave me two choices, clearly regarding Sydney, and quizzically offered a thumbs-up and then a thumbs-down. I shrugged.

An hour later, I was still pretending to drink the beer I had poured from the keg, an effort that yielded a foam-to-beer ratio so pathetic that the guy next in line simply said, "A tragicomedy." I felt like a ghost as I wandered around. I used to throw these parties when I was their age—a keg, plastic cups, hot dogs on the grill, bowls of peanuts and barbecue potato chips at a house you could barely afford. Before long, they would graduate to the parties Syd and I had only recently stopped throwing—a rented tent, a hired DJ, a catering team with a bartender and servers passing out hors d'oeuvres with names like mushroom polenta and crostini, and much talk of chutney and sun-dried tomatoes. I never really enjoyed either. Both styles of parties required a cleanup job all out of proportion to the purpose of the event. Kelsey grabbed my arm.

"Come. It's time to meet the mystery guest."

She put her arm inside mine and led me through the front door. As she did so, I instinctively felt I should pull back and simultaneously looked around for her husband. After the incident with her in my car, I felt uneasy when she opened a door across from her bedroom and told me to shut it behind me. Then she opened the adjoining bathroom door and moved out of the way. Barreling toward me, slowed considerably by the poor traction of the hardwood floors he would soon make it his job to ruin, was a golden retriever puppy. No more than two months old. Glorious.

"Meet Bailey. Bailey, this is Dan. I've told you all about him."

. . .

Being the professional speaker in our family, I gave the eulogies at both my father's and mother's funerals. I didn't cry. But years before The

Drift, my Irish setter of seventeen years, Isaac, had found it difficult to sit down. He limped when he walked and moaned in his sleep. I took him to the vet, and while it should have been perfectly obvious, I was shocked when she told me he should be put down. She told me he was in great pain and if I loved him, I would not take him home. She put us in a room and gave us a few minutes to say good-bye. Every single night that I walked in the door, he was over the moon about it, like he had thought he was never going to see me again. And now, I was about to make a decision that would ensure he didn't. I hugged him and when the vet came in (How do these people do this every day?), she looked away for a second, and with her voice cracking, said, "You two seem like old friends." Five minutes later, I left with just his leash. I sat and cried in my car for an hour before I could drive home. That night, as I lay awake, sleep out of the question, I realized not many people could pinpoint the exact day their youth ended. But mine ended that day. At the office, I did my best to be all business. But everyone saw through me. Kelsey came in one afternoon and said, "First, I'd like to say on behalf of everyone we are so, so sorry. Second, and this comes from me, you have to get better. Like now. It hurts my heart so much to see you like this, Dan. It's freaking me out. Nothing is supposed to ever get to you. That's kind of the whole point of you."

. . .

I played with Bailey for the rest of the party. Suddenly I was so glad I came. I only stopped playing with him when Kelsey's husband came in and said he just couldn't figure Kelsey out. One minute she is telling him they have to separate and the marriage is not working, the next she comes home with a dog. He stroked Bailey behind the ear and shrugged in the time-honored way of a confused but loyal husband.

It was almost midnight when Kelsey, Bailey in her arms, walked me to my car.

"He is fantastic, Kel. He will bring you so much joy. And Dez is going to love having a dog."

"I got him for you, Dan."

"Meaning what? I get to visit and play with him?"

"Meaning I got him for you. You'll see."

I still beat Sydney home by an hour. I sat outside on the deck with a book of Billy Collins poetry. His writing is deeply wise and funny, but I kept reading the same lines, comprehending nothing, as she made her way through the garage, the TV room, the breakfast nook, and the kitchen. She saw the lights on outside and opened the sliders carefully to avoid letting Hadley or Gatsby outside. This told me she was not that drunk. An indication she was at a rendezvous and not a party.

"I didn't bother calling you back because I figured you were in the air."

"You get your papers graded?"

"Some. Then Aggie called and I met a bunch of them at Confetti's."

As I let her lie settle in, we sat in silence and listened to the sounds of the evening. The occasional coyote lament, the constant katydid chatter, the vague rumbling of thunder on a humid, summer night. I had planned on a full-on interrogation. I had set traps and was prepared to recount evidence. I wanted to extract a weeping confession in which she would beg me to forgive her. But I said nothing. She said she was exhausted and was going to turn in, and I asked her to sit down. I said I had a question for her. Even a tad drunk, she was full of apprehension. She sat back down slowly and took a deep breath.

"Want to have a date night Saturday?"

"A date night?"

"Yes, a complete lack of spontaneity. Planned sex. We dress up for dinner, I get you flowers, I lull you into a trance with witty conversation, and I get you all nostalgic by talking about can't-miss things like our wedding, the beach house in the Outer Banks. We, in short, act like the couple we once were and are supposed to be and I think still are, underneath whatever this is. A date. Saturday. Would you be available, Mrs. Cahill?"

"And you're going to eat? Like, off the menu?"

"I'm feeling Fettuccini Alfredo with a side of cholesterol."

"And dessert?"

"Two. One to take home in case I want a snack after sex."

"Can we stop at a karaoke bar after dinner?"

"Absolutely not. I want you back, but there are fucking limits!"

And I heard the first genuine laugh I had heard since The Drift had entered its denouement. It would be the last time I would ever see her go to bed happy.

. . .

I was thinking go big or go home and was Googling places like The Copper Beach Inn, The Griswold Inn, or The Water's Edge—all swanky, romantic, and on the shore an hour from our home. A couple of them had live music, and all of them had the kind of New England charm I was looking for. I was on the phone pricing suites when Sydney emailed me that she had made a reservation at Grant's in West Hartford.

Okay, wait. Grant's is nice and all, but we'd been there a hundred times, it was more of an upscale-before-a-movie-or-play place. It wasn't what I had in mind for this epic date night. But when I mentioned the choices by the shore, she blamed the drive and said she'd rather sleep in her own bed. I told myself venue was not the point and to just go with it. We both had to work, so we agreed to meet at the restaurant.

Sydney was nervous from the start, and I gave her the benefit of the doubt. This was, for all intents and purposes, a cease-fire. Of course it is going to feel strained. But I thought once we got into it, alcohol-aided, we could get past the hesitation. But it was soon clear that her nervousness was not motivated by the occasion. I was deep into the plot of a funny work story, full of surprise twists leading to an unexpected ending, laced with hilarious moments, when I realized she kept look-ing behind me. Then—and this would annoy anyone, but for someone who is paid outrageous money to tell just this kind of anecdote, it is the worst—she interrupted my carefully crafted ending, stood up, and waved wildly.

Well, what do you know? The soccer boys, unencumbered by spouses or girlfriends, were at a large table. Syd went over to them instantly and came back ten minutes later. She didn't ask me to continue my story. She said they had asked us to join them and she had said no, but then she added, "Unless you want to?"

This charade lasted another twenty minutes. At one point Jamie went to the restroom and had to cross the room, and she literally stopped talk-ing midsentence and watched him until she caught his eye. Ah, young love. A few minutes later, Morris, the soccer ringleader, said he had to borrow Sydney for a minute to settle a bet they had about what hap-pened at one of their play-off games. She was gone for so long, the waiter asked if I wanted him to cover the entrees. When I saw her put her arm on Jamie's shoulder while she listened to Jack act out a soccer story, I felt something give way deep within me. Everything was suddenly crystal clear to me. I got icy calm. She began to return to our table and at fifteen feet away, she got scared. She had never seen this look on my face. Never.

"What's wrong?"

"Nothing. I'm leaving. I'm going to give you what you clearly want, which is to sit next to your boyfriends."

"Oh for Christ's sake, don't make a . . ."

"You shut the fuck up. Do you think I'm an idiot? Clearly, you don't love me anymore, and it's very obvious you don't respect me, to pull off a stunt like this, but I never thought things would get so bad that you would question my intelligence. Am I supposed to believe this is a fucking coincidence? You are such a child. Did you leave a note in his fucking locker so he'd remember to make a reservation?"

I stood up and took a roll of bills out of my pocket. Incongruously, I kept my voice clear and low, but my hands were shaking. I peeled off several hundred dollars and dropped them on our table. Then I took a few hundred more and threw them in the general direction of the soccer boys.

"Here's for your dinner, and their dinner—pay for everyone's fucking dinner! You can leave me, you can have all the money, you can fuck around with your boys, but you will not treat me like this. Shame on you, Sydney. Enjoy your night."

It took everything I had to not stop by their table and start swinging, but they made it easier by looking down. The whole dining room was dead silent, so I guess I was louder than I realized. I stopped by the hostess stand on the way out and apologized for disrupting the evening for their guests.

She never came home that night. When we first decided to move in together years before, Syd had made two rules: No Going to Bed Angry and No Leaving. You could leave the room and gather yourself, but you couldn't leave the house. These were idealistic rules to begin with, and even before The Drift, we had to break the first rule because "I'm not admitting I'm wrong, and I am so tired!" But the second rule was sacred. Unless I was traveling for business, we always slept in the same bed. That night, around 2:00 a.m., I knew she wasn't coming home, and I didn't want her to.

The next morning I fed the cats, made my breakfast, and took my coffee to the den. Like any other Sunday. As a professional speaker, I had long ago mastered the art of compartmentalization. I knew that no one cared if my plane got in at 3:00 a.m. and I got no sleep before my keynote. They cared about this keynote, their keynote, and they weren't interested in excuses. Every day in my office and on stage, I had to be the guy they came to see. I had to be sharper, smarter, and funnier than I was the last time they saw me. I had to project the person they not only wanted me to be but also that they thought they could become. "Ninety percent of people," Lou Holtz said at a conference I spoke at, "don't care about your problems; the other ten percent are glad you have them." So I didn't think about the fact that my wife was unofficially missing in action; I wrote two staff sales meeting agendas and reviewed the sales forecast for the coming month.

I was powering down my laptop when Sydney's car came down the driveway. It was nearly 3:00 p.m.

She had a speech ready. Far be it from me, given my vocation, to not allow a speaker to present their prepared material.

"I know you think I've been sleeping with the entire soccer team and the mascot. It's not true. Selma gave me the name of a therapist in Avon. She says he's very good. I hope you'll agree to go. If not, I understand. I know I have had a part in this, Danny, but I can't tolerate what you did in that restaurant. Will you go to this therapist with me, please?"

"Where did you sleep last night, Sydney?"

"In a hotel. In Syracuse. I got it in my head that the only safe place was to go home. To sleep there and have Aunt Ellie make me feel better, and I got as far as Syracuse and realized it was stupid and I was tired, so I got a hotel and drove home this morning. I know it seems preposterous. I know you don't believe me."

It was so preposterous that I did believe her. Syd was from Buffalo, and after her mom died, her Aunt Ellie had essentially been her guiding force. I was picturing their home and how we spent Christmas there every year. How much I loved Ellie and her husband, Porter. How much I looked forward to seeing her funny and accomplished brother every year and his vibrant and intense wife. I loved Sydney's whole family, and I suddenly realized this was a package deal. I was going to lose them as well. People pick sides, and family has no choice whose side of the aisle to sit on.

The headhunter in me wanted to ask her to name the hotel she stayed at and produce the receipt. I thought I could put an end to this charade right now by calling the credit card company and requesting the most recent charge. If none existed, then she clearly stayed with someone. It was the prudent thing to do. Before I could say anything, Hadley leaped on her lap. She hugged him fiercely and asked him if he missed

Mommy. And the rage left me. I didn't need to ask a therapist how we came to this. This most nurturing of women had nothing to nurture. And all the love I had for her couldn't fill the void. I wanted her to be happy, and yet I knew we would never be happy without children. So why not face facts and move on? Every day in the office, I repeated the same mantra over and over once we had done all we could do to solve a business problem: "It is what it is." Clearly it was time to walk away. I rolled my den chair over to her. She seemed so profoundly tired, and I didn't care if it was because she had been with someone else all night. I stroked Hadley's shaggy coat, then gently cupped Syd's face in both of my hands.

"Let's go see this therapist guy."

"Yeah?"

## CHAPTER 11

# Accidents and Lawsuits

**Athol112@Yahoo.com:** So Danny, this month alone I have had two guys turn down offers because they wanted more money, and I just had a guy take a counteroffer after accepting my client's offer. My jobs were so much better. Sigh. I just wish they wouldn't go on interviews and waste everyone's time if they weren't sure they wanted a new job.

**Danny:** It would be nice. Ever been to marriage counseling, Athol? Some people go to marriage counseling in a sincere effort to fix issues, to find a way back to a happier time. Some go so they can later say they made one last effort. Some go so they can say things in the safety of a session that they could never say at home. Don't you think counselors wish people wouldn't come to the sessions and waste everyone's time?

**From "A Live Webchat with Danny"**

. . .

I was dressing for my weekly session with my therapist, Russ, and I needed to get the amount of mineral ice right. Too little, and I would be in agony sitting on the stiff-backed Berkeley wing chair that faced his own, separated by a coffee table that was graced ominously with a box of Kleenex. Too much ointment and not only would we both smell it and try not to mention it, but also my eyes could tear up, creating the illusion of a facile breakthrough. The landline rang and even though Russ was one of the few people in my life who had that number, it was unheard of for him to cancel a session less than an hour before it began. It was probably Dane. Yep. I hit the Ignore button and let it go to voice mail.

Dane is the owner of the gym where I got hurt. The owner of the leg press whose faulty mechanism compressed and fractured my spine. The owner now living in fear that I was going to sue him. When he first called, I was impressed. He seemed genuinely sorry the accident occurred, but then he kept calling, asking me about the prognosis and was there any long-lasting damage that would affect my work, and I realized what he was after. As a business owner, I understood. All entrepreneurs are one crazy lawsuit away from financial ruin. And he was right to worry. Whenever I told a client or candidate or friend about my accident, they would say, "Oh, you should sue his ass! I know a guy, he'll get you millions!" But I shrugged it off. Dane was a great guy who ran a clean and well-equipped gym. I just wanted to get better. I loved that Russ never brought up my back unless I did. It was amazing to me how much trust I had in Russ now, considering how circumspect I had been that first day when Sydney and I began our brief foray into marriage counseling, sessions in which we took all the shards and fragments of The Drift, handed them to Russ, and waited impatiently for him to apply some glue.

. . .

I've sat through enough off-Broadway auditions to know that Russ would never get the part of "The Therapist." He was too obvious. The distinguished greying beard, the cardigan with patches. He was a pipe away from the director saying, "Next."

But within a couple of minutes, I found myself drawn to him. His mind was penetrating, and he found angles and picked up on emphasis quickly. His voice was smooth and deep, and when he nodded, he looked right at you and held the look, and you understood that he really, really heard you. But even this I fought. It was just his training; this came with practice.

It took a few visits for us to get the backstory that would support what Sydney and I both felt intuitively with Russ. This guy had been there. Not just as a therapist. This guy had fucked up in his life. His abiding kindness and empathy had been forged in folly and futility. I would later learn he was a recovering alcoholic, married more than once, and just remarried in his early sixties. When you are in the presence of a truly recovered addict, you sense their inability to judge others, their awareness that tomorrow is a line of credit the banks could call in at any moment. He had a peace about him, one that he had earned. There was nothing you could take from him that he hadn't already tried to throw away. He had not one trace of shame left in his body. I wanted to trade places with him and know what it felt like to have nothing to hide.

Sydney gave him her full-wattage smile. I was at a distinct disadvantage. She had been seeing Selma for nearly a decade. She dropped a few therapy-speak buzzwords to let Russ know she was no amateur. "If it would help," she said, she knew he needed a certain amount of exposition. Would he like her to give a synopsis? Russ sort of half shrugged and half nodded. It wasn't really what he had planned, but he could tell Sydney was not about to be stopped. It took me years to recognize this reality. Russ did so immediately. Maybe this dude could help after all.

Sydney needed all men to like her. I knew this, and yet I couldn't help being wary that she would turn him against me. I should have given him more credit. Sydney began with her backstory, and it was impressive how mindful she was of our fifty-five minutes, and how much territory she quickly covered. Her upper-class background that became a middle-class background when Grandfather lost his company (Was this why she loved and wanted nice things but tended to trivialize their importance when money came up?); the divorce of her parents; the ugliness and evil of her abusive stepfather; her turning to sports and her emergence as the popular and pretty girl that everyone loved; her mother's disappointment at Sydney's choice of first husband; the subsequent unresolved rage she'd felt when her mother committed suicide just before the wedding; her courage in leaving him without a backup plan (leaving out conveniently that she'd known I was waiting in the wings for her); her working as a waitress while going to graduate school; and her love for her tenured job at the community college.

She wrapped up by saying she loved our life, that she felt blessed every day by having friends, neighbors, and family who loved us. She said all couples have issues and marriage was about finding a way through them. She never mentioned our failed fertility, her soccer friends, her drinking, or the twelve hours she would routinely sleep on weekends. She never mentioned she loved me. She beamed at Russ, but he wasn't looking at her, he was looking at me.

Russ turned to me and waited. I said nothing. It got uncomfortable. He waited. I smiled. Don't fuck with me, buddy, this is Sales 101. The one who talks first loses. Silence always freaked out Syd.

"Honey, I think Russ is waiting for you to give some background."

"I'll pass."

"Danny, I don't think that is helpful. He gets a frame of reference by knowing how you grew up, and in the spirit of reciprocity, and *fairness*, you should . . . "

"See, here's the thing. Sydney likes to go back. I don't. I was raised poor, and I get how that created certain problems. And advantages too. That's where my drive comes from, right? But I've now been wealthy longer than I was ever poor. It just seems so lame to go back there. I don't see how it helps. Marriage counseling-wise. All due respect."

Sydney gave Russ a flagrantly conspiratorial "you see what I deal with?" look. But he gave her nothing back. He was focused on me.

"I understand. A lot of people come in here and see the first few sessions as not just beside the point but painful to recount. But later they realize that they're necessary steps to finding your way back to each other."

"You just 'feel, felt, founded' me! That is wild! It's a sales close. A classic. 'I know how you feel, others have felt the same way, and what they found was if they bought my product they were happy.' Therapy through sales principles. Who knew?"

"Russ," Sydney said, while glaring at me, "I'm sorry. I would say he's not normally like this, but he actually is never not like this."

"No, he's right! When I learned it, they called it something prettier, but a sales close is exactly what it is. Okay, so let's be salespeople and bottom line this deal. Why are you here? What's the problem?"

I could tell he wanted me to engage, but Sydney was having none of it. We were here on her terms, and that is where we were staying.

"We're here because Danny is incapable of real intimacy and because he is suffering from a particularly acute midlife crisis."

On my online subscription site there is a feature called "Ask Danny." No one ever stumped me. But when Russ asked me if I would agree with Sydney's assessment, I had nothing.

"If she says so."

"That's a child's answer, Danny. If you think I'm wrong, then just say so."

But I didn't know the rules of therapy yet. I thought we would come in here and couch our feelings, protect our secrets. Let this guy in but only so far. We're a team. It's us against the world. I didn't realize that Sydney saw therapy as a chance to say things she couldn't say to me outside. I was always impossible to argue with. I had the unbeatable combination of an airtight memory that could recall specifics that contradicted your position; a quicksilver mind that could produce responses, some unworthy and below the belt; and a hardwired need to win at anything where a score was being kept. Sydney had the same need to win but couldn't match my polemical skillset, so therapy, where one person speaks while the other suffers in decorous silence, was perfect for her. Russ would protect her. I was worried it was a setup, and it was. Russ was still in sales mode, qualifying his prospects.

"Was there a triggering event that brought you in or have you found yourselves, over time . . . drifting?"

"You should know that we found each other by breaking the trust of the relationships we were in at the time, and I think that has created trust issues for us that we never resolved."

"To be clear, she was married at the time. I had a girlfriend. I'm not saying that makes me better."

"Then why did you say it?" Sydney huffed.

"Because I think it makes me better."

Russ asked if there had been a violation of trust recently. Sydney said no. I said yes. Russ waited. I made my case that she appeared to be sleeping with one of the soccer/mountain-biking boys and that recently, for the first time, she had not come home. She countered that she was driven away by my humiliating rant in the restaurant. Sydney unequivocally said she had slept with no one since we were married. I shook my head like that was nonsense, and yet felt a flood of relief.

"Well," Russ said, noting the clock on the table with a tilt of his head, "we're at the end of our allotted time."

Now what. Penalty kicks? Russ rubbed his eyes. He was tired of people like us. Who could blame him?

"So, look, I'm semiretired. I used to do this forty-five hours a week, now I do half of that. If one or both of you already knows you want out, and you want to use sessions like this to do it, I'd say save your money, save my time, grow a set, and break it off. You'll survive. If you want to work at it, well then I'm in, because I think there's a lot of love in the room. Any questions?"

"Uh, just one. What fucking room are you in?"

Russ laughed. Sydney slapped me on the knee and asked Russ to evaluate our chances.

"You don't like each other right now, and I get that. You're treating friends far better than you are treating each other, or even yourselves. So let's leave it at this. When it was good, was it good?"

Such a simple question. Sydney nodded, started to cry, and buried her head in my chest. And I looked away from Russ and felt my face give way.

"So fucking good. You don't know."

"Well," Russ said, nudging the Kleenex box our way, "that's the room I'm in. See you next week."

. . .

I sat in Russ's waiting room and thought about how different things were now. I'm a punctuality freak, and back then Sydney was always late, so we never saw this waiting room, we were always slamming the car door and sprinting up the steps and apologizing to Russ for being late. I had worried then that Russ would be played by Sydney, but now I just worry about Russ. He has had prostate surgery, and the dog he walked every day had just died. I thought of him as a friend, and after isolating myself from my former world, there were times I thought he was my only friend. But then I realized that was not true, not because I paid him and only saw him in this room, but because only he knew everything. I never told friends everything.

"Every time I see you," Russ began, shaking my hand, "I think, *I should get back in shape,* and then you leave and I think, *nah.*"

As an icebreaker, I told Russ that Dane was stalking me, worried I was going to sue for negligence. He said he knew I didn't need the money but perhaps a lawsuit would keep someone else from being hurt. So I told him about my brother's bike accident when he was fifteen and I was almost nine. A car pulled out as Tony was riding through the Woolworth's parking lot and hit him head-on. He went flying over the bike and landed on the asphalt. He was taken to the emergency room at

Charlotte Hungerford Hospital, where my father—me in tow—sat in fear. We had less than no money, and whatever the hospital was going to charge to fix my brother's broken collarbone and minor concussion, we did not have. The man who ran over my brother walked into the emergency room, introduced himself, fell all over himself apologizing to my father, and then—weirdly my dad and I thought—sat with us in the emergency room. A resident came out and told us it was only a broken collarbone, and then there was an unbearable silence until the man came over to my dad.

"Look, I just have to know. Are you going to sue me?"

My dad was genuinely perplexed. There was no artifice in him. That is why he never stood a chance against my mother.

"Did you do it on purpose?" my dad asked.

"Of course not."

"Then why would I sue you? Try to be more careful."

No one needed the money more than my father. A lawsuit, so easily justified by people who say, "It's the insurance company's money," would have made life a lot easier for my family. But it wouldn't have been the right thing to do. And my dad taught me a lesson that I would go on to willfully ignore over and over—"If it feels wrong, it is wrong."

I looked up at Russ. He was smiling. He believed deceased parents get smarter every year. I told him, "The next time Dane calls, I am going to tell him that I'm not going to sue him and to be more careful with the maintenance of the equipment." It was too late for me to become even half the man my father was, but maybe it wasn't too late to try.

## CHAPTER 12

# *Coincidence*

You should probably tell your spouse that your job isn't going well.
But you don't want to scare them. You should be able to tell your best
friend that you are miserable, but better to keep the social life on the
shallow side. Post happy pictures. So you know who you tell the truth
to? Your headhunter. Because they get it. And because they asked.
We all live a don't-ask-don't-tell existence, until somebody gets bold.

**From Danny's "Disruptively Honest Interviewing" Session**

. . .

We met with Russ every Saturday that summer. After leaving his office
all bruised and wrung out, we were supposed to spend the day together,
leave the session behind, and not talk about the issues. He even gave us
a code word: blue. If one of us couldn't resist resuming the discussion,
the other one was supposed to say "blue" and the conversation would
stop. We were so bad at it that we had to make a game of it. "Excuse
me Syd, how does it go, something old, something new, something bor-
rowed . . ." and when I was the one guilty of going out of bounds, she
would offer, "Guess who is going to have blue balls this weekend?"

The sessions were edifying, if ultimately doomed. I was in the business of convincing candidates that change would be healthy and wonderful for their careers, and yet I was terrified of the change that would come with losing Sydney. As the therapy went on, I became more convinced than ever that Sydney and I were who we were, that we would walk away from each other, find someone else who wasn't up to speed on our antics and issues, and five years from now repeat the same mistakes. This was such a depressing notion that I dug in. I tried hard in therapy. And for a while, I thought it might be working. We were kinder to each other, we stayed home more, and made love more. And while some of the early stuff was hard to hear, I thought it might be productive.

## Early Summer Therapy Factors That I Thought Might Be Productive and Lead to Breakthroughs

**The Pamela email.**

After agreeing she would never again check my email, Syd admitted she found an email from Pamela—a woman I had known but not seen in a decade who had asked me what was going on. I, in characterizing our fertility issues, made the statement, "Looks like it's not going to happen, and maybe it's just as well. With our issues, I'm not sure I want to have kids with Sydney anyway." I was mortified that Sydney read such a horrible statement. Something I wrote one of those Thursday nights when I was so angry with her.

I wanted her to know it was untrue and just something I wrote out of anger. But I didn't have to say anything. Russ said, "I know of very few marriages, including my own, that could survive someone reading all my emails. We say things to friends that we can't say to each other. Friends are rough drafts. You both need to change your passwords."

**Quiet time.**

Sydney liked white noise. She wanted to have the television or stereo on at all times as background noise. I saw it as craving distraction. A setup for procrastination. I spoke for the first time about my house growing up. My mother screaming she couldn't take it anymore, breaking dishes over my father's head, and threatening him with a knife. I would go outside, even in frigid weather, and sing some pop song at the top of my lungs to drown them out. I craved quiet.

**Listen. Don't fix.**

This I didn't get. I thought there were three types of people: the kind who make things happen, the kind who let things happen, and the kind who sit around saying, "What happened?" I took great pride in making things happen, on not confusing motion with progress. So when Sydney cried, I wanted to know what was wrong and offer solutions. She told me, and Russ nodded—so it was now the undisputed truth—that she just wanted me to listen, and hold her, and offer nothing. She'd figure it out, or maybe she didn't even need to change whatever it was she was crying about. She just needed to be listened to.

**She was supercompetitive with me.**

We're married. It's not supposed to be a contest, and by the way, if it is, I am *so* winning. If I called her and said I just got a standing ovation, she would respond that she just had some student tell her she was the best teacher she ever had. Just the year before, we ran the Litchfield Hills

Road Race together. Sydney had trained hard for it. I did it on a lark, because I was always in some sort of decent cardio shape, even though I hadn't been a serious runner in years. We agreed we would not run together "as a couple" because Syd had a time in mind and didn't want to babysit me. I finished four minutes before her and then hung out at the finish line to cheer her in. When she came around the corner, I yelled, "Bring it home Syd!" and she gave me a furious and hurt look. She was crushed that I was already done.

Russ looked at Sydney, and she nodded. She said it was true, petty, and something she needed to work on, and I thought, *Really? Wow. Maybe, just maybe, we can do this.*

Not so much. The conversations so far were the easy stuff. The kind of things you can cop to without any real effort. You put it in under the we-all-have-our-foibles category, and you sincerely agree to work on making the requested changes. But Syd was biding her time. Once she had the lay of the land and thought Russ would deflect and salvage any misstep, things went south fast.

## Late Summer Therapy Factors That, Proving Too Tough, Were Deal Breakers

**Money as hardship.**

Sydney said she understood that my impoverished childhood had created my drive for the security of money. "But isn't time the most precious asset? He's never home. He pursues money indefatigably, and I'm grateful for what it provides, but if he's not home to enjoy what he's worked for, what's the point?"

She told Russ, tearfully, that I didn't understand that she would live with me in a cardboard box. She wanted me, not what I provided. Russ nodded solemnly, as if she had just described me waterboarding her on the front lawn. And I knew at some level she believed it. But I remembered instantly the sad story she had told of her mother's fear that she wouldn't find a man "to take care of her in the style she was brought up in." The pride she took in the art and furniture in our home. The way she would slip me her credit card bill each month, no explanations offered. I paid all the bills. Her salary as a professor—other than for her car insurance and groceries—was hers to do whatever she liked with. It occurred to me that she didn't even know how much Russ charged. I remember her friend Aggie, one especially cold winter, asking how much it cost to heat our home every month and Syd's blank expression. It was so easy for her to sit in our therapist's office in our toney town—with no financial cares in the world, with no earthly clue what our tax bill was or how much we had invested, or even what our monthly nut was—and from her privileged perch tell me my values were out of line. The room was deathly quiet when Russ asked me to comment, and even I was surprised by my bitter reply: "It is easy to decry the value of money when you are given an unlimited supply of it."

In the car on the way home from the session, Sydney offered to call the contractor and kill our home improvement project. We were finishing the basement in a big way—adding another bedroom, a bathroom, and a home gym with commercial flooring and a lifecycle exercise bike, a row of dumbbells, a power rack, and surround sound for the entire downstairs. We were two people in a house already too big for us, and without children we had no reason to do the project other than we needed something to do with our time and money. I shook my head and asked her what color the sky was.

Two days later, in a sales contest battle that was fiercely waged, Kelsey beat out Bill and Greta for two tickets to the Pilot Pen tennis tournament. This was the local WTA event that attracted all the world's top players and was a tune-up for the US Open. Kelsey knew nothing about tennis except that I played it and followed it closely. She asked me to take the afternoon off and go with her. The contest was strictly for my employees, and I had kept tickets for one weekend session for Sydney and me when I'd gotten the box seats. So although I knew it would get people talking, I said yes. I wanted Kelsey's breezy energy, I wanted to see professional tennis and the amazing skills of Venus Williams and Lindsay Davenport through her nascent eyes, and I wanted to complete my conversation about money too. As we settled into our seats, our age difference was apparent immediately when she rubbed oil on her face while I layered on sunscreen. I asked her if money was important to her.

"Is that a trick question from my sales manager? Three words—Jimmy Choo boots! And, oh yeah, that mortgage thingie and feeding my daughter—but mostly the boots."

I didn't laugh, and she caught on immediately that my mind was a mess. It was hard to know whether she was superhumanly intuitive or whether we had some singular bond. Or both. She asked me something no one else ever had.

"What I don't get is how you still care about making money when you already have so much of it. I get that you once were a plebe like me, but that was, no offense, G-Pa, a long time ago. But every day you go at it so hard. What is that?"

I pictured my dad pulling any one of a dozen sad excuses for cars, all at least fifteen years old, into the gas station. I pictured the smoke pouring out from under the hood, the car dying before it could be properly parked, and the mechanic's pitying, irritated look. They didn't have the term white trash yet in our postwar mill town; the term was "raggies." The Cahills were known raggies. My father would often be unable to negotiate payment terms to fix our car, and we were regularly forced to walk home. The older I got, the farther ahead of my father I would walk. I didn't want people to think I was with him or of him.

"Money is how adults keep score, Kelsey. You get treated better when you have money. You would see me very differently if I didn't have money."

"No doubt. Then you'd just be a hot guy I would use for sex and ignore your texts 'til you gave up."

"That's Justine Henin, by the way. World number one, and her gorgeous backhand? A gift from God. And that would be Venus Williams."

"She's freaky. Those legs go on forever! Okay, so three tennis questions. One, why does it go from 30–15 to 40–15? If the score is kept in increments of 15, shouldn't it go to 45–15? And why is 'zero' the same as 'love' in tennis? Zero and love being the same thing is a very depressing notion."

"I have to fall back on my mom's 'just because' since I have no idea. What's the third question?"

"Are all these players lesbians? Is that wrong to assume since the stands are filled with them? It's like we're at an Indigo Girls concert."

Between matches, we went to the food court. Kelsey said it was very difficult to eat french fries in front of me without feeling judged, but I was her guest and not her boss this afternoon, so she was going to do it. I paid the bill, and she pointed to the waitress and shrugged.

"You always overtip. You have no idea what you just gave her, do you? You gave her a fifty on a bill for $23.50. People who are rich are usually the cheapest people ever. But you're not like that, and I get it. I'm just like you. I want money, so I don't have to waste any more energy worrying about money."

That was exactly right. Why couldn't I articulate that to Syd, or Russ, or myself? By this time, Kelsey had been working with me for four years, and she seemed to know me at a level that people who had known me my whole life did not.

When I dropped her off back at the office, she asked me what I was reading. Kelsey was an autodidact and overly sensitive—given how insanely smart she was—about her lack of formal education. She lived in fear that some VP would call her on it and refuse to work with her. It never happened. She compensated by reading every night while her husband watched television. I told her to read Kundera's *The Unbearable Lightness of Being*. I told her it reminded me of her—that for a few minutes today I felt what the characters felt in the book: existence giving way, ceding ground to something without weight. Something better. I thanked her for the tickets. Just before the moment, which was lasting too long already, gained any more momentum, two of my employees came around the corner, and Kelsey threw the door open and yelled, "Whassup?" to them. She never looked back. I was glad she was gone and sorely missed her at the same time.

**"He is what he said he was."**

Syd never took her eyes off Russ while she laid out what she termed a key issue. When she met me, the match seemed surreal. I had just gotten my MA in English at night while working full-time as a headhunter. She was doing the same thing at my school's archrival. She wanted to write, and I already had some off-Broadway credentials as a playwright.

Early in our friendship phase she came to one of the productions in New York City. When she and her first husband walked into the theatre, she saw me talking to Jerry Stiller and Anne Meara, who were on the board of advisors for the fledgling theatre. At the time Stiller was on *Seinfeld*, and standing next to him was his son Ben, not yet a megastar but well known enough. Sydney said she saw me and thought, *He isn't even overwhelmed. He expects to be here.*

Sydney wanted an audience. She was a performer at heart. At one time, she wanted to be an actress or singer but now saw teaching as a way to have an audience every day. When she saw me speak and felt the raw energy and emotional reaction I managed to draw from people, the way I "stalked onstage," she was drawn to me. Sydney was an athlete. She knew physical and competitive excellence in college and was unhappy at how sporadic her training had been since. She knew I was committed to fitness to a degree she had not been able to capture as a working adult. "I thought, *He has done what I want to do. He knows how to do it. I need to get closer to him.*" Russ interrupted her. He reached for a notepad. A rare move for him, signaling a significant thread.

"I'm not sure what you are saying. Did you want to be *with* him, or did you want to *be* him?"

"I really don't know anymore. All I know is when we were first together I would get up with him to work out first thing in the morning. Then after a while, I would tell him to go without me. But, and I'm not proud of this, I would get angry with him. Why do you need to work out every goddamn day at six in the morning? Why not stay in bed with me? Why can't we lounge around and relax, make love lazily?"

It took all I had to not point out that most mornings she was dead to the world from the wine she drank the night before. I spent many mornings after I got home from the gym waiting for her to get up and start our day. I was bored out of my mind! But I knew what she was saying was hard for her—and intractable.

"And when we were first married, I was so impressed that he didn't have my procrastination issue. He could just say, 'I'm going to write' and disappear into the den for a couple of hours. Meanwhile, I would do anything to avoid grading papers or writing a chapter for the textbook I'd been working on for a year or more. All the phone calls, the deal making, the strategizing. I knew he was amazing at it—I was in his business—and I knew running two businesses took energy, but I thought he would calm down. I thought it would be less exhausting to be around him after a while. I started out wanting to be like him, and then I morphed into trying to get him to change, to be more like me."

"So let me get this straight." (Russ waved his hand in a vertical motion signaling me to dial it down.) "I presented myself as the person that it turns out I actually am. I remain passionate about the things I said I was passionate about. And contrary to all the other couples who sit in these chairs all week, bitching that their spouse has changed or is a phony who turned out to be the opposite of what they purported, my big sin is that I am who I said I was?"

"I'm sorry, Danny, the very things that used to attract me to you make me crazy now. To me, you're not committed, you're rigid and lost."

"But that's not fair!! Can't you see it's about you? Instead of facing your failures, you want to take the easy way and blame me! You're the one who's not who you claimed to be!"

. . .

My father had a major stroke on New Year's Eve a decade earlier. For fifteen months he did his rehab exercises, went to speech therapy, and squeezed the rosary beads he asked my mother to get from the attic. He never got better in any measurable way. He could speak but could not be understood, and the left side of his body was completely useless. Already suffering from arthritis before the stroke, his inability to move intensified his arthritic pain, and he suffered greatly. He kept a pad on his chest and wrote notes. I visited him every Sunday, and something about not having an actual dialogue made it safer. I could ask anything. And get a note back. We were freed up.

"So, Dad, if you had to name one thing you would want me to remember, the one thing you would want me to know about life? What have you learned?"

To my amazement, he didn't hesitate. He took his pad and pen and scribbled furiously, and then handed me the note. It read. "Take care of your teeth."

I thought, *Really? That's all you've learned in sixty-eight years? Maybe this isn't as tragic as I thought.* But I just nodded and pocketed the note. But I never could fool him. He knew he had disappointed me. A nurse came in to give him some meds, and I went to the restroom. When I came back, he had a second note ready for delivery. I keep it in my office now. I never take it on the road with me for fear of losing it. It has become my life's creed. It reads: Blame No One. Expect Nothing. Do Something.

. . .

**Marriage on a need to know basis.**

"He wants me to see him as this ubercaretaker who will protect me. And he knows I want that too. But he wants it both ways. He doesn't want me to have to worry about anything, but then he resents me for not appreciating what he does for us. But how can I? He won't tell me anything. He wants you to think everything comes easy to him, and the second you do, he takes you to task for believing him. He gets me to buy into his construct and then is furious when I do so."

Russ looked at me. I would have taken the Fifth if constitutional rights weren't forfeited at his door when you walked in.

**The conditions under which my love is unconditional.**

"He would never say it, and I know how this sounds given I benefit from all of it, but he has this way of making me feel that what he does is more important than what I do."

So wrong. I never did a seminar without telling people the world was crazy. My wife, a brilliant teacher, should be the one making millions. Speakers? Headhunters? Grossly overpaid. This was where the Saint Sydney moniker came from. How could she not know that? But did I ever tell her?

"We're at this horrible point where the more attention he gets and the more success he has, the more I want to make him pay a price, to bring him down a peg. I say mean things, and I know it's worse when I drink. He holds everything inside, and part of me just wants to break him open. He hates weakness in himself, but in others too. I know he hates it when I complain about my body and then eat junk, I know he thinks my drinking is ruining our sex life, I know he thinks it's hypocritical to tell him how much I love my students in one breath and then whine about how burned out I am on teaching the next. But he doesn't get that it's normal. It doesn't mean I don't love him or I am unhappy. My love is unconditional. I don't think he believes that."

"I don't. Because it's not. Pets, yes. Children, sure. Adults? No chance."

The session was so draining, and Sydney said she understood if I

wanted to go play golf and get away from her. But I had a better idea—
a drive to my older sister Hanna's house. She is two years older than I
am and took fertility drugs at around the same time Sydney and I were
trying the more traditional route. Her third treatment was successful,
and now her twin marvels, Mason and Martin, were almost a year old.
Hanna was my hero long before her sons came along. She had put herself through school in her late twenties, built and sold her own video
arcade business, and then embarked successfully on a new career in
insurance technology. She was kind and wise and smart, the new family
matriarch. We both wanted kids, but she had none of my angst or fear.
She had the courage to see it through.

As we drove up her steep driveway, she came out of the house and
waved, looking a decade younger than she had before the boys were
born. They had rejuvenated her in a miraculous way, and I thought Sydney and I needed a reminder of what was possible. All the anger I felt at
Russ's office dissipated when Sydney scooped up both boys, took them
to what was once the living room (now given over to a toy store's ware-
house), splayed out on the floor, and began a series of voices, tickling,
puppetry, and farting sounds. Mason laughed so hard he was in spasms.
Hanna knew all about the therapy we were going to, and she knew we
must have come straight from there. She saw me watching Sydney and
kissed my head, exactly as my mom used to. She told me to hang in
there. I shrugged like it was no big deal. Like I didn't know what she
was talking about.

**Coming clean.**

Before we left for our final meeting with Russ a week later, Sydney had
to go back in the house to get a sweater. There was a chill in the air.

Summer was giving way. School had just started, which meant getting to know a new class of kids for Sydney. My company's fiscal year-end was September 30th, which meant I had to make a year's worth of decisions on tax planning and budgets in the next couple of weeks. We needed resolution. After Sydney's proclamation about unconditional love left me not just unmoved but fighting to hold on to a splenetic list of minor offenses as evidence that she was flat wrong, I decided I needed to get out of my own way. I knew this was about me more than her. I thought she'd gone out on a limb the previous week to say things that were painful and potentially relationship-ending for us, but she was either that brave or in that much pain. I told her on the way to Russ's office that, if it was okay with her, I had a little speech prepared, and I wanted to go first. I reminded her how painful it was for me to give speeches and not get paid for them, and she smiled, but I could tell she was anxious.

"So you guys know how much I hate talking about the past. I hate the idea that things that happened so long ago can affect me today. That seems so weak to me. But ever since last week, when Syd was so honest, I started remembering being little and how critical it was for me to be okay with my mom. I would perform little skits for her, and sweep the floor for her, and hold cold compresses to her temples, and fetch the standard Italian woman's breakfast—coffee and toast and cigarettes. And so I caught on to the game. If I did well in school, I'd get attention. If I walked to the laundromat for her, or ran to the neighbors to borrow money, then she would be nice. And I got the message, you know? Do well and people will like you. If you don't, they withhold their affection. You have to produce. So I learned to get to practice early for basketball because being late was Coach Haden's pet peeve. My boss John Hobson said all rookies needed to work until five, so I never left before seven.

If I looked good, and if I could afford to take women to the best resorts or get the closest seats, if I made sure they had orgasms before me, then they would stay. If my speech this year was different and bigger and funnier than last year, then the crowds would cheer. If I was the best boss ever, my employees would be loyal. If I ever stopped producing, if I ever slowed down, if I ever had nothing left to give, then I would be left alone. Before today, I would have told you, 'Sydney has to have things her way, she's difficult, and I've learned to just give her what she wants.' But that's not true. Oh, I grant the request all right, but then I seethe. I punish her. And I'm so sorry for that, Syd. So look, here it is. I've never been able to tell anyone, 'I need you.' My personal zeitgeist is about not needing anyone. I've sold myself on the notion that we should *want* to be with each other, we shouldn't be dependent on each other. But that's not true. That's crap. I need you, Syd. I need you so much."

The silence was painful. I don't know if Russ was waiting for a response from Sydney or if she was waiting for him, but I couldn't have felt more naked. It was like when I finished a seminar and asked if there were any questions and no hands went up. Were there no questions because I had covered everything so well, or did I bomb so badly they just wanted to get the hell out of the room? Then Russ patted me on the knee, and he had a smile that was familiar to me. It was the smile I had when a rookie recruiter—who months earlier was helpless and fumbling and lost—executed my closing strategy perfectly on the phone and secured the deal with a client; the smile that says, "This is why I do this; this is worthwhile, this matters."

"I can see you approve, Russ, but I didn't say it to get your approval, although that would be just like me."

Russ was happy, and I was happy that Russ was happy, and I felt cleaner somehow, but Sydney didn't seem happy. She was clearly affected by what I said, but she was too solemn. The way she was nodding reminded me of a kid on a rock ledge over a river who was being dared to jump off. She was trying to assure herself it would be fine, that she couldn't turn back now.

**Coming clean. The sequel.**

Sydney leaned forward and crossed her arms around herself like she had stomach cramps. She said she knew how hard that was for me, and she believed it meant that Russ was helping us, that we could find our way back. But I had inspired her, and she needed to come clean herself. Something about the way she had to gather herself filled me with what headhunters know as "deal-breaker dread."

"The important thing is, it's over, but I have been involved with a guy on the soccer team. I did leave the marriage. I know I denied it to your face, over and over. I lied each time. I'm so, so sorry."

Russ. Thirty-five years of listening to this garbage. Poor Russ. He closed his eyes and looked up at the ceiling. Another summer lost.

"I owe it to you to answer any questions you have for me, Danny."

"You mean like who it is? It's no doubt Jamie. If you're expecting a litany of questions about where and when and what sexual positions, I'll pass. I know the playbook."

"If it matters, we never actually had intercourse. I know you don't believe that, but it's true. He wouldn't cross that line."

"'He wouldn't' is precious little solace. You must be losing your touch."

Russ stepped in. He had regained his balance. He said it was important to step back and realize what an opportunity this was. The worst was over. What Sydney had yearned for me to say, she'd finally heard; what I had lived in fear of was finally out in the open. He asked Sydney if she was sure she had broken it off. She said she swore it on her life. Russ looked at me and said he knew I was thinking that Sydney has simply repeated the pattern that brought us together, that I was feeling foolish, that my shame-based upbringing had been triggered. But he said I was wrong. He had seen people change, had done it himself. Trust can be restored. He said he could even give me the formula: Truth Over Time Equals Trust.

He said compared with any couple he had worked with, he knew we loved each other deeply. He urged us to take a time-out, to be kind to each other—and do absolutely nothing, take no action, in the near term. He asked Sydney if she could do that, and she nodded furiously. They both stared at me.

I wanted to tell them that it wasn't until this moment that I had realized how much I was capable of fooling myself. I really had believed her denials. I thought she was probably getting her ego stroked and was no doubt—when alcohol-fueled—bending boundaries of marital comportment. Sydney was a world-class flirt. But as I started to feel the same motion sickness I felt when peer-pressured into a roller-coaster ride, as I felt the jabbing pain in my gut (someone else has fucked her while I was home worrying, someone else was inside her), as my world lost whatever was left of its footing, I knew I had never accepted what was so very obvious. Kelsey had told me I had to know at some level that Syd was cheating, and I did know, but I found a way not to believe what I knew.

Instead, I looked at the clock and mused aloud that time indeed did fly when you're having fun. I handed Russ the check for the session. Then I summoned every ounce of energy in my body.

"Sydney, I want you to know that I realize that had to be an incredibly hard thing to say. That took guts."

. . .

Anyone paid to conduct an arcane study on Post–Therapy Betrayal in married couples would have given us high marks over the next few days. I came home early from work. Sydney was home and had made a meal with the cleanest of macronutrients sans the patronizing commentary. We played chess, a wonderful way to pass time without having to actually converse, and when she trounced me, as she always did, there was no trash-talking on her part, and I refrained, for obvious reasons, from my usual excuse that she had cheated. When she brought out her papers to grade, I asked her if there were any standout students this year, and she read me a few samples from her Composition 101 course. She in turn asked me about the deals I was working on and listened intently when I explained the dynamic between the client company and the prospective candidate. When CNN led off its weather segment with a monster hurricane predicted to hit the Outer Banks where we vacationed every year, we followed the story, and then reminisced fondly about the first time we saw wild horses running on the beach past our blanket. We went to bed together after I made my rounds, making sure the cats were inside, turning off all the lights, and locking the doors. Sex was out of the question, but I held her and told her to sleep well, and then Gatsby jumped on her chest. She stroked him until she went under. But we were not at peace. We got no catharsis from her confession. We were numb. We knew this couldn't go on, that it was wholly false, but we didn't know what to do.

Every night during that terrible fortnight after Syd's confession was painful when we went to sleep. I was hurt, of course, and angry, for sure, but what I felt most was a loss of power. I couldn't make it go away. It was out there in the world. The person I loved most had humiliated me. She had a choice to protect me, and she chose otherwise. Russ told us that when trust was broken, it was not like a house fire where everything had perished. It was like a broken arm. It could heal. The last thing I remember thinking when we gave each other a cursory hug and turned over that night was that I wanted to believe we could restore what we once had, but for some reason I just couldn't. What was wrong with me? Some nights she seemed so lonely that I wanted to tell her to call Jamie, to go to him, to do whatever she needed to do to stop looking that way. And she could see I was lonely too.

. . .

"Are you on your cell?"

"Yeah, I'm in the car."

"Well, the call dropped just when you were getting to the good stuff. Are you saying you are going to join a swingers' club? I mean, I get wanting to get back at her, but that's not quid pro quo, that's quid pro whoa!"

After a couple of mind-numbing weeks, I had taken to driving around after dinner. It was fall in New England, the foliage full and magical, and we were still at a point where Sydney couldn't question anything I wanted to do. She knew I didn't want her to come along, and she was glad to get the chance to breathe. She didn't know that on one excursion I called Kelsey, ostensibly to talk about business or to ask about Desiree, but soon I told her everything that happened in therapy.

"No. Jesus. Verizon needs more towers in the Farmington Valley. I was saying I wish I had the courage of my intellectual convictions when it comes to sex. I was saying I understand the idea of a swingers' club. I can see that from their perspective it's more honest. They concede that you can love someone deeply but get sick of them sexually. It's pure biology. Hardwiring. So they get together at scheduled intervals, exchange partners, you get that need met, as does your partner. You drive home together. No games. No yearning. No duplicity. We long to sleep with others and yet judge others who do; we say we are being faithful, but it's only out of convention, or the fear of getting caught, or our moral framework. Swingers don't have to flirt. They separate their needs. It's more honest. Right?"

"You're asking the wrong person. I flirt with inanimate objects, and I'm unfaithful. I'm kind of my own category."

"The point is I understand an open marriage. I wish I were capable of it. But I'm not. When I love someone, I want sexual possession. I want them to want only me. Even though I know that can't be sustained."

"Do you believe her when she says she is done with Soccer Boy?"

"I do. How pitiful is that? But there'll be another soccer boy someday, right? Or a colleague, or friend of a friend. There's always someone better looking, younger, faster. It's who she is. You tell me Kay, if you decided to make your marriage work, could you stay faithful to Jay?"

She said she had to call me back and hung up immediately. I was about to text her to tell her I was wrong to call her, it was not her concern, go be with her daughter. But instead I pulled into a Dunkin' Donuts, not to buy my tenth coffee of the day, but to use the restroom for the tenth time that day. By the time I pulled back onto Route 6, my phone was buzzing. She had switched to her cell phone, and the sound was scratchy with a slight echo.

"I went to a lawyer. We drew up the papers. I'm filing for divorce. And before you panic or say anything you might regret, it has nothing to do with you, or you and Sydney."

"Well, of course not. Why would it? What was the tipping point, since you've been talking about this for two years?"

"Nothing as dramatic—no offense to Saint Sydney—as your therapy trauma. You really want to know?"

"Sure. If you want to tell me."

"I said something *so* funny that even I was amazed I thought of it, and I got nothing from him. He didn't get the reference. I am married to a dumbass. We all have our lines in the sand."

I reminded her, after giving her the abrupt laugh she sought, that her husband was a manager of a large medical device manufacturing plant who managed dozens of people and a multimillion-dollar budget. He was a former officer in the army, and he was educated and bright and fairly funny in his own right.

"He doesn't get me. He never will. I'm too young to settle. Looks fade—I get that, but I am going to be funny forever, and I can't waste it on him. I'm serving the papers, Dan."

"When?"

"I don't know. I wish he would give me what you have now. I wish I could find him cheating. Then I could file, and he'd be the bad guy. I tried not having sex with him for a really long time, but I check his browser history, and he just amps up his porn usage."

"What would you do if you weren't afraid, Kelsey?"

"Fuck, I knew you couldn't get through a whole conversation without one of your seminar aphorisms. I know! But it's so easy for you to say. I have to think of Desiree, and her not being in the same house as Mommy and Daddy, and you know how I am with money. I don't even know what our bills are, or even what bank we have our mortgage with. I just make placements and cash commission checks. And he does the cooking and laundry and all these little things that you don't have to worry about because you have money."

Right. I had heard this before from other friends during The Drift. The wealthier I became, the less empathy people felt for me. "Buy new feelings" was the unsaid suggestion. You're too rich for us to ever feel sorry for you in any real way again. I was silent for so long that Kelsey asked me if I was still there.

"Can I go so offline that you might fire me? Please keep in mind I am about to become a single mom and really, really need my job!"

I was tired of driving. I pulled into a parking lot shared by a Friendly's restaurant and a Walgreens. I didn't bother telling Kelsey she could speak freely. She knew no other way, and she was well aware she was at no risk at work. Her favored status was already causing deep unrest among the senior people. She was the youngest person to ever make junior partner.

"Why isn't this a good thing for you? You've been unhappy with her for so long. Can you even remember the last time the two of you did something together that made you feel happy?"

I could.

Two years before, Sydney had decided her grade school friend Karen would be perfect for my just-divorced college friend Bruce. I didn't get it. It seemed to me Bruce would be licking his wounds after a brutal second divorce, and Karen lived in Cleveland. The logistics made no sense. But once Syd hatched her scheme, and had Karen out for a long weekend and just happened to ask Bruce to stop by, it was clear I was completely wrong. Bruce called me the next day to see if she liked him. I told him

I wasn't sure since she hadn't left a note in my locker, but I had a study hall with her coming up and I'd ask. He hung up and called Syd. They talked for an hour, with Karen sitting on the arm of the chair listening in. They went out that night. Bruce flew to Cleveland the next weekend, and every weekend after for three months. They were engaged at Christmas, and now Sydney and I were on our way to Buffalo for the wedding. Only being the best man and the maid of honor—essentially our finder's fee for the hookup—could make Sydney down her Xanax and risk flying.

In fact, it was only as a way to distract Sydney from her terror that I asked her what her thoughts were about the toast. Karen asked us to do it together.

"I figured you would handle it. Toasts are your thing. You haven't come up with anything yet?"

Welcome to my world. I had spent, at that time, a decade being paid obscene fees for speeches I hadn't written until I got on the plane. I'd scribble an outline and wing it. I would still do this today if associations didn't demand PowerPoints that they could copy in advance for the attendees.

I played with some word tracks and some rhythms in my head, and then I wrote a few lines and numbered them. I handed them to Sydney.

"Okay. Here's what we're going to do. Memorize these key phrases, and just keep in mind the overall intention of the scene."

"Which is?"

"The more you argue with me, the funnier it will be."

And in the next ten seconds I realized why I loved her so much. She was fearless. She looked at the lines, which had to seem meaningless, and then nodded her head. She was all in. We never discussed the toast again nor did we rehearse.

The next day as everyone settled in at the reception, the DJ said it was time for the toast, and for those who didn't know, Sydney and Danny were the ones who introduced Bruce and Karen, and therefore were going to do the toast together.

"Hi, I'm Danny and from the moment I met Karen, I said to Sydney, 'I think she'd be great for Bruce. In fact, my gut is if we got them together, they'd fall in love and get married,' so it's no surprise to me . . . "

"Wait, wait, what?! It was *my* idea and *you* said it was a stupid idea!"

"Uh, no, honey, that's not how it happened. But listen, the point is . . . "

"The point is you said they'd never make it to Christmas!"

"No, no I believe I said the holidays can be a depressing time."

"Back the bus up, you said Bruce would get sick of flying to Cleveland!"

"No, no I said travel can be arduous . . . (sotto voce) Honey, there are people here."

"You said Karen loved teaching art too much to give it up for Bruce!"

"Well, okay, that I did say, but I think it was because I flunked art history, and I was repressing something. Can we not do this right now . . . "

"You said, and I quote, 'One of them will get cold feet.'"

"I really don't remember specifying a body part. Look. Can we at least agree that no matter how it came down, your best friend and my best friend have found each other, are crazy in love, and that, by raising our glasses, we hope they end up with a marriage just like ours?"

"Oh sweet Jesus, let's hope they do better than that!"

We killed. Sydney never rushed it, stayed in character, and nailed every line. It was us at our best. We would never be in sync that way again. Our farewell appearance as "the couple meant for each other."

Kelsey's voice was getting softer, wispy. She was tired. It had gotten dark out.

"Well, I can't decide. Either she's a spoiled brat or you are very different to be married to than you are to be with at the office all day. But I've known you for almost five years now, and I'm giving you the benefit of the doubt. You've been good to me . . . "

I bristled at allowing her to bad-mouth Sydney, even as I knew by calling her and telling the story of Syd's betrayal I had brought it on. I told her the truth was always in the middle in these situations. But Kelsey was in full umbrage-on-behalf-of-Danny mode, and I shamelessly soaked it up.

" . . . you don't judge me. You're the only person in the world I can confess these shitty things I've done to and be completely honest. I see how you treat people and how kind you are, and you make me want to be a better person, but lots of people make me want to be a better person. You're the only friend I know I won't lose if I choose not to become a better person."

My car had been off for so long that I was starting to shiver. I noted the time and told Kelsey I was sure she had to put Dez to bed soon and I had to drive home.

"Me too. God, I must have gone through a quarter tank of gas sitting here. I have the carbon footprint of Shaq."

"You're sitting in your driveway?"

"No, when I switched to my cell, I said I was running to the grocery store. I'll make up a story. I drove around for a while but I just pulled over."

I laughed and told her I'd done the same thing. We were ridiculous. Then she said she was hoping the Walgreens she was next to would have the things she would need to cover her story. And then I saw the interior light of a car door come on, and across the parking lot, Kelsey stepped out of her Passat. Nearly the entire time we were talking, she had only been a few rows away in the crowded parking lot. Neither of us was anywhere near home.

"Kay, look up and to your left, about a hundred feet, near the restaurant."

Her look was an unlikely mixture of shock and certitude fighting for space on her face. She came to my car, and I started the engine so we would be warm. We didn't say anything for a few unbearable moments. What was this?! What did it mean? We stared out the windshield. It was like we were at a drive-in where no movie was showing.

"I can't believe this. Out of all the parking lots, and all the Walgreens, in all the towns . . . "

"You have to pull into this one? I know you're too young for *Casablanca*. What a waste of a reference."

"Do you seriously think this is a coincidence? That we both just happened to decide to drive around, that without knowing where we were, we both ended up in the same parking lot at the same time, spending two hours talking about our broken relationships?"

"Something occurred without any apparent causal connection. I'm pretty sure that would be the definition of a coincidence."

"If Sydney drove by right now, do you think for a second she would think this wasn't planned? That it was innocent?"

"No. And I wouldn't expect her to. It's hard enough for me to believe it."

"Well, I don't think it is coincidence. And I don't think it is innocent. And I think it does mean something. Just saying."

"Me too."

"So what do we do?"

What was the bottom line? How was she going to capitalize on this? How would this new information, our meeting, help her seal the deal? No one I ever trained had her closing skills.

She was nearly twenty-seven now. It was no longer her youth that drew me to her. She was a mess. Selfish and shallow, yet capable of posing serious questions and thinking deeply about them. Every day I saw her present a phony self to the world, and yet in my private office she unveiled an authenticity people twice her age couldn't match. She covered her insecurities and fears with bravado and action. I knew she was damaged and engaged in a lifelong battle with demons not yet understood or revealed to her. Did I want to help her win it? Did I think I could save her?

We hugged. We didn't kiss. She made a joke that the last time she went parking with a guy he at least tried to feel her up. She went to her car, and I beeped the horn and pointed to the Walgreens. She made a pistol out of her thumb and forefinger and pointed to her head, and then strolled toward the automated entrance door.

When I walked in the house, Sydney was on the couch in the family room. She looked worried sick. She asked me if I was okay. I said I was fine. She started to follow me into the bedroom, and I was suddenly concerned that she would smell the hug and freak out. I went into the bathroom, and she waited on the bed while I washed up. I told myself I had done nothing wrong, and her suspicious look irritated me. She didn't have the nerve to ask me for details. And as I got into bed and saw the digital clock/calendar on my bedside table I could see why. It was a Thursday night.

## CHAPTER 13

# Betrayed

Now I have to tell you about my dream. I really don't want to, because I detest it when books or movies have dream sequences. The protagonist falls off to sleep; cue the New Age music (completely alien from the rest of the soundtrack), and in case we are too dumb to realize *he's dreaming this*, dissolve slowly to the dream while we see our dreamer toss and turn. In a book, it is often worse, because they don't even tell you it's a dream until you get far enough in to realize nothing is making sense—*oh . . . he must be dreaming*. That's when I skip ahead until I see we are back to the land of the living. I have never, by doing this, missed a single shred of information of value. Henry James and I would have fist-bumped on this point since he said, "Tell a dream, lose a reader."

Syd loved to talk about her dreams. I find most women do. Many mornings at the office I would be loading up the coffeemaker and some woman staff member would say to me, "I'm pissed at you. I had a dream last night about you. I was, for some reason, back at girl scout camp, but I was my age and dressed for work, and you were supposed to give a seminar, but you were in a sleeping bag, and I was trying to get you out of the sleeping bag, but you kept saying 'let me sleep in until the marshmallow roast or I'm going to fire you.' You were so mean to me. What do you think that was about?"

Nothing. Dreams are a random firing of neurons. They're boring. Please don't tell me about any more of your dreams.

But Syd would start most mornings recounting being chased by monsters or trapped in a burning building. Someone was always in pursuit of her. They were "so real" that she was often sweating or hyperventilating. They were always about to stab her, shoot her, or strangle her. I would wake her to calm her down. Then she would tell me the excruciating details of her "straight to Netflix" dreams, fall back into oblivion, and I'd be up all night.

Maybe my real issue with dreams is that I never dream. Or if I do, I don't remember them. Dubitable friends, and even Russ, would tell me I do dream but am choosing not to remember. "Hell," one friend said, "my dog dreams."

I spent most of my adult life dismissing the meaning of dreams and even accusing people of manipulation, of using their dreams to say something they didn't have the guts to say while simultaneously preserving the built-in excuse that they were "just dreaming." I thought dreams were lazy thinking. Nothing of meaning could come from these fragments. So as a person who finds dreams a waste of time, why would I take you this far into my world and risk losing you to a dream sequence?

Because then I had the dream. Because the dream was my tipping point.

The first remembered dream of my life. And everything had to change.

Vietnam was all anyone talked about the summer I turned twelve. It is hard for people to fathom today, when we take the never-ending War on Terror for granted, when some American involvement somewhere in the world has become a given. We have more access to information than ever; still, no one I know would be able to tell you how many marines died this year in Iraq, but when I was twelve, the aggregate count of Americans killed in Vietnam was the first thing discussed by Walter Cronkite and David Brinkley each night on the evening news. But America then seemed divided into two camps: Either you thought North Vietnam's regime had to be vanquished to prevent the spread of communism, or you thought the war was insane and was in no way mission critical to our security or to the preservation of democracy. Young men either wore their hair long, listened to the entreaties of John Lennon and other peaceniks when they held their bed-ins or sit-ins, and actively demonstrated as "draft-dodging conscientious objectors," or they kept their hair short, modeled themselves after their fathers who served in Korea or WWII, and signed up to "kill some gooks."

My brother was a hybrid. He listened to heavy metal rock and did drugs and wore tie-dye and said things like "groovy" and "solid." A total hippie. Then he enlisted. My father then recast him to the rest of the family as a hero; someone fighting to keep us all safe from the communists who were practically at our door. He was never sent to Vietnam. He got lucky and was stationed in Korea. He would call once every other week, and my father considered the call sacred. We all had to be home and gathered around the phone. "Your brother is calling from the War," my father would yell out to me as I played in the yard. I would roll my eyes, come into the house, and ask my father when the North Vietnamese had invaded Korea. He would cuff me in the head and hand me the phone.

Some months later, just before summer started, my brother was transferred to El Paso, Texas, and my father announced we were taking a family vacation and driving to El Paso to see him. There were many levels on which this was unacceptable to me. First and foremost, I was a star in Little League, and I would miss four games! Then, add on the idea that I would be with my family, who seemed to hate each other on most levels, in a car, for three days straight! Not happening. And then there was Tibby. My first dog. We got her when I was a baby, and I adored her. Other kids had teddy bears or blankets. I had Tibby. When reminding my parents that we couldn't afford the trip didn't work, when pointing out that our car often broke down in town and was therefore unlikely to make a 2,000-mile trip didn't work, I played my ace. Who would take care of Tibby?

I volunteered to stay home while they went on the trip, and my mother laughed. "We're going for two weeks. I can't leave a twelve-year-old home for two weeks by himself. No, Danny." Now my mother knew I didn't cry about anything. She had wired me that way herself to make her life easier. So when I suddenly burst into tears and said Tibby would starve to death, she gave me the full treatment. She called me over and told me to sit on her lap. She said she knew I loved Tibby very much and she would never do anything to hurt her or me. She said she had already made arrangements with a kennel. They would feed her and give her water and, "Guess what, honey? They hire these students who are studying to be animal trainers at places like Disneyworld to play with the dogs during the day, so don't be surprised if when we come home Tibby knows a few tricks to show you!" I remember having the presence of mind to ask her why Disneyworld would hire people to train dogs when there are no dogs in Disneyworld other than the fake ones like Pluto, but she changed the subject instantly. She promised me,

"God strike me dead," that Tibby would be fine, and we would pick her up the day we got home. When I asked how we could afford a kennel, her eyes narrowed, and she pushed me off her lap. "Are you saying you don't believe me, your own mother?! Is that what you are saying to me?!" I assured her it was not; I just wanted Tibby to be okay. I said I was sorry, but she was done with me and told me to leave her alone.

So a few days later, off we went to El Paso. And now the dream. I want to point out that I didn't go to bed consciously thinking about the El Paso trip. I wasn't triggered in any way by events that day. I fell off to sleep.

*Suddenly I was back in our 1970 Impala.* We were still a few hundred miles out of El Paso. I couldn't believe how big and dusty and boring a drive through Texas could be. It was the third day of our sojourn, and my mother had already threatened to kill everyone in the car, including herself, and I can speak for my sisters in saying that would have been fine with us too. Our collective complaining from the backseat hit a feverish pitch, and I heard my mother whisper to my father to get off the next goddamn exit and find something for these idiot kids to do. At first my father, eager to get to El Paso and give the Medal of Honor to my brother, protested, and then he stopped midsentence and pointed to a sign and smiled. It was as if he was a dying man in a desert (well, I guess he sort of was) and saw an oasis. The sign read: Go-Carts this Exit, Fun for the Whole Family

I asked the man (he was probably seventeen) who gave us the three-minute speech on how to use the brakes and what to do if we hit the wall of tires and spun off the track ("Y'all just stay in the cart and I'll be there right quick and we'll get you going again."). I asked which was the fastest go-cart, and he pointed to the emerald-green one and winked at me. We had to wait until two more families arrived before they would let us out on the course to make it worthwhile for them, but that simple business judgment was killing me. When a car pulled up with a few more kids, I greeted them and asked if there was anything I could do to expedite their getting their helmets on. I started giving them the CliffsNotes version of the lecture we got—but to no avail. They had to go through the same ordeal. My parents sat on a picnic bench with a big umbrella and sipped Tab soda. None of us had ever experienced that kind of heat or seen that kind of topography. As far as the eye could see, the world was flat and brown. Awesome for go-carting! Finally the families got locked in, and the minimum-wage adolescent running the place waved the checkered flag.

I'd like to say, for the record, I was way, way ahead when it happened. I never considered my sisters serious competition, but I was concerned about this wiry local kid who tried to pass me on the first turn until I banked him off the six-foot-high pile of tires that lined the course. I recall being vaguely irritated that I didn't ask what the course record time was before we started. And then it didn't matter.

Doreen was the baby of the family. Decades later, when she was struck by multiple sclerosis and couldn't work, when she was later forced to go into a rest home in her early forties having been shortchanged on all of life's joys and most of its experiences, I felt nothing but fondness for her. But back then, Hanna and I were annoyed that Doreen was raised with none of the discipline that we were. She got away with murder. Now I can see that my parents were simply exhausted. (Often in those teen years, my father would wake up, walk into the kitchen where I was eating cereal, and cuff me in the head. When I asked why, he would say he knew I was going to fuck up at some point that day, so he might as well get it over with. And I would have to nod, since I did have specific plans to fuck up that day.) Doreen got whatever she wanted. She cried; they caved. Simple. And so what, right? Until you are on a wide-open go-cart course in El Paso, and unlike New England tracks that were shorter and where the carts had built in governors that prevented high speeds, these carts could exceed fifty miles per hour. The wall of tractor tires that lined the course pre-vented you from being able to break through and end up on the adjacent highway, but still, a ten-year-old girl with poor hand-eye coordination should not be allowed on the course. She was borderline for the height and age requirement, and when the kid running the place suggested, "The little lady ought to sit this one out," she wailed big time and embarrassed my mother. Shame ruled our world, so my mother sold hard.

"If she goes slowly enough, I'm sure it will be fine, and we'll all be watching." And then she lied. "She's done this before back home."

I can't say I heard or saw it. The helmet was so tight it was hard to hear anything besides the motor of the go-cart. I only realized, as I made the turn that led into the stretch, that no other carts were on the track. I pulled over, and what I saw seemed so surreal that I thought it was some sort of desert mirage. The small mobile home/trailer that served as the office and concession stand for the go-cart place was at least fifteen feet beyond the tractor-tire-lined walls of the course. As you pulled off the course when the ride was up, there was a narrow lane lined by conventional car tires. You pulled over, turned off your engine, the kid came over and took your helmet and said, "Y'all have a nice day and thanks for coming."

Doreen was impaled on the large towing hook at the end of the trailer. She was three feet off the ground hanging off the hook, her leg speared like a piece of sushi. Her go-cart was upside down in the middle of the parking lot. The small tire wall near the entrance was completely knocked down. Everyone was screaming—nobody louder than the minimum-wage kid running the place. My mother was incapable of panic. My father was bent over the concession counter stretching a phone cord calling for help, and my mother dragged the picnic table over to my sister like it weighed five ounces—Tabs and paper plates flying—so my sister could lie on it. My mother ordered the other parents to find towels, and while she was waiting, started tearing her own white tee shirt apart. It was the only time in my life that I saw her put shame on hold.

While the scene was shocking, I already knew what had happened. When I had passed Doreen on the course, I could tell she kept confusing the brake with the gas, and on one pass, I could see the kid waving the checkered flag to try to get her off the course. She told me later she'd slammed on what she thought was the brake and froze. She couldn't lift her leg off the gas or steer. And she headed right for the parents' picnic bench. At lower speeds, the wall of tires would have stopped her, but she was maxed out for the entire final straightaway, and when she hit the smaller tire wall near the entrance, the cart went end over end and into the air. My older sister and my parents both claim—so I have to believe them—that the cart flew over the picnic table, the seat belts finally gave way, and Doreen slammed into the side of the trailer. The cart kept going, and on her way down, the hook speared her leg.

A half hour later, the fireman removed the hook, with her still on it, and put them both in the ambulance. Just as they were loading my sister into the ambulance and my mother was giving instructions to my father, one of the parents interrupted and said she wanted my mother to know they were going to get together as a group and say a prayer to Jesus for her little girl, and my mother stared her down without comment. My father thanked the woman, and my mother gave my father a look that said she would never forgive him—for the idea to stop, for the accident, for the need for the trip, for Vietnam even, but mostly—for saying thank you to that woman. My mother rode with Doreen, and we followed them to the hospital in our car. I would never again see my father drive over the speed limit.

Three excruciating weeks later we drove home. Doreen needed the entire backseat to extend her wrapped and braced leg. We needed to stop every couple of hours so my mother could re-dress the huge wound. Doreen cried most of the trip. Hanna cried because she had to sit in the backseat with

Doreen's leg on her lap and couldn't read or move without Doreen screaming in pain. I whined incessantly about how undignified it was for a boy of my advanced years—six months from being a legitimate teen—to be sitting on his mother's lap for hours at a time. By Tennessee, I calculated I had spent more time on my mother's lap on the trip than I had my entire life. When I pointed this out, she said, "Well, enjoy, it's your fucking swan song."

All the way home my parents argued about money. I gathered that my father had taken an emergency loan, not his first, from his factory's credit union, and my mother had done what she loathed to do, asked her estranged aunts for money. This was before health insurance, and with no notice we had to pay for Doreen's surgery and find a place to stay for three weeks while she recovered. My brother got us some discounted military family housing, and while for most people the spare apartment would have been mortifying, it was cleaner and bigger than our house. So the conversation—when they weren't telling us to shut up—was about who was to blame, and how we would pay the money back.

Out of respect for the situation, all the frayed feelings, and the proximity of my mother's ire (I was still on her lap), I waited until New Jersey to ask. I was proud that I held out that long!

"Can we pick up Tibby from the kennel on the way home?"

"No."

"Why not?"

"Jesus H. Christ. Where would we put her? On your sister's leg? We'll get her tomorrow."

Her spatial concerns being unimpeachable, I waited until we were home and unpacked. It wasn't even 2:00 p.m., and when I asked if we could go get her, my mother assured me they were closed. I went to the phone book and pointed out the hours of operation. She melted down and told me to stop being so selfish. And then she went cold on me. "We'll get the goddamn dog when I'm good and ready."

When I asked again first thing the next morning, she started on a story about how she had called the kennel and they'd said they were fully booked . . . but my father could take it no more. He was shaving with the door wide open in our tiny bathroom off the kitchen, and he slammed down his straight razor into his cup of shaving soap and his voice shook. "Jane. Enough. Tell him." My mother took me outside and told my sister Hanna to stay inside. Oddly, I remember worrying that Tibby might be sick, but it never occurred to me, with my trust in my mother so absolute and sacrosanct, that what I was about to hear was utterly predictable to even a kid my age if I had possessed a lick of sense.

"Tibby is not at a kennel," she explained. "We couldn't afford a kennel. You know that. And there was no one to take care of her, and even if there had been, she would have been tied up all day on that chain in our tiny yard. It's cruel, Danny, to treat an animal that way. You can't say you love her and want to be cruel to her, right? So your Dad spoke to some friends at work who live in Goshen, on a farm. Where she could run. No chain. And they are nice people who love dogs. So they have her."

I was still processing. I still didn't get it. I thought that was fine. Good call. So she'd had a nice vacation on a farm—sounds like she'd had it a whole lot better than we had. "So now let's go get her and bring her home!"

"We can't, honey. We gave her to them to keep. She's their dog now. They have little kids who needed a dog. We'll get you another dog someday. But we decided this was best for Tibby, who is getting on in years. Don't you want what is best for her? Don't you love her enough to want what is best for her?! Did I not raise you right?! You stop your crying right now and answer that question, little man. Are you really that selfish?"

"No. No. They can have her. I just . . . I love her; she's my dog!! Don't I get to say good-bye?"

"We don't think that's best. It would just make it worse. I'm sorry, honey."

That night, just before it got dark, I looked out the living room window and saw my father take Tibby's chain off the tree in our backyard and put her bowls in the trash can. He was crying. I went outside and waited for him on the porch. As he passed me, I told him it was okay; "I know it wasn't you." He seemed utterly miserable.

And who knows, I might have been all right in time. Kids forget, right? They get distracted. Surely this was my mother's plan. And it might have worked. By the third day, I felt guilty about crying or complaining about Tibby when my little sister was in such agonizing pain. I pictured Tibby running in from the yard and inadvertently slamming into my sister's brace. I was trying to sell myself, but while kids forget, kids are cruel, too. I don't even remember what Hanna and I were arguing about, but on the fourth day we were going at it hard, and I called her stupid for whatever minor trespass she'd committed, and she scoffed.

"I'm stupid. Oh that's rich coming from you! Do you think Tibby is really on a farm? Are you really that dense?"

I was so clueless. What did she mean? Where else would she be?

To her credit, Hanna said never mind, but I was relentless. Then I got physical and started jabbing her and calling her stupid, and she finally snapped.

"She was put to sleep, you idiot. There was never a farm; there were never any friends of Daddy's who magically needed a dog. They took her to the pound the day before we left. She's dead! Your dog is dead!"

I slapped her and pulled her hair and told her to stop lying. She broke from me and ran into the kitchen and opened the drawer where my father kept all "his papers," which was code for all the bills we were behind on, and after a few minutes of digging, she pulled out an envelope, and threw it at me. The letterhead address said Torrington Animal Control. Even I knew that was a euphemism for the dog pound. I pulled out the document inside, which was a yellow receipt. I scanned quickly. My father's signature. My dog's name. The date—the day before we left, and the term, "euthanized by gas." And the amount. A donation asked for but not required. Ten dollars. It only took ten dollars to kill my dog. It must have seemed like such a deal to my mother.

Then I woke up. Thirsty. My shirt soaked. My head pounding. So that is dreaming, huh, that's what I've been missing? You can have it. The problem was I didn't know if it was a dream or a memory. I certainly remembered the trip and my sister's accident. I remembered giving Tibby away. Did I make up the rest? It didn't feel like it. But how would I know? Throughout the entire day at work, I remembered it all over again, and every time, it was more vivid. Every time, I felt such rage at my mother. But I also knew I could be tricking myself. The fact was I had just found out my wife was cheating on me, my world was in flux; it would make sense for me to project my anger and loss of control onto my mother instead of onto Sydney. Maybe I needed to believe my mother had violated my trust in a monstrous way in order to forgive what Sydney had done.

. . .

I left work early and drove an hour to New Hartford to talk to Hanna. Considering how much we fought as little kids, it was amazing how close we had become. Like my dad, she was incapable of deceit; like my mom, she was tough minded and strong willed. When she saw how distraught I was, she asked her husband to watch the boys, who never left her sight, and we sat in her family room. I recounted my dream, and when I got to the end, she started to cry. I hadn't seen her cry in thirty years, including at both our parents' funerals, where she welled up but never let go.

"It's not a dream; it's true. I didn't know you didn't remember it. I just thought we were never going to speak about it. Do you hate me?"

"Oh, God, no. Hell, I would have used it against me, too. I don't know how you waited four days. I just want to know, what did I do? I have no memory of what came next."

"Really? Wow. You read the receipt, and you calmed right down. You went outside and didn't come back in until Mom got home. You walked up to her, with no expression, and you handed it to her. Then you sat down and watched TV. Mom kept waiting for you to go nuts, but you never did. Then you stopped talking. You really don't remember this?"

"I stopped talking? For how long?"

"God, I want to say months, but that couldn't be because you had to go back to school at some point. But for sure, a few weeks. You wouldn't speak. They weren't sure you could speak. Mom actually pinched you while you were sleeping to make sure you could make a sound."

And it started to come back. I was remembering it all now. They took me to a doctor. There was nothing wrong with me. I had just lost faith. It was actually my mother's idol, Cary Grant, who brought me back. He was on television. It was in his last, post-movie days. He wore longish white hair and heavy Woody Allen glasses but still couldn't hide his good looks. My mother was saying she read somewhere his real name was not Cary Grant—that when he grew up in England he'd had a different name. My father said he remembered that too—that Grant was once a gymnast before he was an actor, but he couldn't recall the name either. And I couldn't bear it any longer. To know something and not share it was as impossible for me then as it is now.

"Archibald Leach." My parents stared at me. "That was his name before he changed it to Cary Grant." My mother signaled to my father not to react. She said, "Thank you, dear, you're right. Such a clever boy I have."

Hanna asked me whether she could hug me and I told her I didn't need a hug and she said that was not why she was asking. So I hugged her. She asked me if I was going to be okay, and when I didn't answer, she said if I was going to stop speaking now I should remember it's already been done.

I drove home and realized I should probably give this some time. Did it mean I was no longer capable of trust? Did it mean I had some hardwired fear that anyone I loved would eventually betray me, and if so, then what would be the point of ever being with anyone?

But I didn't give it time. Something was extinguished.

I sat Sydney down and said we couldn't resolve the situation without a trial separation. I needed to leave. I made it clear that I wasn't trying to punish her but that I couldn't think clearly and see her every day and hope things would heal. I even told her about the dream. Thanks to her years in therapy, she sensed its import even more than I did, and after hearing the whole thing, she agreed a separation made the most sense. We held hands quietly, and, no doubt recalling her alcoholic mother's own freakish choices, she said softly, "God, our mothers fuck us up, don't they? Maybe it's just as well we never had kids."

"Do you believe that?"

"Not for a second."

We went online and started searching for furnished condos. I left two days later. Never to return.

## CHAPTER 14

# Sex with a Younger Woman

There are two ways people tell lies. One is to say something that is not true. Your candidate says he is making $150K when he is actually only making $120K. He figures you can't check since he is working. The other way people lie is to withhold information. To conceal. This is much more common in the real world. And it is more damaging because of its insidious nature. Here's the thing you need to know about people if you're going to be a great recruiter: Nearly everyone will conceal (and people who conceal don't think they are lying), but most have a hard time saying something false when asked a direct question. From those who can, there is no defense.

**From Danny's "This Just In—Candidates Tell Lies" Seminar**

. . .

Today was a big test for my back and my recovery. I passed some conventional milestones. I could rotate fully left and right and stand on one foot pain free; my chiropractor was happy that I could hold "child's pose" for thirty seconds, and I could now sit in a chair with no brace or pillow. My hips still had a severely limited range of motion, and I still couldn't pass the test I found the most embarrassing. They would have me lie on the floor and attempt a "bridge" position, where I thrust my hips forward in what appeared to me to be a comically sexual way. At the first tentative thrust of my hips, the spasms returned, stabbing wildly, and the inflammation would radiate for hours. I didn't ask my doctor what I really wanted to know. Would I ever have sex again?

And then I remembered how I handled it the last time I had wondered if I would ever have sex again, and I thought it might just be for the best if my back never fully healed.

Money makes hard things easier. I took a six-month lease on a fully furnished condo in the Farmington Woods complex, just a few miles from our house. The owners, the Warrens, were an elderly couple who spent their winters in Vermont and came back to Connecticut for the warmer months to be around their grown children and grandchildren. All I had to move were my clothes, but Sydney came with me anyway. We were in solidarity. She asked me if I wanted to take my spring clothes or golf clubs. I shook my head and said we'd have it all figured out by then, and she squeezed my hand.

Our deal was simple. Get some space. You only get divorced once, and before we throw it all away, let's give it some time. She told me I could come by any time to see the cats, and if I was concerned about her not telling the truth about the soccer guy, I could come by with no notice. She had nothing to hide anymore. She was waiting for me to tell her she could do the same, but I said nothing.

She had one rule, and she had to ask me something first. "Was there anyone else? It would be perfectly human," she said calmly, if you had slept with someone else, or if you moved out to be with someone else," but she wanted to know now. I told her, truthfully, that I hadn't slept with anyone else since our first date and, at the same time, concealed the brewing storm of Kelsey. So she rolled out the rule. "We are still married. This is a trial separation. We cannot date anyone else—even casually—during the six months." She said if at any time either one of us decided we wanted to either date someone else or simply give up the ghost and file for divorce, we would do so with civility and kindness. No craziness, no horror show. Let's never be that couple. Then she sat on the couch and waited for me to make a move. When you're married, you know the look. You don't have to initiate sex; you give the look. But seated under the family portrait of the Warrens in this very strange place of theirs, that idea suddenly struck me as beyond sad. All I felt was fear. I shrugged, which she mistook for lingering anger, gathered herself, and gave me a hug at the door.

I reneged on our deal in three weeks. Cowardly, I began a trial separation with one woman while simultaneously embarking on a trial union with another. I was afraid of getting too involved with a woman I knew to be unstable and petrified of losing the woman who had hurt me. I'll spare the buildup, the near misses and gamesmanship, the suggestive emails, the caving in to the taboo first kiss, and the breathy thrill of the illicit that is part of its attraction. I'll get to what sex is like with a twenty-seven-year-old woman for a man embarking on middle age.

"Okay, wait! What is that?!"

"What?"

"That, that thing you're wearing!"

"What—you mean my thong?"

"I have never seen anything like that. Does that hurt to wear?"

"No. Are you telling me you have never seen a thong?"

"Uh, I would have remembered this. This is amazing. Look, you can slide it over for easy access."

"Look at your face. You're hilarious. It's also called butt floss— you've never heard of that? God, I have so much to teach you. You like?"

"Like? I wouldn't put it in the same class as fire, or the wheel, or elec- tricity, but it's a solid fourth among great inventions. No, no . . . leave it on for a while."

In a cheating survey by the dating site Victoria Milan, they reported that over fifty percent of cheaters found their spouse or significant other more attractive than their lover, only thirty percent of men cheat with younger women, and only twenty-five percent of lovers are in better physical shape than the spouse or significant other. But cheating survey after cheating survey found one common thread: Cheaters found their lovers to be more caring and better listeners. Cheaters found their lovers made them feel more appreciated.

I knew if people found out about us, they would assume it was sim- ple: middle-aged guy and the attractive young woman he happens to manage. A younger model. Like any cliché, there is some truth to it. Kelsey was not only gorgeous but also as enthusiastic about sex as she was about everything she did. Sex with a new lover is an extension of the dinner conversation on a first date. All your old stories are new again, and all your old jokes get laughs. You are charming because the information is new to your date. Similarly, all your old bedroom moves get the ultimate do over. It is not that no one has ever touched her in that way. It is that you haven't. In a marriage you tell yourself and others the sex is better because you know each other's body so well. Married sex is more efficient! Illicit sex is wonderful precisely because you don't know each other's body; you must find each other's hot buttons, and you can't get right to it. Its inefficiency is central to its allure.

But the surveys get it right. I wasn't trying to prove to Sydney that two could play at her game. I wasn't out to fuck a younger woman to make sure I was still "viable." By the time I was separated and Kelsey was divorced, I felt like we were each other's confidant. We understood each other. We told each other the truth, even the ugly truth. We could easily have stayed that way—friends deeply bonded—and looking back now it's easy to see that we should have, but we had to know what it would be like to be together, and being together meant having sex. Would she find me lacking next to her young and fit ex-husband? She had been with older men in her various affairs and found them all wanting in stamina and energy. ("Hot talk, followed by alcohol to get up their nerve, and then Limp City") And what about me? I had my concerns too. Was she going to be all talk? One of those hot-looking women who were unresponsive in bed? Young women are concerned with how they look naked; mature women are concerned with what they get when naked. And was it worth it? We had to work together every day, and the minute our clothes came off, we were putting her livelihood, her relationship with her peers, and her partnership equity stake all at risk. And if Sydney found out, I would be putting half of everything I had spent decades building at risk, not to mention sacrificing my integrity and sense of self in the process. All for sex?! Really?

Really. We had resisted our chemistry for nearly five years. And circumstances now handed us an opportunity. I had by then spent over a decade closing deals by telling candidates who were afraid to take our job offers, "If you take the job and it doesn't work out, you won't regret it. We don't regret actions taken. We regret being afraid to act."

Once we officially, in short order, became a scandal, certain married friends of a particular age called me. And while they initially followed protocol and showed concern about my state of mind and future, they quickly asked about the sex.

Your biggest fear turns out to be your friend. The young guys you think you can't hang with actually help you out.

*According to a survey of American* and Canadian sex therapists in *Esquire*, most intercourse lasts between five and seven minutes. Factor in guys in their twenties who still haven't outgrown premature ejaculation, and it isn't uncommon for women to complain that their men lasted two minutes.

During one of our first few nights together, after a couple of hours in, sheets soaked and nearby furniture overturned, Kelsey managed to ask, "Okay, what am I doing wrong? How could you not have come by now?" The fact that I, and I'm sure most guys my age, could finish whenever they liked, was not her experience with her peer group.

*"Fore" better and worse.* The young guys are fine with oral sex as long as they are on the receiving end, but even before Kelsey, the talk among the girls at the office was how foreplay, and specifically receiving oral sex, was not in the young guys' carnal canon.

I always found the giving of oral sex to be the most intense and grat-
ifying part of being intimate. Bringing someone to a long, slow release
seemed to me life's sweetest joy. Kelsey shared that, in a hookup, allowing someone to go down on her required a level of vulnerability and
trust she often couldn't muster. But she didn't have to deal with it very
often, because most men didn't offer.

> ***The Porno-ization of modern sex life.*** My generation's rela-
> tionship to porn was relatively infrequent (stags, SpectraVision
> when bored out of your mind in a hotel, a couple of drunken
> nights with your mate when trying to spice things up), but
> Kelsey had grown up in the digital age, where porn was ubiq-
> uitous, seen for the first time in your early teens, and available
> on any computer.

I learned about sex and then compared what I knew to what I saw
when I watched porn. Kelsey first learned about sex from porn. I remember being shocked during one of our Associates Dinners to hear that
most of the couples in their twenties and early thirties often "greased
the skids" with porn. It was how they got lovemaking started, a part of
their nightly routine as common as brushing their teeth. Syd and I had
decided we would never have a television in our bedroom so that we
would never be that couple who watched CNN instead of touching each
other and so that we could do our reading. But Kelsey's crowd all pow-
ered up the flat screen mounted directly in front of the bed, selected the
pay-per-view, picked a category (MILF, threesomes, girl on girl, black
on white), turned off the lights, and waited to get turned on.

Kelsey and I didn't watch porn. She told me that she wanted to start over sexually with me and that the women in porn were way too hot for her to allow me to see. This was code for Kelsey's concern over her breast size. They were lovely and perfectly matched her body type, but next to the preposterous enhancements in porn, she felt insecure. She repeatedly talked about getting an enhancement with her next commission check. But even though we eschewed watching it, I was immediately subjected to porn's influence in our sex life.

It began with some edification. There were entire sexual positions with which I was unfamiliar. At one point in the proceedings early on, when Kelsey was on top of me, she suddenly lifted off me, turned around, and squatted back down on top of me. I asked her what she was doing, and she said, "You don't like reverse cowgirl?" (A perfect name! Who names these things?) Of course, anatomy and geometry being limited, it turned out that most of the stalwarts I had practiced were either still in vogue or simply renamed. (Sixty-nine and missionary seemed impervious to rebranding; although Kelsey was too cool not to shorten it to "mish.")

I also had to get out of my comfort zone in regard to talking during sex. Without a fundamental grounding in porn-speak, I always considered myself open and communicative during sex, but it soon became apparent that my style, forged in romance, was beyond quaint to Kelsey; to her it was nearly bizarre. While I would encourage the way she touched me with affirmations like "yes" or tell her how sweet she felt or tasted, she flabbergasted me with comments like, "Fuck me, motherfucker." At the time, this was too intoxicating for me to think through. Kelsey had come so far as a recruiter in five years in part because she was a savant at mimicry. I would write her scripts and rebuttals and arguments, and she would mimic not just my words but my attitude and tone. It made perfect sense that she would grow up watching pornography, marry a guy who loved to watch it, and learn to mimic the responses that men wanted to hear. I'm sure it no longer even required conscious thought, and part of it, no doubt, was a genuine, freewheeling form of sexual expression. It never occurred to me, trying to play catch-up, that she might not be truly feeling but simply figuring out, as she did all day at her desk, who it was you wanted her to be and becoming that person for you. All I knew at the time was that the intense sex I had known in my marriage had been recast in this new, bolder vernacular. It was the opposite of the deeply satisfying but, by definition, rote sex one has in any marriage. I never knew what would happen next.

I found parts of the Porno-ization terribly sad. The first of these I dismissed as the young person's equivalent of the "How do you want to handle contraception?" conversation. We had done the obligatory making out on the Warrens' couch and decided we should take it upstairs. When I sat on the bed to remove my shirt, she knelt down on the floor between my legs, well aware of her tantalizing proximity to the business end of five years of torture, and said matter-of-factly: "Just so we're clear, I don't do anal, don't come in my mouth, and absolutely not on my face. From here down (she pointed to her neckline), go crazy, but I'm not shampooing my hair for you. It takes like three hours to dry." I knew Kelsey only knew how to couch fear in humor. I made her get off her knees, sit next to me on the bed, and hugged her. I told her to relax. I would never hurt her or disrespect her, and she laughed out loud. But she couldn't hide her relief.

While I tried to stay open-minded about the unsentimental education Kelsey's Porno-ized experience could provide me, there was a line in the sand I couldn't cross. Kelsey wanted me to choke her as she reached orgasm; as if this was common knowledge and I was a Luddite asking her how to launch a browser. She couldn't believe I had never heard of the practice of intensifying a climax by being simultaneously choked. She said she would show me how to squeeze, not her windpipe, but the carotid arteries on the side of her neck, cutting off oxygen and accumulating carbon dioxide, and if timed right, sending her to another realm of pleasure. I told her this didn't feel right to me. I associated choking with hurting, the exact opposite of giving pleasure. I told her that I understood where it all came from. Porn was made by men for men. "She wanted it rough" is the first line of defense for every domestic abuse case in the news. And I even understood the primal side: being taken in a dominant way is the most common female fantasy. But she had to see, at some level for her, with her history of molestation, that including this practice in our sexual repertoire was kind of fucked up. She held her ground and said I was overthinking it. "It feels good, and I like it. That's all I know."

Chastened and worried that I was not measuring up to what she wanted, a few nights later, as I hovered over her in essentially a plank position, slowly, then more quickly, bringing her to orgasm, I leaned back and moved my hands to her throat. She nodded, took my hands and placed them just so, and then instructed me how hard to press. When she was close, she signaled me by digging her nails into my forearms, and I pressed firmly. There was no doubting that her experience was deep and different than what I had seen in our short time together. But I was completely confused.

I rolled off her and went to the bathroom to gather myself. I was furious and couldn't understand why. I washed my face with cold water and went back in to face her.

"I won't do that again. I can't. If that's what you need, that's fine. I'm sure you can find a long line of guys more than willing. But that's not me. I can't hurt you while I try to love you. I can't. I'm sorry."

"Oh, babe, no! Dan, I don't need that. Jesus, you're shaking. It's nothing. Bounce back."

"Isn't what we do okay?"

"It's ridiculously phenomenal. I was just trying to impress you. I'm just trying to live up to the hype so you don't change your mind about me."

We felt guilty because we were having sex, and we often had sex to feel better about feeling guilty. Her ex-husband was still very much in the picture. He wanted to make it work. They had a little girl. He and Kelsey were a young couple with a big upside—what was her problem? While other young couples with a toddler stayed home all the time, they still partied and went out. He did most of the cooking and even babysat overnight when she went on all her "company events." Kelsey had by then created a firewall of friends who would claim she was with them, or colleagues who would say they were at a hotel together, pitching clients in the morning. He assumed Kelsey's insistence that they weren't meant for each other was just her usual lack of foresight and impulse control, and he thought if he gave her time then she would see how scary the real world was without his baseline of support. So he often came over to spend time with Desiree, and Kelsey could hardly say no, especially when she was coming over to see me at the Warrens'. She wanted more time to go by before she told him she was moving on with other men so it wouldn't adversely affect Desiree, and I was in no position to call her out. I didn't want Sydney to know. Kelsey and I had open talks about how I might be making a mistake and want to go back. "You love Saint Sydney. I know." And neither of us wanted the office to know and have my authority compromised or her legitimate claim to senior partner status tarnished in any way. We spoke openly about living a diversion that might end any day, and every time we said it, each of us waited for the other to say that it was nonsense. That we were real.

The most mind-altering part of sex with Kelsey, the part that kept me up for hours, making me question whether I had truly wasted huge parts of my life, had nothing to do with the sex itself.

There was a client, a forty-five-year-old "player," who Kelsey openly referred to in her office bullpen as "dreamy!" In a department meeting, it got back to me that Kelsey had said, "I would totally do him!" This was common Kelsey-speak, and normally I would let it go. But now we were together, in our convoluted way, and I told her I wasn't going to tolerate this kind of disrespect. She apologized and told me she knew where to draw the line and while she was just kidding in the first place, she would be more careful. Two days later she emailed me from her bullpen that she had been sent back a fee agreement with problematic language and could I stop by her desk at some point and help her craft a response? When I got to her desk, she was in the restroom, but her she had her email up. In the inbox was an email from the aforementioned "player" of a client with the subject line "What's up, Hot Ass?"

The mark of a great liar is that they fully expect to be caught on occasion, and they are never thrown by it and always prepared. Kelsey said hearing about what she said and seeing the email must have been horrible for me, and she was truly sorry. She said it had always been a problem for her, as a born people-pleaser, to shut a guy down. She said she had downshifted her tone with the guy, and his email was in response to her cooler vibe. She said it wouldn't happen again and that he, or any other guy, hadn't meant anything to her since our first night together. I didn't know at the time that this situation would repeat itself, with minor variations, a dozen times over the next year.

I did know at the time that this minor betrayal, coming on the heels of Syd's drawn-out major betrayal, was unhealthy for me. I couldn't make myself believe Kelsey, and I was mad. So I did what I had learned to do: I got a book and sat opposite her on the couch. Kelsey stared at me. She turned on the TV and waited. I didn't know what she was waiting for. This was how I rolled when angry. We would now be cold and distant with each other for several days. There would be no touching, no light moments, nothing beyond a transfer of facts necessary to keep home and hearth functioning. My anger needed to be given its time. In a few days, or maybe even a week (with Syd), one of us will soften, touch the other one affectionately, something funny that happened at the college or at my office will be offered to entertain, and that night, love would be made tenderly. Rinse. Repeat.

Kelsey didn't know the rules, and even if she had, could never have abided by them. After a few minutes, she sighed, turned off the TV, and moved over to my end of the couch. She took the book out of my lap and started to unzip my pants. Being aroused while sulking was new to me, but I pulled her hand off my zipper and replaced the book on my lap.

"Don't cock block me." (It took everything I had not to call a time-out and write down *cock block: another perfectly descriptive term I had never heard before*.)

"Kelsey, stop. Look, I don't . . . I'm still angry. Don't you get how upsetting that was to me?"

"I know, but I said I was sorry. We talked about it. It was, like, twenty minutes ago. Now I want to have sex, so move the book."

"No. Look, I think you should go home."

And she started laughing. She said I was about to get an education. She said it was only fair, given all I had taught her about salesmanship and deal making, that she be the one to school me about the wonders of hate sex. She said, "Having sex when you're angry is fantastic and the one thing you *should* be doing. One, it is the fastest way to lose the anger, and two, if you channel your anger into your fucking, it will be intense and wonderful.

"I don't want you to stop being angry at me," she said as she dropped her clothes where she stood, and hovered over me, like a bully on a playground. "I want you to fuck me like you hate me. Yeah, I read his email, and it turned me on a little, because I *do* have a hot ass — what do you think of that, Boss Man? That piss you off? Show me!"

An hour or so later we were in bed. Holding hands. Her face was chaffed from my late-day beard, my back bleeding from her scratches. Voices hoarse and tired. Soft kisses on the ear. Silly laughter. I couldn't remember a time in my life when I had gone more rapidly from angry to truly over it. How many days and weeks had I spent sulking, suffering, punishing? Only to arrive at the same place. Kelsey was shaking up a core belief of mine. I thought it was shortsighted and weak when someone would make a poor choice (break a diet, leave work early, take a vacation when broke) and justify it by saying, "Life is short; we could die tomorrow." My mantra was forged from the opposite notion. Life is long — what if tomorrow comes and you have to deal with the consequence of your poor choice? Which is more likely? Over time, I had been rendered incapable of living in the moment. Kelsey only knew how to live in the moment. Why wait for makeup sex when you can have hate sex now? Suddenly, her lack of impulse control, which seemed so dangerous, was now not just a virtue of hers, but one I needed to learn. I had constructed my life so that there would be no surprises, nothing I couldn't see coming and be prepared to handle. And yet Syd proved that the surprises came anyway, and control was illusory. Kelsey had another way. Let things happen, see what happens, pick up the pieces. At the time, it not only didn't seem crazy to me, it seemed like genius. After all, my way had gotten me right where I was.

My archenemy, shame, reared its head sexually as well. Kelsey, who by now I knew had a cavalier relationship with the truth, could also be wonderfully frank. So one postcoital night, as she sucked on a joint, and drank the Cakebread chardonnay she always seemed to need to get in the mood, I asked her for the downside. What do the young guys have sexually that I don't? I loved that she never hesitated. "They get it up faster. Especially the second time. Other than that, babe, forget it. No contest."

The next day, I went into the Warrens' medicine cabinet for the first time, looking for mouthwash that I would replace the next time I went shopping. And there it was. A prescription bottle of Viagra was on the counter. I looked inside, and there were around ten or twelve pills. I reasoned he didn't keep an actual count. He'd never miss one. I jumped online and got the basics. One hour before sex. Lasts for four hours. Don't take more than one. Don't take with nitrates (whatever they were). Don't drink much. Take on an empty stomach.

The next night, Kelsey texted me that she was on her way over, and I took the pill. It said it would take sixty minutes to kick in, but when she walked in and hugged me, just her touch solicited a hardening so pronounced she laughed and said, "Miss me much? Settle down!" Most nights, we opened the wine and went straight to bed. Of course, this night she had just had a huge fight with her ex and needed to download. I kept staring at the clock over her head on the mantle and nodding periodically. This was followed by a realization that she hadn't eaten since noon, and I rustled up dinner like a short-order cook on probation. Then she got a call from a candidate and excused herself to talk business, while I literally stared at my crotch, as if looking at it would keep the stuff from wearing off. I went into the bathroom and stroked myself and nothing happened. Does it work if you're the one doing it? Is that not the saddest question in the world? But a few minutes later she was off the call and took my hand and led me upstairs. And I flunked a test.

Oh, not the Viagra. It was amazing, and I fully understood why it had turned the pharmacological world upside down. As if being with a beautiful twenty-seven-year-old didn't reinvigorate me enough. Jacked up on sildenafil, I felt a level of power and certainty that I had once taken for granted. Taking Viagra for the first time is very much like going to the ophthalmologist for the first time in years and being fit for the right prescription. You remembered what it was like to really see, the way seeing was meant to be, and you realized you hadn't even known what you weren't seeing. But I didn't tell Kelsey I had taken it. I should have. Russ had convinced me that I had to stop letting shame dictate what level of the truth your partner could handle. I withheld things from Sydney if I thought they would embarrass me or diminish me in her eyes, and I told myself they didn't matter anyway. I would never lie about big things. But that distinction was not mine to decide, Russ would say (and Syd would nod furiously), "This is why she doesn't feel true intimacy with you." It backfired anyway. Kelsey knew. When she left that night, she turned at the door, "Look, I know I'm not exactly the one to be all judgy about chemicals, but tonight wasn't as good. It was unnatural feeling. I guess I don't turn you on."

Most nights, even during this short period of sexual rediscovery, intense elation, and gnawing craving, I was alone at the condo. Part of the thrill of an affair is how little time you have, how you have to escape, plan, and lie to carve out time. My lies were no longer minor and designed to avoid shame; now they were monumental and designed merely to get me what I wanted. But what did I want? Kelsey asked me if I was just trying to get back at Sydney. Sydney would call me and ask me if the time was helping, was I healing, did I think I could ever trust her again? I told her I didn't know—not to punish her, but because now I didn't know if I would ever feel trustworthy again.

Many of my mentoring clients were on the West Coast, and one night at the condo I had a long torturous conversation with a top-producing recruiter who was in a slump. When producers are in slumps, they take shortcuts. They stop doing the cold calling that got them where they were, and they rely on old clients, who are very nice to them, but don't give them much business. We circled around and around. "If you keep doing what you're doing, you'll keep getting what you're getting," was my grand finale, and I was about to shut him down when there was a banging on the door. Not a neighborly banging, a "come out with your hands up" banging.

Sydney stormed by me and asked me straight out if I was alone. It was remarkable to me, given how I could have just as easily not been alone, that I was offended by her question. When I told her of course I was, she searched the house. I followed her and absolutely badgered her. Had I ever frisked her on a Thursday night when she came home in her party dress? Had I ever demanded to go through her purse or see her phone? Go ahead! Look! I'm a guy living in a stranger's home because my goddamn wife made a mockery out of our marriage. You put me here, but you go ahead and search. Of course, I was able to do this so fearlessly because the housekeeper had been there that day, and all traces of Kelsey were gone.

"I've been calling you for two hours! Who have you been on the phone with for two hours?"

I grabbed my phone and showed her the phone number, then I went to the recruiter's website and showed her that the numbers on my phone matched his profile number. And then I played my mother's martyr card and told her I had to work two jobs because I have to maintain two houses, because my wife has two sets of rules she lives by. Then I asked her to leave. She started to apologize, to tell me the house seemed so empty and sad, that it was funny considering how often I traveled, but she never knew how safe it made her feel to know I was coming home. She said the cats missed me, and she missed watching me torment Gatsby with the red dot of the laser pointer. She asked me if I missed her, and I said yes, and it infuriated me that I wasn't lying, and in the moments that followed, I got more and more angry. I knew it wasn't Sydney I was mad at. I called Kelsey and explained what happened. She blurted out that we had dodged a bullet, which only intensified my anger. But now I had a new way to deal with anger. I pleaded with her to come over.

"Okay, I'm not sure if it's considered proper hate sex protocol if you're mad at someone other than the person you want to have sex with . . . Dan, Dez is asleep, there's no way I can get there."

I backtracked and told her I'd calm down and was sorry to call so late. She went pin-drop silent, and I told her this couldn't go on. We had to make a decision. Everyone was getting hurt. She agreed but told me for right now that I needed to go to sleep. But I couldn't sleep, nor could I conjure a highlight reel of those electric early days with Kelsey. Instead, my mind returned to the way Sydney would curl up with me on our couch in the family room with a blanket. Snuggling led to kissing,

kissing led to touching, one of us would grab the remote and power off, while the other swept the couch cat-free, and later, just before we would realize we were starving, Syd would look deep in my eyes and say, "Boo, you made me stupid. I don't have a thought in my head, except I love you."

And so the answer, to my long-married friends who wondered what sex with a younger woman was like, was that it was remarkable, wonderful. It was not only not making me feel better, it was also making me feel worse, and that was precisely why I was seeking it. I didn't want to feel better, even for a moment.

## CHAPTER 15

# My Center Gives Way

Rummy put down his fork, folded his hands under his chin, and glared at me, the effect doubled by the gold cuff links he always wore and his voice, which as always was too loud for the room. Rummy thought whispering was for losers.

"No, you will not fucking do that! And if I don't change your mind about doing that before we leave here, I swear to Christ, I will beat you to such a fucking pulp you won't be able to speak to her. I don't care how old I am or how much muscle you have! I will not let you ruin your fucking life! And I say all of this with love, brother, you know that."

The father of the perfectly lovely looking family at the table adjacent to ours cleared his throat to get Rummy's attention in hopes he might remember where he was. Rummy simply stared him down.

Rumford Giles Harrison. A fancy name for a regular guy. He was as bright and literate as anyone I ever knew, but most people were too busy being indignant to notice. He had a coarse and vulgar style of communicating. He took crap from absolutely no one, refused to suffer fools, and yet everyone who knew him knew he had the biggest, softest heart on the planet. Once you made it into his inner circle, you were there to stay. He would do anything for you, give you his last dollar, and more to the point of this meeting—would tell you the truth. I had other friends I could have talked to, but Rummy had been there. Rummy was a legend in the recruiting industry. In the 1980s, when fees were a fraction of what they are today, he was a legitimate million-dollar producer. And he was fearless and in your face. He would cold call the presidents of potential clients' companies and tell them they had a choice. They could use him to staff their firms, or he would label them a source company and make it his personal mission to headhunt all of their top people. "I work with all companies," he would tell people who were offended by the approach. "This call is about giving you input as to the direction I take. Front door or back door, the choice is yours."

Like me, his success led to people asking him to speak at conferences. That's how we met. His seminars were brilliant. He would give you specific verbiage on how to handle the most difficult objections and scenarios recruiters faced. I was blown away by his confidence and sheer salesmanship. But you had to get past the language, and most people couldn't. Half of the attendees, usually the young guys like me, thought he was fantastic. A hero. But the older men and many of the women would either walk out on his sessions or give him low evaluations. Rummy didn't care. "It's how I talk. Fuck them."

On the outside, Rummy was all ego and bluster, but he was a true student of recruiting. He would humbly come to my sessions, sit in the front row, nod furiously, and laugh with the rookies. I never felt more flattered than when Rummy came up to me after a session and said, "Kid, you fucking got something special. I got ten pages of notes. I thought I knew everything. The only thing I don't get about you is, how can you be so funny without saying 'fuck'?"

Rummy was now nearly sixty and struggling with the kinds of health issues one would expect from a guy who spent his twenties and thirties on the road. Rummy personally interviewed all his candidates, drinking, smoking cigarettes, and managing what we then called "an executive cocaine habit" (you don't buy it, but you never turn it down). Rummy made his living on the phone and refused to change with the times. He had no email address. In the years to come, he would eschew Facebook and LinkedIn. He had made his money and was not about to worry about "networking." He would have laughed at the notion of how many con-nections or Facebook friends you said you had. "Those aren't friends," he once told me, "those are contacts. You get like three friends in life." I was grateful to be in Rummy's inner circle. I needed someone who wouldn't lie to me; because while I was well aware of how much I was lying to others, I was unclear about how much I was lying to myself.

"You cannot tell Sydney."

"Rummy, you don't understand . . . "

"Here is what will happen. Not maybe. For sure. You know what, Mr. Famous Speaker? I'll give it to you in your language—what do you call those thingies? The computer version of the overhead projections they always get pissed at me for not having? PowerPoints! Right. Here is the PowerPoint presentation of your life if you tell Sydney you are seeing this chick."

### Slide One: You Will Lose Most of Your Money.

"Not just half, most. Because lawyers will get involved. You grew up poor—you really ready to go back? Because from where I sit, no pussy is that good."

**Slide Two: If She Gets a Good Lawyer, They Go After Your Business.**

"You get divorced, but you're still partners with a woman who fucking hates you. Please, don't interrupt. Let me finish my PowerPoint presentation. How do you think your little work pedestal is going to hold up when the staff, especially the women, find out you poached the youngest and the hottest? They'll be jealous and angry, and not because they feel bad for Sydney—although that's what they'll tell you—but because the idea that you would throw everything into chaos for a piece of ass threatens their own marriages! They will have a hard time trusting anything you say. You ready to throw that away? I've never seen a staff that trusts their boss like yours, and I know you earned it, but it will disappear instantly. They would have taken a fucking bullet for you and now they're going to want you to just take that bullet."

**Slide Three: Your Center Cannot Hold.**

"I forget who said that. Who? Yeats. Right. Well the dude was dead-on. That little chick of yours will not be working for you much longer. Shut the fuck up. Let me tell you how this ends. Do you think Sydney would allow her to stay if you reconciled? Do you think the other partners at your firm who have been with you forever are going to be okay with their new boss, the owner's new wife, if you hitch your star to your little femme fatale? Or how about when you find out your little hottie has not given up the habit of fucking around on her guy, whether it's you or her husband, who she clearly threw out to clear the decks for you? Think you'll be okay with that? I can't tell you which iteration this will take. I just know I have seen owners of search firms take up with their recruiters for thirty years, and at the end of the day, the owner stays, and the other party leaves. Bank on it."

### Slide Four: We're Sitting Here a Year or Two From Now and You're Sick—Sick in a Way You Have Never Been.

"You blew up your world and for what? You'll be alone, depressed, with less money than you have had in two decades, and the last thing, the very last thing in the world you'll want to do is be with someone else. You'll have friends—oh not me, buddy boy, but you'll find them—who will tell you that you can start over, you're a great catch, there's someone they want you to meet, and you'll shake your head and you'll be thinking, at the fucking cellular level, you'll be thinking, *If she's so nice, why would you wish me on her?*"

### Final Slide

"All of this awaits you—I fucking promise you—the minute you sit down and tell Sydney you are fucking a girl in your office, who, by the way, anyone with a fucking head on their shoulders can see is Sydney 2.0.

"Now tell me you're not going to tell her, or I will take your car keys like you do mine when I want to drive drunk, because it is that fucking stupid!!"

Rummy had come to these conclusions the hard way. Less than a decade earlier, Rummy's wife had taken up with "some punk," an electrician twenty years her junior, who Rummy had actually introduced to her. Rummy was outraged—and heartsick. He fought her tooth and nail, spent a fortune on lawyer's fees, and went on strike at work, refusing to earn another dime until she no longer benefited from an ounce of his labor. He would call me and bitterly recount her every sin, and I would try to point out that going broke was not the solution. He was furious that he would have joint custody of his two beloved daughters. If she wanted the punk and wanted to pretend she was twenty-eight, why should she get to pretend she's a mother too? When I tried to point out, gently, that Rummy wasn't being fair, that he had told me many times of hookups at conferences with women he barely remembered, which were the inevitable results of scotch- and cocaine-fueled "happy hours," he pushed back hard.

"That is completely different. She never knew about any of those women. I was careful, I respected my family!"

"So if instead of taking up with this 'punk,' she'd told you twice a year she was going to Vegas for a girl's weekend, but really that was a cover for her fucking Chippendale dancers, then you wouldn't have had an issue with it?"

"Okay, that's a bad example, because those Chippendale guys are fucking gay, but I get your point, and no, it would not be okay. Don't look at me like that. I'm a guy. It is different for a guy. That's a biological fact."

*Only*, I thought, *it is not biological*. During my long nights at the Warrens', I found it comforting to research the history of infidelity and to try to find books on recovering trust. This led me to the work of Helen Fisher (author of *Why We Love* and presenter of multiple TED talks) and her scientific approach to the study of romantic love. She came to her conclusions by studying the brain with FMRI analysis and by measuring chemical levels. She found that women struggle with fidelity the same way men do. "Who do you think these men are sleeping around with?" she asks. The oxytocin levels, the same chemical we get from drugs and alcohol, rise during casual sex in women and men, and the craving and obsession and "horrible dependence" our lovers cause is the same for us all. Fisher contended that love is not just an emotion but better understood as a basic drive, broken up into three elements: lust, romantic love, and attachment. We are attached deeply to our spouses but crave the dopamine increase that comes with lust and the novelty of new love. When we are in lust, we have sex all the time, and that leads to romantic love, where we think about the person constantly, and everything reminds us of that person, and we are blind to their flaws. Eventually we become attached and feel the rewards of sharing a life and knowing a person deeply, but within two years we cannot feel the same intense elation or spike in our dopamine levels by seeing that person—let alone by having sex with them. Fisher says we can choose to act any way we want as intelligent adults, but the truth of her research—a truth that when I heard her say it made me pause the video, sigh deeply, and realize I had become a statistic—was this: "You can crave one person while being attached to another person." *You can love someone while loving someone else.*

"Look, you know I have nothing against fucking young women. I tell all my divorced or soon-to-be-divorced friends to fuck young women. You know why? Not because of their bodies, but because they aren't angry yet."

"They're not angry because they haven't been with guys like you and me yet, Rummy."

"Oh, fuck that. This is about Sydney and the soccer player. You are fucking pissed. I get that. I was there, Danny, but it will wear off. You and Sydney are fucking made for each other, I've seen the two of you together—you fucking love her! This is not about the hot girl at the fucking office!"

"Excuse me, gentlemen . . ."

Oh no. The family man has decided, or been shamed into it by his wife, to man up and ask Rummy to watch his language. He should have just gotten the manager to get us thrown out, which has happened plenty when I dine with Rummy, because this approach never works.

" . . . I'm here with my family trying to celebrate my daughter's birthday, and we don't think it is fair to have to hear this locker room talk while . . . "

"You better be here to celebrate a birthday, otherwise the funny hats and noisemakers are flat weird. But you didn't see me, while trying to have a serious, potentially life-changing conversation with my friend here who happens to be in crisis, you didn't see me asking you to keep it down when you sang 'Happy Birthday' in every conceivable fucking key. Tell you what, hotshot, you go back to your table and tell them you told us off and don't say another fucking word, and I'll resist the urge to hit you so fucking hard that when you wake up your shirt will be out of style."

The family man cleared his throat and, like others before him, some-how intuited that in 1974, Rummy had been an amateur boxing cham-pion and that despite his age, if you crossed him, you could get hurt. He nodded and returned to his table.

"Kelsey."

"What about her?"

"I'd appreciate it if you started calling her by her name."

"Oh Jesus, you are in deep."

"I have to tell Sydney. I can't stand the guilt."

"You want to show her you're better than her! That you told her after a few weeks, but she jerked you around for so much longer."

"No. That isn't it."

"Then you want to tell her because you somehow think it will get her back?"

"Is that it? I don't know, Rummy. I just know I don't want to be the guy I apparently am."

"Then do this. Tell Kelsey you need to stop. For now. You need to play this out the way it was intended. You're going to tell Sydney that you crossed the line but that you are stopping. You're going to respect the rules of the separation. Now you're even. Start over."

"Amazingly, that actually sounds like a plan. That actually feels right."

"But don't under *any* circumstance, tell Syd that it is Kelsey. She can handle a revenge fuck. She can't handle Kelsey. Promise me."

Rummy pulled out his wad of cash—he never used credit cards—and even though he drove an hour to help me, he refused to let me pay. He called the waiter over, handed him a few hundred-dollar bills, and instructed him to pay for the lunch of the birthday family. Paradoxically obstreperous and altruistic, he made it clear the waiter was not to say who paid for their lunch. As we waited for the valet to bring our cars around, my head was spinning. Who should I tell first? Kelsey, that we needed to take a break? Or Sydney? Did it matter? Rummy gave me one of his bear hugs and made one more prediction.

"Have you gotten to know the kid? The five-year-old?"

I explained that I had only seen her at the office. She only knew me as her mom's boss.

"Well," Rummy said, handing the valet a twenty, "if Kelsey's as smart as you say she is, that's about to change."

. . .

When you tell someone they are fired, be prepared. At best, they will distort reality; conveniently forget their own lack of results; and imply they were sabotaged by the office culture, the seating chart, the speed of their computer, or the training. At worst, they will attack you personally. I never fight back. I remind myself that when this meeting is over, I am the one who still has a job. I get cold. The whole meeting takes five minutes.

**From Danny's Manager Training "How to Fire"**

. . .

I got a chance to practice what I preach because a few days after my lunch with Rummy I had to do a manager's retreat in Palm Springs. Nearly everyone who brings me in to speak on a repeat basis invites me to stay at their home, rather than a hotel, but I would rather die. Hotels allow me to rest in silence while I gear up to put on the cloak of the Danny persona they are paying to see. I conserve energy at hotels, and being surrounded by strangers is somehow more comforting and less sad than being welcomed into someone's home. But I made an exception in Palm Springs for Nick and Janet.

Nick was a semi-retired retained search recruiter who moved to the Coachella Valley from Chicago to play golf full-time and work when he felt like it. He was twenty-one years older than Janet. They seemed happy, and, like Sydney and me, their childless world was offset by the cats they adored. I could be myself around them, and Nick went out of his way to make sure my visits were not about work. Janet was sweet and hilarious, and they were the first couple I would cite as "happy while childless" during the years before Sydney and I attempted to start a family. Now I was interested in them for another reason.

I couldn't bring myself to tell them what was going on with Sydney and me, but after dinner, when we sat around talking in their living room, Nick abruptly fell asleep after his second glass of Scotch. It wasn't even 8:00 p.m. Janet shook her head and said, "Welcome to my weekday world." She said it was worse on the days he played golf. Even though he took a cart and played first thing in the morning, he would often come home at noon, eat lunch, and sleep through the afternoon. She said it was funny: From the time she'd met him, when he was thirty-nine and she was eighteen, she couldn't keep up with him; and then at fifty-nine, it was like someone threw a switch. He couldn't stay awake. She sighed and said she couldn't imagine what the next twenty years were going to be like, and just then he rolled over on the couch and his shirt hiked up, exposing his burgeoning belly. She woke him and ordered him to go to bed.

I always felt dehydrated after long plane rides across the country, but the desert air made it worse. I was standing at the sink downing bottled water in shorts and a tee shirt, petting the kitten that was a new edition since my last visit, when I saw Janet looking at me in the reflection of the sliding glass doors. She couldn't tell I could see her, so she was unguarded. And she looked me up and down. I got what I needed in that moment. I decided I never wanted Kelsey to be looking at a younger guy the way Janet was looking at me right now.

I checked my email before bed to see what I had missed at the office while traveling all day. If I needed any more evidence that Rummy's strategy was best, my first email was from Sienna, one of my senior recruiters, saying she was sorry to bother me when I was traveling, but she was too old for these kinds of games. She and Kelsey had had a teleconference pitching a client that afternoon. He was the kind of twenty-eight-year-old that could only become VP of sales in a software company. In that industry, once you get an app ready to take to market, you have six to twelve months to make an impact or the company will fail. So, generally, they hire the guy with the highest energy, ego, and testosterone level. Sienna said she was embarrassed during the call because it quickly devolved into the candidate and Kelsey shamelessly flirting about going out and partying when she came in to meet the C-suite. It got even more uncomfortable an hour later when Kelsey told Sienna she was going to drive in and come back in the morning rather than take the train with her. To me, Sienna said if Kelsey wanted that kind of reputation, it was fine, but it didn't reflect well on the company's brand and, "To be honest, Danny, I just want to shake her. I thought you should know. It's your company; it affects you too." Was this code for "we all know what is going on with the two of you, and maybe you should know about this before you blow up your marriage"?

It was after 11:00 p.m. on the East Coast. I called Kelsey and told her I needed her to make babysitting arrangements so we could have a serious conversation when I got home. But I had trained her too well. She said she knew that meant bad news, and she would rather have the bad news now than wait all week and wonder what was coming. "Fair enough." I told her, "I need to put the brakes on. Maybe for a while. Maybe forever. I owe it to Sydney, my marriage, and myself, to do what I agreed to do—go through the trial separation without being influenced by anyone else." I told her I intended to confess to Syd that I had violated the agreement but would not identify the person or discuss specifics.

I waited for Kelsey to attack. But Kelsey deserved more credit. She told me that she understood and that she wanted, more than anything in the world, for me to be happy. If that meant me going back to Sydney, then that was fine. She had hoped, in the short time we'd had together, that I would've seen that we could be great together, but clearly I only saw her as some mixed-up kid I now regretted getting involved with. Before I could protest, she said she had to go, but she wanted me to know that while there may have been a time when getting me to choose her was some sort of silly childish challenge that she had to pull off, winning that challenge actually validated her in some pathetic way, now that I had actually let her in. She knew me—not the speaker and the big boss—but me. She genuinely loved me—enough, in fact, not to guilt me into staying by doing some song and dance about how she gave up everything for me. "I'm not like that, Dan, I hope you know that." And she hung up.

. . .

"Just tell me, is it one of my friends?"

Sydney then named two colleagues from school that she said she always got a vibe from when I was around them. I had the nerve to feel umbrage that she would think I would sleep with the women she worked with. (I would never do such a thing; I would only sleep with a woman I worked with.)

All the way over to what Syd referred to on the phone as "my house" when she invited me to our house, I worried about how I should approach her. She hugged me warmly—I'm not sure she knew any other way—and led me to the formal living room as if I didn't know where it was. The pictures on the mantle of the two of us had been removed. She told me she assumed I wanted to tell her that we were done. Her voice was firm, but I could tell it was bravado. I laid out Rummy's strategy:

- I want to confess that I strayed from the agreement.

- I regret it, and I will recommit if she will allow me to, and if going back to Russ would help, I'd do that as well.

- I'm not taking the position that she cheated on me first, so what I did was okay, or that my cheating didn't count because we were in some fashion separated. We had a deal. I violated the deal. I'm sorry. I'll understand if we can't go on and there is too much damage. But I am here because I want to respect the original intention of the separation.

- Lastly, despite all evidence to the contrary as of late, I loved her.

"Uh huh. Did you fuck her?"

"After everything I just said, that's what you want to know?"

"No, I also want to know who it is, but we can start with 'did you fuck her?'"

"I'm not going to tell you who it is. It doesn't matter."

"Did you fuck her? I am your wife, and I deserve to know."

"I never once asked you about specifics with your soccer boy, and I was living here at the time."

"I didn't fuck him."

"How convenient and well thought out—you get to confess but retain your virtue. I don't believe you. And Syd, it doesn't matter. The intent is the same."

"It matters to me!! Do not tell me you love me and refuse to answer me! I can't sleep. I can't eat. You've been torturing me. I *knew* there was someone, but I trusted you. 'Danny isn't like that,' I kept telling myself. You say you want to make this work. Well if you do and you are not lying, then you will tell me right now. Who is it? And did–you–fuck–her? You owe me that!"

*Don't you love Tibby enough to want what is best for her? Did I not raise you right? You stop your crying right now and answer that question, little man. Are you really that selfish?*

"Kelsey. It's Kelsey. It could never have been anyone else. And yes, we did what adults do."

Rummy was so right. She fell back onto the sofa, took one of the throw pillows, and held it to her stomach as if to staunch a bleeding wound. Had it been one of her colleagues, women her age who were long suffering in marriages or just divorced, she would have taken it in stride, would have been magnanimous and compassionate. It might even have released her from her own crippling guilt. But Kelsey . . . the woman Syd said she understood so well because, "I was her"? This was the wrong answer. This would not stand. My center, given my answer, would not, as Rummy had predicted, hold.

## CHAPTER 16

# "This is Called a Dead Lift"

When I scanned my card to enter the gym, an alarm went off. It had been so many months since my compression fracture that my membership had lapsed. I purposely came two hours later than I used to so that I could avoid my 5:00 a.m. crew seeing me in my reduced state. I didn't know their last names, didn't know where they lived, had in fact never socialized with them outside of the gym, and yet somehow "my crew," and their judgment, mattered to me.

My doctor insisted I get a personal trainer to watch my form and supervise my comeback. Colby was twenty-four, and he conceded he had never trained anyone my age and mentioned blithely that I was his dad's age. I had to buy new workout gear because my usual tight tank tops would have looked ridiculous. I now knew what the new members felt every January when they walked in for the first time, empowered by their resolutions, and looked around at the regulars. They felt intimidated, and we didn't help. We gave them the look that said, "Really?

Dude, I give you three weeks—max." Colby had no degree in exercise physiology. He was a jacked kid who took a certification course. But I couldn't judge him. At twenty-four, and in his profession, he could justify his vanity. But for me, it was about being in crisis and being out of control. Kelsey and I were suddenly just workmates again, and I had no contact with Sydney while she sorted out her feelings. So I did what I do when I am in crisis and out of control, the same thing I am doing here with Colby: I try to get my body stronger. My body I can make do what I want. Or at least I once could. That's where Evan came in.

. . .

"Evan. I want to see you about something personal, not biz, and I'm probably going to shock you. Can we talk offline?"

When Evan nodded solemnly, I realized he thought I was going to tell him about Kelsey, which told me she had been telling people at the office, and—putting aside her breaching my trust—Evan now thought I was going to tell him I couldn't work with him knowing he had slept with my girlfriend. But I was not mad at him about Kelsey. Oddly, I saw him as part of her "before life," when she was mixed up and acting out because she was trapped in a bad marriage. Now, in my bizarre view unsupported by any review of the facts at hand, she was with me, and all had changed to a higher plane of being. I had a different agenda for Evan.

"I know, and do not judge, that every year about this time you and your buddies do steroid cycles."

Evan leaned back and angled his head to the side. What was this?

"I want in. If that's okay. I'm just in that 'tear it up' mood, and I figure at my age, I could use some help."

"That's it? That's what you wanted to see me about?"

I nodded, and Evan jumped out of his chair, insisted we "bring it in," which I then learned meant a kind of half hug that I saw guys do at the gym as a sign of greeting, and began making a shopping list.

" . . . So our testosterone base will be Deca and tren; we'll do that for eight weeks and in the middle, we're going to need some Winstrol to cut us up—otherwise we'll retain a shitload of water. Then near the end, we'll do some clen, and that will make us fucking pop. Once we come down from it all, we'll need some Clomid and some Proviron for PCT, otherwise we'll have raisins for balls . . . Boss this will be so much fun!"

"Do I have to use needles?"

"No, no, it's all oral, which is tough on the liver, so make sure you go to a health food store and get some milk thistle. But Boss, listen to me, there is no point in doing any gear if you are not going to eat. You have to throw away that diet of yours and eat!"

"What's the percentage of increase in calories on one of these cycles? What's the ratio of protein to carbs?"

"No, no, fuck that noise. That's the whole point. You can eat anything, and you only get bigger and harder! Pizza, cheeseburgers—you have to feed the beast when you're in beast mode, or you are just wasting the juice. That's part of the fun! Go big or go home!"

"So how big can we get in eight weeks?"

"We'll look like Greek gods! Or even cornerbacks!"

Google and WebMD must make doctors crazy. We get a symptom, start a search string, and without the benefit of medical school or any clinical experience, we know exactly what we have and what drugs we need. Within fifteen minutes of Evan leaving my office, I knew everything about anabolic steroids.

I skipped over all the parts about how there were certain scientists who questioned the efficacy of steroids in a transparent attempt to dissuade teenagers from trying the compounds. Kids aren't stupid. Steroids work. I saw it every year in Evan, and they see it every month in their gyms. Without steroids, you can safely gain one to two pounds of muscle a month. With steroids, you can gain twenty pounds of muscle in a six-to-eight-week cycle. Your strength increases fifty percent, so if you have been benching 200 pounds, you will be benching 300 pounds by the end of the cycle. Keep in mind, average weight lifters are thrilled if their bench goes up twenty pounds in the course of a year! I was starting to get a placebo effect just from reading, I felt like getting under my desk and bench-pressing it!

Oh, yeah. There are side effects of anabolic steroids. Sigh. And a few convenient justifications:

- Lower sperm count. (But it has no effect on orgasm or volume. I can live with it.)

- Infertility. (For me at this point, it's a value-add.)

- Enlarged breasts from excess estrogen. (Evan says the Clomid counters this!)

- High blood pressure. (Okay. Busted here—my dad died of a stroke. I should not do this.)

- Roid rage, high levels of intensity. (Bring it. Have we met? It will probably calm me down.)

- Hair loss from DHT conversion. (Everyone knows bald is sexy. I would rock that look.)

- Liver toxicity. (Uh, yeah, that's not good. But I don't drink, so my margin, liver-wise, should be high.)

- Shrunken testicles. (Hmm . . . on the other hand, your penis is unaffected, so the contrast might look amazing!)

So your body already makes everything anabolics give you. But when you go on a steroid cycle, you add synthetic derivatives of testosterone to your body that it doesn't need. These exogenous doses, often ten to a hundred times the levels your body is used to, then signal your HPTA axis to shut down, essentially saying to your testes, "I got this, take a nap!" That's why they shrink. Protein synthesis, the ratio with which your cells build protein, increases, and the muscles, with training, grow large. And potentially, so does your heart! And when the cycle is all over, and you've taken all these risks to artificially enhance your physique, you come off your drugs and hope to God that your natural testosterone cycle reboots. Sometime it doesn't, and sexual dysfunction can be permanent. (So you might sacrifice the only thing you really need to be hard in your body for your look.) The "PCT" (post-cycle therapy) Evan told me about is supposed to ensure this "reboot," and it always has for him. But he is a child by comparison.

And no matter what else happens, you will literally piss it all away. Within a month or two, all benefits of the cycle will evaporate, and you will look the way you did before. This is why some guys do a second "cutting cycle" just before the summer when the shirts come off. The cutting cycle features agents like clenbuterol and Winstrol. Both have been known to cause cardiac damage, and there have been reported cases of sudden death. (On the other hand, you do look good in that wide-ass coffin!)

I summoned the willpower to exit out of my browser and get back to work. There were two emails waiting. Kelsey said she hoped I noticed she had been very productive and professional during our relationship intermission and, now, deserved a reward. She wanted me to meet her at Paven Park—a neutral site during broad daylight—on Saturday, so that I wouldn't feel like she was making moves on me, just to chat about how we were each feeling. There was no anger, no tantrum about not being able to work, no romantic reminders to evoke guilt. Then there was an email from Evan asking if he could stop in. Had he changed his mind? Had his dealer been arrested? Maybe it was all for the best. What was I thinking? He tapped on the door and popped in. I waited.

"So . . . don't get pissed. I just wanted to say that, I don't know, if you are doing this for her, you don't have to. She's really into you. Remember, I said not to get pissed."

*So he knows. The whole office knows.*

"A little credit please? I'm doing this because I have been working damn hard to get in shape, and now I want to push the envelope. That's all. Okay?"

Evan fist-bumped me.

"Jacked and stacked. For real!"

But I didn't have a clue who I was doing it for or why. I just knew I was going to do it.

. . .

"And this is called a dead lift. That's because you lift the bar from the floor, so it's literally dead weight."

"Colby. Let's hit the pause button. I filled out a four-page questionnaire from you, and in it I detailed my workout history and my injury history and why I am here. Did you read it?"

"Uh, I kind of scanned it."

"Well. Why don't you go read it, and I'll wait here. Go!"

I looked around the gym. It had always been a sanctuary for me. The only other entity I knew to be the same with every encounter was my dictionary. Words never let me down. I could trust words. And there were so many words that I could never learn them all. You never finished your journey with words. The gym was a close second to my dictionary. If you did your exercises in the correct form, with the proper intensity, and with enough frequency, you would get predictable results, no matter what else was happening in your life, and yet you were never finished. You could always improve. But as I looked around, I saw this was no longer true, if it ever *was* true. Now the gym was fraught with danger. With my injury, I once more had given absolute trust and in return had been burned.

And when did this happen? Everyone on the gym floor was wearing headphones or earbuds. When did it become impossible to work out without listening to music? The two-minute recovery time in between sets was when the guys I came up with would chat about the week's NFL matchup, or arch their eyebrows in the direction of the girl doing lunges and make a comment about the tautness of her ass. The gym was a social place. Marriages originated in the gym! You didn't need an introduction, you didn't have to come up with a pickup line or buy a drink, and you knew she'd be here tomorrow. You could get to know each other. Now the gym is filled with robots. No one talks to each other. They stare at the ubiquitous TV screens hung overhead in twenty-foot intervals like a sports bar. And without fail, they rack the weight and check their phones. God forbid they be untethered for the full hour of their workout.

There is nothing wrong with any of this. It only seems wrong to me because my sanctuary has been razed. They have built a new one, and while they have kindly grandfathered me in, I no longer belong.

I was about to leave when Colby tapped me on the shoulder.

"My bad, dude. I went to my boss to complain about your attitude, and he told me I have never been in the shape you were in for years before your injury. He slapped me around pretty good. So maybe you could forgive the disrespect, and we could start over?"

Overt and transparent manipulation. Delivered calmly and with humility and even the appropriate lowering and softening of his voice. Well played.

"Personal trainers don't make any money, Colby. You ever think about being a recruiter?"

## CHAPTER 17

# Rainbow Sprinkles

Infidelity did not seem to agree with me, but limbo seemed to be worse. After a lifetime of not dreaming, I dreaded going under, because all I did now was dream. Not just the occasional rerun of my mother's betrayal with Tibby but a recurring nightmare of someone breaking into the house during the night and harming Sydney. I should be there to protect her. And Gatsby and Hadley. We kept the kitty litter in the basement, and there was a cord-drawn lightbulb at the bottom of the stairs. Syd, a cat whisperer who missed her calling, had taught Gatsby to jump up, grab the cord with his paws, and hold on long enough for the light to come on. I kept replaying his trick in my homesick dreams. I kept seeing Syd's face when I told her I had been with Kelsey and Kelsey's face when I told her I needed to think things over. I wasn't sure who I was betraying or what exactly I was grieving.

The Farmington Woods condo complex is the largest in Connecticut. Something like twelve square miles of quintessential New England woods. It is populated by two groups: rich, elderly empty nesters no longer able to keep up with a large house, and divorced people of means who still wanted the country setting sans the snow blowing and the lawn cutting. All day long, they could be seen power walking in expensive sweat suits or carrying towels and coolers to the "quiet pools" where no children were allowed. But I joined their ranks only at night, often heading out my door at midnight and walking all the way to the golf clubhouse and back, returning at close to 3:00 a.m., and sitting in the Warrens' overstuffed recliner until the gym opened at five.

When Kelsey looked up from her book at Paven Park, she made an unsparing assessment and spoke the truth.

"You look like shit, Boss. You look like you haven't slept."

"Zig Ziglar? Are you trying to impress me by reading sales training books?"

"You said he was awesome and I should read him." Kelsey tossed the book into a bag at her feet that was larger than I had ever seen her carry. "But he talks a lot about his beloved redheaded wife, so I'm finding him kind of annoying. Did you steal your 'fear of loss' rant from him? I don't care—I steal from you all the time. Just curious."

Everyone resists being sold. It's human nature. So we use the Fear of Loss Close. It would be a nice world if people made decisions for their own personal gain, but they don't. They make decisions and finally commit when what they really want is taken away from them.

Kelsey was hurt, and when she was hurt, she went after your weak points. She knew I was a stickler about attribution when I quoted writers and speakers, and that I hated it when word got back to me that some speaker had used an anecdote of mine or stolen one of my word tracks. In reality, everyone in the speaking business was guilty of what Daniel

Gilbert (author of *Stumbling on Happiness*) later termed *kleptonesia*—
recalling something you heard from someone else as your own thought.
It went like this: The first 500 times you say it, you say, "I heard Danny
Cahill say last week . . ." The next 500 times you say, "Someone once
said . . . ," and for the rest of your life after that you say, "I was just
thinking the other day . . . "

"Maybe I need to leave the firm, Dan. This is fucking hard. Going
back to what we were, pretending nothing ever happened. I don't think
I can do it. I'm not trying to put a gun to your head. I'm just saying,
maybe it's best. I would need you to tear up my non- compete. I have to
make a living. I'm a single mom now."

"Could you at least look at me? Are you trying to add to the punish-
ment by looking off into space?"

"Get over yourself, Dan. I'm trying to keep an eye on Desiree!"

"She's here?! An ambush is completely uncool, Kel. What happened
to the heartfelt harangue about her not getting to know me until we were
committed and how confusing it would be for her and how you were not
going to allow any boyfriends to be in her life . . . "

"Excuse me, did you say boyfriend?! Is that what you are? This is
news to me. I didn't get out of my marriage for a boyfriend."

"I know, why would you? You had plenty of them while you were in
the marriage!"

"Mommy, can I go on the swing, please?"

She was so much bigger than the last time I'd seen her just a few
months earlier at the office. I smiled at her, and she wrapped her arms
around Kelsey's thigh and buried her head. But she was smiling when
she took cover.

"Remember Mommy's boss, Dan?"

The shout-out helped. Dez showed her face and nodded. I waved. It felt idiotic.

"Wanna go play on the swing with me?" she asked.

"No offense Dez, but you don't look big enough to swing me very hard."

"No, silly, I get in the swing, and you swing me!!"

"Oh, no, no, I don't think that's the deal. I mean, I only do this like every four decades, and I was really looking forward to you swinging me."

Kelsey started to say that her boss had stopped by to talk about work, but I stood up.

"Tell you what, Dez. I will swing you for a while, and then you can swing me, deal?"

Desiree nodded with the utmost seriousness, which would have probably ruined me in and of itself, but it was a setup. She was just getting started. Before I got two steps toward the jungle gym and seesaws and swing sets, Desiree did what she had been taught to do—she reached out her hand to me. I was forty-seven years old and had never held the hand of a child. I was unprepared for the effect. Her hand was so small. How did she manage with such hands? In the sixty feet to the swings, I learned more about kids than I'd ever known. No one had ever been able to articulate to me why you exhausted yourself for them, gave up your plans for them, cashed out every chip of your previous identity for them, only so they would outgrow and even resent you for having done so. Why would you do such things? But now I had a sense. I'm not sure I was ever as profoundly sad as when we reached the swings and I had to let go of her hand.

Fifteen minutes later, Desiree was imploring me to swing her higher, but I was scared to death of her falling on my watch. From a distance,

Kelsey made a "push, dude" motion and was laughing at my absurd lack of temerity. I got a true glimpse of parenting when Desiree started chatting up a fellow five-year-old. Parenting is mostly waiting. Her pal's mother stood nearby holding her youngest in her arms.

"Your daughter is beautiful. God, she's like out of a magazine."

"Oh. Actually . . . thanks. She definitely takes after her mother."

"No, I can see you in her for sure."

Now see, this is when lying doesn't get the credit it should. Mostly people lie to make themselves look or feel better. But sometimes telling a lie is the kindest gesture you can make. Sometimes it is even an act of love.

Back at the bench, Kelsey was packing up. Now I understood the big bag. Moms have to travel with a serious amount of kid gear. Because you never know what might strike their fancy at any given time, you simply pack everything. Kelsey's conscience had gotten to her.

"Dan, I'm sorry. You're right. It was an ambush, I should have told you . . . "

"Hey, I get it. Where you go, she goes. That's the drill."

"No, I could have gotten a sitter. It was on purpose. I'll cop to it. I wanted you to meet her. I guess I wanted you to see what our world could be like."

Kelsey told so many lies that, when she was honest, it was amazingly effective. She was a fighter and didn't see it as a fair fight. I knew how good it used to be with Sydney, but I didn't know how good it could be in the future, because I hadn't met the most important part. I felt a tug at my knee.

"Can we get ice cream?"

I was never very good at saying no to women I cared about, but I was completely defenseless when it came to Desiree. I told Kelsey to sit tight and that we'd be right back. She threw her car keys to me and pointed out that my Porsche didn't have a child's seat. It was a win-win for Kelsey. She had admitted her bad behavior, and the plan was working.

Because I had no previous experience being alone with a child and had never conversed with one longer than a minute or two, I spoke to Desiree as if she were my age. People would later remark on this and point out that it was good for her development and vocabulary, as if I had a strategy. But I was simply clueless.

"Are you going to get sprinkles on yours?"

"That really is an existential question, Dez, and I'm glad you asked. Sprinkles or no sprinkles? Does the ice cream lose its intrinsic meaning if we get sprinkles? I mean, you didn't ask me to go out for sprinkles, did you? No, you specifically said you wanted to get ice cream, but what good is the ice cream without sprinkles? Is there any value to being a purist? I mean, tastes evolve. It isn't a matter of one versus the other. Why be so absolute about it—know what I mean?"

"Yeah," she nodded sagaciously, as if she had already worked this out and I needed to catch up, "especially rainbow sprinkles, right?"

"That's what I'm saying! Exactly. Why can't everyone else just get that?!"

Kelsey pulled into the parking lot in my Porsche. She got out and swaggered toward us. She knew exactly how hot she looked with the top down and knew that no one who saw her had any idea it was not her car. I noticed that Dez had residual chocolate ice cream on her face, and suddenly I knew what to do. I took one of the few remaining clean napkins we had left, bent down, told her to stay still, moistened the napkin with my own saliva, and wiped her mouth clean. She closed her eyes and was perfectly relaxed. I did a Dad thing. It felt completely normal and the exact opposite of a gross chore. Why hadn't someone told me about this magic? Kelsey asked Dez if she had fun with Mommy's boss, and when Dez nodded without equivocating, I felt a swell of pride. She asked her if she had thanked Mr. Cahill, and we both confirmed that she had, though I really didn't recall—and then she ruined me. She took no prisoners. Showed no mercy.

"What kind of ice cream did Dan get you, Dez?"

"Existential. With sprinkles."

And then, according to plan, Kelsey loaded up her car and took the magic away—fully aware that I knew where to find it.

## CHAPTER 18

# Leaving Limbo

**Diagnostic #10—Has Your Body Told You to Leave Your Job or Relationship But You Are Hard of Hearing?**

Are you listless? Eating or sleeping too much? Or not enough? Have you lost interest in everything? Are you self-medicating with alcohol, drugs, or sex? Does your lower back or neck ache every day? Is sarcasm your first line of defense? Are you aware of how unattractive that is?

Here's the bottom line: Pain is your body's way of demanding change. Sometimes our bodies tell us what to do before our brain catches up. You need to listen.

**From "Ten Diagnostic Questions on Deciding to Leave or Stay" in Danny's book, *Harper's Rules*.**

. . .

Thank God the crying jags began. They brought me to my senses and got me out of limbo.

If you've never had one, crying jags are not like the crying you do at the end of a Lifetime movie where despite the ravages of chemo, the lead actress still looks incredibly hot. Crying jags are not the silent crying you do at funerals, and they're nothing like the proud tears that run down your face at your son's graduation, marking the inexorable passing of time. No. Crying jags are special.

They sneak up on you. Some would say they are like the downpours that come in the late afternoon on a humid day. And while they are indeed as torrential, the analogy doesn't hold because on those days you can feel the humidity building, the rumbling of the thunder, the sudden stillness in the air before all hell breaks loose. Crying jags give no such warning. And there are no rainbows.

The first one made complete sense to me. I was driving back from Healthtrax, a health club where Sydney and I had often played mixed doubles years earlier, but I didn't play tennis that morning. I had stopped by at Kelsey's invitation to watch Desiree take swim lessons. For Kelsey, this had long since become a draining mommy-chore; the pool area was stiflingly hot and the chlorine smell was overwhelming, with Dez yelling, "Mommy, look, I'm floating!" every two minutes. But it was my first time, and since I still hadn't learned to swim, I was truly impressed, both with her progress and her ability to express joy with seemingly insufficient cause. She slapped the water with her hand, and even though the move lacked purpose—it didn't even splash anyone— she would crack up, which would make me crack up. Joy for joy's sake. What does that feel like?

On a back road on the way home, I heard a car horn, looked to my left, and realized I had just passed Sydney going the other way. Within seconds she rang my cell and wanted to know what I was doing off the beaten path. I told her I had played a singles match at Healthtrax, but her lack of follow-up told me she didn't buy it. My regular club was miles in the other direction. She knew Kelsey lived in the area. But she chose not to accuse me, and we agreed to chat soon.

Several minutes later, as I waited at the busy intersection in Farmington that was the gateway to the Litchfield Hills, I felt it come on. There was a rolling feeling in my stomach, and then a rushing feeling in my face, then a few heaving breaths where I tried to fight it, and then a cascade. I could hear myself emitting wailing sounds, and I was so curious that I actually lowered the rearview mirror to see what I looked like. It was grotesque to me. The guy behind me went around me, waving his arm, and I didn't blame him, but I was not safe to drive. I pulled over to the side of the road and put on my flashers. I've never carried a handkerchief in my life, and I had always counted on Syd when I needed a tissue, so I wiped my face with my jacket sleeve. Crying jags are messy.

I pulled it together and figured it was a simple guilt trip one-off. The aggregate consequences of my choices. I had fallen into a limbo. At first, I avoided both Kelsey and Sydney and took as many speaking gigs as I could to get out of the office and have time to think and decide what I was doing and what I wanted.

But meeting Desiree had allowed for a creeping, incremental rationalization. I wasn't sleeping with her mother; I was watching her swimming lessons. I wasn't committing to anything; I just met them for lunch at the mall. But within a few weeks, the loneliness of weekends at the Warrens' condo spent pacing the rooms and looking at pictures on the walls of people I had never met, being the only person solo at a movie theatre on date night, and my new vampire habit of walking the grounds of the complex most of the night took their toll. Kelsey would invite me over to play Candyland with Desiree. "Kel, she cheats. No matter what the dice say, she just fucking puts her player on Candy Castle. It isn't right!!"

"Dan, she's five. She doesn't see it as cheating; she just wants to win."

"Well, hell, let's just put some Patriots season tickets in a trust fund for her and be done with it." I would have a glass of wine while Kelsey drank the rest of the bottle, and I would go home. Only soon I wasn't going home, but I wasn't honest enough to update Sydney. How could I?

Sydney shocked me one day by calling me at the office and asking if I would just listen and not talk for a few minutes. She told me she wanted me to know she had given up drinking. She didn't mention programs or methodologies, but it was clear it was organized and she was dead serious about it. She said that it had to be hard for me to hear, given how many times I had suggested she do so and how many of our issues I thought stemmed from her drinking. "But you can only do it when you are ready to do it." She said she hoped it wasn't too late for us, but even if it was, her sobriety was her life's top priority. She said, "That must sound selfish," and I told her it was anything but. I told her I knew she didn't need my approbation, but that I was proud of her. She wanted me to know that in group sessions she had heard some horrific stories of lying and cheating and cruelty. She said she'd found herself reassuring perfect strangers that their sins and issues came from pain that they had been carrying their whole lives, that it was not a judgment on their characters; that she was known in the groups for being the voice of reasoned empathy, but that she now realized she had offered more compassion to these strangers than she had to me, and she was sorry for that. I said, "That means more to me than you will ever know."

I held the phone in my hand long after the call was over. Did Sydney want me back? Or did she just want to vanquish Kelsey? And if we tried, could we really put both our transgressions behind us? Or would we punish each other, quietly, in stealth mode, forever? And what of the issues that drove us both to leave the marriage? Didn't we just create a big diversion? Won't those issues return? Won't they be worse?

. . .

We send you on an interview, and the VP, your future boss, is late. He doesn't apologize. He takes calls and looks away while you are talking, his mind wandering. He tells you he will send you the health benefits package to review, and even though you told him you had special needs due to your child's condition, it doesn't arrive. The job itself is great, and when the VP calls to give you an offer, he is complimentary, deferential even. He seems to have all day for you. What to do? Which is the real boss? Welcome to one of headhunting's cardinal rules: The way someone manages the hiring process is the way he manages, period.

**From Danny's "People Reading" Seminar**

. . .

Two days later, while waiting for the CEO of the company that had flown me in to finish his remarks and introduce me, I felt a crying jag come on. Crying jags don't care what you think you are thinking about; they have no respect for who is watching you or what is going on—they come when they damn well please. I ran to the restroom, took off my suit jacket, turned it inside out, and cried into it to muffle the noise. Mid-jag, I realized the AV guy had already clasped my wireless lavalier microphone to my tie, and it was possible that 350 people were hearing their motivational speaker sobbing. I ripped the power pack off my belt and thanked God that the light was still in the red "off" position.

The jags began to increase in intensity and frequency: most mornings on my drive in to the office; at the gym; during a spin class where it was mercifully dark and we were all sweat-soaked anyway; and while doing research online for the weekly email newsletter that went out to thousands of recruiters on my subscription service. When you feel you are fully concentrating on something having nothing to do with them, the jags hack your heart, breach your nervous system's firewall, and wreak havoc. Once, I was even caught. By Kelsey, no less. We went to great pains at work to be business-as-usual. She had found out through her network that a candidate she was about to place was lying about his work history, and she bounded into my office to get strategy on how to expose him without losing the deal. I had just finished a jag. When one came on at my desk, I would close the heavy glass door to my office, face my high-backed black leather swivel chair toward the wall, turn the speakers up on my computer, and play a training video until it passed. Thinking I was safe, I turned to her, but my red eyes and distorted face were ridiculously obvious. I waved her away and sent her an email saying it was not about her. She wrote back that she knew part of why I loved her was because she called me on my bullshit, and that me saying crying at my desk was not about her *was* bullshit.

I was going to call Russ, but I knew what he would tell me. The jags were issuing me a warning: Make a decision, and we will let you be. Stop living in limbo, and you will stop fearing the shame of random crying.

And since when did I have a problem making a tough decision? I was known for it in my office. Walk into Danny's office with a problem, and you walk out with an answer. And, forget that I did it twenty times a day running my search firm. It was in my DNA! I had a history! When

I had managed to get a play produced off-Broadway at a prestigious one-act festival, the artistic director called and told me he had seen the rehearsals and he liked me and my play very much, but my director (a film actor who had never directed for the stage), was incompetent, and I had to let him go or he would pull the play. The problem was the director was the guy who had taken my play and shopped it around for me. His stated motivation for helping me was to launch his directing career! I couldn't betray him. I told the artistic director I wasn't going to fire him, and if that meant my play was pulled, well, so be it. He told me I was being foolish but called me back an hour later and said the play was on. A few years later, my boss, the owner of my company, was starting to burn out. He was losing focus and hardly ever coming into the office because he knew I had everything handled. I went into his office and put the proverbial metaphorical gun to his head. Sell me the business, or I walk and start my own. A month later, at twenty-six, I was the owner of my firm and on the hook for a ten-year buyout. When I fell in love with Sydney, and I thought everything that happened before was just a prelude to our life together, I was all in. No crying jags. So with my history of making the tough calls and making them work, what was going on? Where was this limbo coming from? And how could I get out? The first answer was easy.

Limbo came from the moments I would spend with Kelsey and Desiree and feel like we were meant to be a family. Small moments, so manifest to others but revelatory to me: the way Dez would walk around the house singing "Dora the Explorer" (and I would find myself humming the lame tune in my car); or how she would lie on Kelsey, who was lying on me, while we watched *SpongeBob* on Nickelodeon; the way Dez made me feel when Grey Mousey (I suppose her version of a blankie or teddy bear) went missing one night, and Kelsey greeted me at the door with the news. "Holy shit, we have to find Grey Mousey. I'll distract her. You need to tear this fucking place apart. She'll freak the fuck out." I did. I found Grey Mousey just as Dez was figuring out he was missing and was two octaves above Fay Wray in the beast's fist atop the Empire State Building. I walked down the stairs to present him to her, and her tears ended instantly, her face beamed, and when she said, "Dan found Grey Mousey!!" a decade of standing ovations paled in comparison to the pride I felt wash over me.

And the best moment of all was a show playing nightly, at 8:30 p.m., with no previews. Kelsey would tell Dez it was time for bed. At first, I was only allowed to tailgate. I got a hug good night, and they went upstairs together. But then I got a backstage pass. Kelsey asked me if I wanted to put Dez to bed, and when I protested that I didn't know what I was doing, she motioned that I would figure it out.

I carried Dez upstairs, she got into bed, and she handed me a book to read to her. She knew the story by heart but wanted to hear it anyway. This offended my sensibilities so I asked her if she wanted to hear a real story, and she said yes, and while I started to fashion a Salingeresque opus about a boy lost in Central Park who meets a magic . . . what? Homeless person? No, that wouldn't be good, that could be scarring. It has to be an animal, but an unusual one. Unicorn? No, it can be unusual without being fantastic . . . stick with a genre. Oh, never mind . . . she's fast asleep.

Now I am a romantic, and I had always deeply enjoyed watching the women I loved sleep. They seemed at peace and safe, and I knew that was partly because of me and how I made them feel. But a child sleeping was new to me. This was a sleeping child I had spent an evening with;

who I had tucked in and got a glass of water for; a child I had stood at the sink with while she rinsed her mouth after brushing; a child I had told "awesome job" when she handed me her abstract crayon drawings—this was uncharted territory. They say you are old when every experience you have reminds you of a similar experience. When was the last time I had experienced anything new? It was illuminating to know that putting a child to bed was not a chore but a privilege. Standing in the doorway watching her sleep with Grey Mousey pressed up against her impossibly fresh face beat hands down the Jon Stewart monologue that Kelsey would yell up that I was missing and that I had previously counted on watching every night.

And it wasn't just the notion of an instant, turnkey family. It was also about Kelsey.

She was the funniest person I had ever met. After a lifetime of making other people laugh, I found, to my surprise, that I wanted to be her audience more than I wanted to entertain her. We literally would—to use Albee's *Who's Afraid of Virginia Woolf?* phrase—take our wits out for a walk after dinner, strolling the neighborhood with Desiree, and making up stories about each neighbor. Her mind went to unusual places, and I could point to anything—a bumper sticker, a small wading pool in a yard—ask her what it said about the people in the house, and she would juxtapose wildly disparate ideas effortlessly into something hilarious. Then she would challenge me to match her, and if I did, she would say, "I hate it when you out funny me." And she listened. You might think, being a guy paid to speak that I was pretty used to that, but it became clear in therapy that I had developed a deep-seated resentment over Syd's penchant for interrupting me mid-sentence. Sometimes it was because she wanted to respond before she forgot what she was saying, but most of the time, she simply wasn't listening. Kelsey would dial in, nod, and then ask follow-up questions. She asked me to bring over my high school yearbook one night—she was born the year I graduated from high school, and she thought that was meaningful. I told her I agreed. It meant I was too old for her. She found the bellbottom jeans and the long hair and the bug-eyed eyeglass frames too funny, but when she came to my picture, it stopped her cold. And I was reminded how this woman with the unyielding, even inherent, need to lie could be so unadulteratedly honest.

"Oh, Dan. You were beautiful. Look at your eyelashes. It's hard to believe that is you. You were amazing. I don't care if you break up with me, I want a copy of this picture and I'm never giving it back."

I knew it was folly to try to convince anyone that my attraction to Kelsey was rooted in her inability to care about things that didn't matter. The walk-in closet in her bedroom was a disaster, with shoes and sweaters and blouses piled four feet high. I would put her on a stopwatch and see how long it would take for her to find the flats she wanted to wear. If she beat her previous time, she would somersault across the room. I hadn't seen anyone somersault in decades. She didn't worry about how the house looked, or whether there were dishes still in the sink when we went to bed. She rallied to clean, cook, and shop as necessary. She had no schedule. The fact that I didn't eat the way most people did and that I would never expect her to prepare meals at set hours made me a bigger catch than all the money in the world would have. She was honest about money, too! "You're rich, Dan. I'm not going to pretend that's not a value-add and that I don't care about the fact that you can provide nice things. But I'm your top producer, and I have always been the breadwinner, so it is *only* a value-add. That's not why I'm in this. And you know it." And I did. I did know it.

So then why not pull the damn trigger? File for divorce. Make a clean break. Let everyone in the world think it is your garden-variety midlife crisis. Who cares? It is not how you envisioned having a family, and having a family was not even your vision all that long ago. But it is now. And you didn't plan it. It happened. Sydney might find her own turnkey, instant family. Or start a new one. There's still time. But whether she does or doesn't is not your concern. Stop the limbo brought on by the lies and the hedging, and in time it will work out. What's the problem? Man the fuck up!

Part of the answer was so awful that I couldn't admit it to anyone. Because it served no one; it offered no solution that was grounded in the real world. But I still couldn't help feeling it: The deeper I got involved with Kelsey and Desiree, the more I missed Sydney.

It felt bizarre to me. I wasn't seeing Sydney. We rarely spoke beyond perfunctory emails concerning finances or mail sent to the house she thought I needed. Our conversations felt strained. I figured part of the strain was because she felt the bizarre feeling too. She wanted to hate me for how I had treated her. She felt foolish giving me more time when I was at the very least seeing Kelsey every day at work and at the worst continuing our affair—and yet we missed each other.

And Dave Eggers didn't help either. This was during the period when Eggers was a cult star who was trying to move past *A Heartbreaking Work of Staggering Genius*. He was running an edgy magazine and had written a follow-up novel, but to most of the world he couldn't shake that amazing memoir. When he spoke at colleges, as he did at

Syd's alma mater, he drew huge crowds. Syd asked me to go. As if we were going on a first date and she didn't want to be dependent on me if the date was lame and she wanted to bolt, we met there. It made me nervous to think of her parking her car and walking to the English Department building. The school bordered on a sketchy area for anyone walking alone—let alone an unaccompanied woman—but I knew if I raised that concern, she would point out she *was* an unaccompanied woman these days. Eggers gave a wonderful, short lecture about the mystery of writing, and soon Syd and I were all in. He was asked to do a Q&A session, and I felt for him when there were no questions and the place fell awkwardly quiet. Sydney came to his rescue, and I was so proud of her. She said she was fighting the urge, which she was sure was shared by every woman in the room, to ask him how his brother Topher, the memoir's hero, was doing. Everyone laughed, and Eggers thanked her profusely for not asking, and Syd said, "Unless you feel like telling me" and everyone laughed again. Eggers, like the rest of the room, was completely charmed by her. She waved me over during the obligatory coffee and cookies break and introduced me to her new famous friend. She called me her husband and listed my playwriting credits with pride. Suddenly we were married again, and everything that had gone down was just some sort of fuzzy dream. She looped her arm in mine as I walked her back to her car. We weren't sure if it was silly or even appropriate to kiss good-bye. So we hugged long and hard. On the drive home, I kept waiting for a crying jag to come on. But it never did. What did that mean?

Limbo did end shortly after, and it was for the same reason it was prolonged. Kelsey. I wish I could say I found the strength to evaluate the pros and cons in a rational, adult way. But Limbo ended by default. I was shamed into it by a series of events that all took place at almost the same time. The best way to stop crying, I found, was to get mad. Fear makes you afraid to act and prolongs suffering. Anger makes things happen.

### Limbo-Ending Event #1

Kelsey and I went to New York City to see a show. We stayed in a five-star hotel in a suite that cost $1,700 a night and looked out over Central Park. We walked around Midtown in the afternoon before the show. I wanted to educate, to explain the ingenious grid design of the avenues and cross streets, to point out how Disney-fied Times Square had become compared to the pre-Giuliani days, but she wanted to stop in bars and hang out. The more she drank, the more she became the girl everyone talked about at the office. Once she reached a certain point, her eyes would change, a switch would be thrown, and she would tell the guy sitting at the bar next to us that he was cute or that she wasn't wearing underwear. That night, after dinner, a two-act Broadway play, and a stop at a comedy club, we came out onto Fifth and Broadway at 1:00 a.m., and as I hailed a cab to take us to the hotel, she said in slurring tones, "What do you want to do now?" Well, I wanted to go to bed, and I didn't mean it as a euphemism for sex. I wanted to sleep. But I took her dancing instead.

### Limbo-Ending Event #2

Those were still the days when most of us had simple cell phones. Smartphones were becoming available but nowhere near ubiquitous. Mine could simply call or text. But Kelsey, raised in constant connectivity, had one of the early smart-phones, where you used a stylus and had some Internet capabil-ities. One of our issues going into our relationship was Kelsey's now-reformed penchant for hooking up with our clients. One of them was a guy nearly my age named Dean, who Kelsey tried to tell me was hardly a threat to us because he was "super fat, and could barely get it up." But she agreed she would cease communication with him; although, she said, we were throw-ing away a perfectly good account, because he hired her can-didates. One day, I went to the fridge to get a snack for Dez. Kelsey's phone was on the counter. Her phone buzzed, and I saw Dean's name flash on the screen before the call went to voice mail. I said nothing, and an hour later, when Dez and I were putting a puzzle together at the breakfast table adjacent to the kitchen, Kelsey checked her voice mail and involuntarily laughed out loud. I felt a puncture in my chest and asked her what was so funny, and she said her mom had left her a funny message. Two days later, when she and some of the other girls in the office went to lunch, I walked into her bullpen. As I hoped, it was empty. I went to her desk, all the while telling myself, "This is pathetic." Her email was up, and sure enough, on the first page, was an email from Dean. The subject line was "Keep your pants on. For now anyway." I opened it and my stomach fell. He had been trying to schedule a rendezvous, and she had apparently been dodgy, and he asked if it was because of "your deal with your boss." Kelsey replied. "I told you, that's a joke." I suppose I could have just taken in the information and ended limbo then, but I was too angry. I asked to see her when she got back and told her I wasn't going to even pretend I had some pretext to go to her desk. I said I had planned it, based on her lie about her mom. And while I was embarrassed to be driven to this kind of tactic — after Syd and the soccer boy and all of Kelsey's own antics I had been witness to over the years — I was not about to go from the frying pan into the proverbial fucking fire. Kelsey was having none of it. "Look, I fucked up, but part of this is on you — why should I cut off all options? You could go back to Sydney tomorrow."

**Limbo-Ending Event #3**

Kelsey and Jay's shared custody of Dez was common enough, but somehow they'd settled on an arrangement where, on his weekends, he would come over on Friday night, they would go out as a family, he would stay over, and he would take Dez to his rented condo Saturday and return her Sunday night. I tried to make the case that this was inappropriate; that when you have been divorced all of five minutes you don't stay overnight. But she stood her ground. She said I had to know by now that if she wanted to sleep with her ex, she wouldn't have divorced him. I had to understand that her priority was Desiree's adjustment to Daddy being gone, that children needed routine and structure, and after her own early scary years before she was adopted, there was no way she was letting Dez feel abandoned or at risk. This was classic Kelsey, giving unimpeachable reasons to defend a position that was clearly not selfless. But it worked on me because the idea of being involved in any way in hurting

Dez flooded me with guilt. Still, I knew what happened when Kelsey drank, how hypersexualized her behavior became, and I wasn't sold on how their nights ended. She tried to reassure me by telling me she had told her ex-husband about us and that he had moved on and was dating, so all of this concern was in my head. She said he certainly wasn't thrilled about being replaced by her boss, but he had a begrudging respect for me and realized after four years that my feelings for her were real. Even this I doubted, and one night after dinner while I was washing dishes and Kelsey was upstairs, Dez walked into the kitchen and stared at me. I asked her what was up, and she said, "My daddy says he hates you." I told her that was too bad, because I didn't hate her daddy; that I thought he was a very good man, and I was sorry he felt that way, and maybe someday that would change. This seemed reasonable to Dez, and she nodded and asked me if I wanted to play Tic-Tac-Toe after I was finished. I nodded and turned away from her, and afraid the crying-jag gods would send a message, I prepared to douse myself in the dishwater to provide cover. He hates me? Of course he does. Welcome to my world.

**Limbo-Ending Event #4**

Diana Krall was the only musician Kelsey and I both admired. When Kelsey used to dance in her living room while vacuum-ing—often hoisting Bailey on his hind legs and twirling him around and even dipping the poor thing—or take the vacuum hose, hold it like a microphone and lip-synch with the lead vocalist, I never had a clue who the band was, let alone the name of the song. But Diana Krall we shared, and so I got us front row seats at the Oakdale Theatre. By the time I picked her up, no more than two hours after work, she was a mess. She claimed she hadn't been drinking, but her eyes were glassy, and she was slurring her words. I knew she hadn't been smoking pot because her eyes got big and red when she did that, and she got sleepy and silly. Instead she was wired, almost agitated. I asked her what she was on, and when Kelsey was accused, she attacked. She started pushing all my buttons on the way there. Maybe being together was a bad idea. Maybe she should work for another firm. Had I ever "poached" a young girl like her before or was she the first? Having learned nothing about arguing with inebriated women in all my time with Sydney, I told her that we would never make this work, given my trust issues, if she was going to lie to me about being drunk or high and that I had no intention of taking up with another woman I had to pour into bed every night. And then, in stark contrast to all my arguments with Sydney, which ended with a mean-spirited or searing phrase, Kelsey indeed separated herself from my realm of experience. She looked at me calmly, slightly sadly, and opened the car door and jumped. We were going approximately eighty-five miles an hour in the middle lane of I-91 in Wallingford. I thrust my right hand out and was just in time to grab her hair. I pulled her back in (by her hair), but the passenger door was wide open, and horns began blaring. When I yelled for her to close the fucking door, she turned to me and started punching me in the face and telling me to let go of her. I had to hold on to her hair to keep her from jumping and hold on

to the steering wheel with my left hand to keep us from crashing, so I had to let her hit my face as I tried to guide the car to
the shoulder of the road. In one surreal moment, I was looking
in the rearview mirror to see if the path to my right was open
and I saw my face being punched in the foreground and in the
background the guy behind me was waving and putting on his
flashers. We made it to the breakdown lane, and the siege was
over. She said she was going to walk home, and I told her to
stop being an idiot and calm down. I took the tickets to Diana
Krall and ripped them to shreds. I told her to close the fucking
door, and when she finally did, I took the next exit and doubled
back to her house. My adrenaline was redlining, and I had to
tell myself to slow down, that if anything was more absurd than
the fact that a mother of a five-year-old would randomly jump
out of a moving car, it would be for me to get into an accident
after surviving such insanity. I turned to ask her what the fuck
she was thinking, but she was fast asleep. When we got home,
I woke her, helped her to bed, and then sat in front of the television, with the sound off, and for the first time mouthed out
loud the words I heard from people my age all the time: I am
too old for this shit.

**Limbo-Ending Event #5**
Limbo ended with no drama. There was no sprint to the finish
line, chest out, breaking the tape. We limped across, exhausted.
In those days, my office had lots of smokers who had to go out-
side to indulge their death-inducing habit. They made me crazy.
People say cigarettes kill you, and of course they're right, but

the problem is they take too long to kill you. If they went out in a group and smoked and one of them took a puff and keeled over dead, they'd all quit. But it takes forty years, and you kid yourself that you'll quit some time down the road before it's too late. They were all in their twenties, so lecturing them did no good. Kelsey didn't smoke cigarettes, but these were her peeps, so she'd go out once in a while and hang with them while they smoked. I couldn't argue that they were being unproductive because they were all exceptional recruiters—Kelsey the best of the bunch. They chatted for ten minutes, finished their cigarettes, and came back in and pounded the phone. Near the end of limbo I stood in the window of our cafeteria area near the entrance and watched her interact with them. Someone said something funny, and they all doubled over laughing. There was a lightness to their exchanges that was at once familiar to me and foreign. I could remember feeling the way they felt, but I was no longer capable of it. Kelsey and I had wonderful moments together, real and true, but I wondered if she ever felt the unrestrained release of her real thoughts with me. Why should she have to love with any reservations? Why shouldn't she feel and think whatever she wanted, without worrying whether she was making me feel out of touch, without me offering, in response to some new experience, "I've already lived that, and I promise you won't care about that in two years"? Ending limbo came to me in a clarified rush, the way ideas did for plays or stories or seminars. And later that night I told her it couldn't work, and when she asked me why, I told her what I knew to be true: "I don't want your youth."

She asked me whether I was going back to Sydney. I told her I had no idea what I was going to do, and she said she thought I probably would, and "that's cool," which was Kelsey's way of saying it was anything in the world but "cool."

. . .

Two Saturdays later, Sydney stood over me telling me to wake up. I was on the green leather couch in the family room, Gatsby curled up at my feet.

"Did I leave the door open?"

"I didn't realize it, but I still had a key in the center console of the car. Sorry. I can't believe I fell asleep."

"You should probably give that back to me. I didn't mean this second. I'm sorry, I'm being a jerk. This is just hard and weird and . . . Jesus, what have you been doing, living in the gym?"

Things were now out of hand. Everyone at work and at the gym was interrogating me. Evan's steroid program had added a couple of inches to my chest, back, and arms, and it was the kind of dense, shredded, dry muscle mass that only drugs can induce. When you watch an action movie and see a ripped actor, and then see him a few months later on TV promoting his next project and he is thinner and smaller, it's because he was juicing for the movie and then came off it.

"I've had a lot of extra time; I spend it at the gym, added calories. Just wanted to see what would happen if I went for it."

"You look like you did when I met you. No, no you don't. You've never looked like that. Good for you, if that's what you want."

This, of course, was Syd's way of saying I looked ridiculous. I handed her the key and sat back down, and Gatsby jumped back up into my lap. His purr was so loud that it softened Syd's face, and she sat down too, and Gatsby abandoned me and crawled up her chest. She nuzzled him and said it was a sweet sight for her to come home to, seeing me sleeping soundly on the couch. I told her it must have made her wonder what year it was, and she smiled. And then an amazing thing happened: We both fell asleep.

Later she made coffee. She took a deep breath and asked me why had I asked to meet? And why did I want to do it here instead of a more neutral setting? All fair questions. And now cue the speech I had prepared on the drive over. I planned to explain that I wanted to discuss *parameters* under which we could *explore* the notion of *restoring* trust, with a *possible* though admittedly *problematic* outcome of starting over. I planned to outline a *process*, involving dating and therapy, by which we could both find a sufficient *comfort level* emotionally and . . . and suddenly the goddamn crying-jag gods decided my prepared remarks were not going to work. I held them off just long enough to blurt out: "I want to come home. I just want to come home."

"You mean it? Yeah?! Yes, honey, I want that too."

Having successfully handed off the crying jags to Sydney the way you lead an annoying guest at a party into a conversation with an unsuspecting victim and then slip away, I had a deep sense of hope and an infusion of energy. I told her it might make sense to sell the house. No ghosts. I promised to stop traveling and end my speaking career if that was required. She promised that her commitment to not drinking was forever and that she understood her relationship with men over the years had been threatening to me. We agreed to stop competing with each other and just *be* with each other; to start saying *to* each other the wonderful things we told others *about* each other. We were getting giddy. We were all in. So I went for it.

"And I don't care if we have to do in vitro five times, or adopt, or fuck it—I will kidnap a kid. How hard could it be to pick off one of the little rug rats at the beach or the mall? We are having a family!"

. . .

Great recruiters close the deal and then get off the phone! They don't let small talk give the client or candidate a chance to change their minds.

**From Danny's "Phone Tips from the Elite" Seminar**

. . .

Less than an hour later, I stood at the door and repeated our plan. I would pay the balance of the lease on the rented condo, keep my obligation to the big Texas conference the following weekend, and when I flew back Sunday night, she would meet me at the condo, we'd pack up my clothes, do a deep clean of the place, and head home. Sydney nodded and took the house key I had returned to her out of her pocket. I thought she was going to hand it to me as a show of good faith, but she held it in a closed fist and told me there was just one more thing. It didn't have to happen overnight, but she wanted Kelsey gone. She said it was impossible for her to stay sane knowing I was working with her every day. She would never feel safe. She said she felt it was a more than reasonable request.

I told her I thought she was absolutely right and well within her rights to ask, and that if I were her I'd be demanding the same thing. But my answer was no. I asked her to consider some things. First, Kelsey was a single mom, my firm specialized in the technology sales sector, and there were no other similar firms that I knew of within a commute; second, the reality is, as Rummy tried to warn me, that she won't stay. It will be too hard emotionally for her and for me, and she will want to move on; finally, I had exposed myself legally, and even though I didn't believe for a second that Kelsey would ever act on it, there were bound to be hard feelings, and she could make a case for wrongful termination. Given my status in the industry, this could be very damaging. Sydney listened patiently and smiled.

"Nonsense. You feel guilty. You should have stayed away from her, and now you can't be the one making her pay the price. You completely absolve her of the way she planned and plotted this. And worse, you still care that much about her."

"That too. I'm sorry Syd. I can promise to end the relationship, but I won't fire her. I don't think it's right."

Syd put the key back in her pocket and told me she agreed with Rummy. "She won't stay. Not if you're really done with her." She opened the door and told me to knock them dead in Texas and that she looked forward to me coming home. I asked her if that meant she was good with me not firing Kelsey.

"If we're going to trust each other, one of us has to go first, so I will. I accept you won't fire her."

## CHAPTER 19

# *Faith*

The third rail of seminars is to never talk about religion, so this is as close as I'm going to get with you guys. Some of you are not committed to a sales career. You are waiting for enough good things to happen to you to justify committing, but call it what you want—fate, spirit, God—here's how He/She/It works: You commit first, and then, because you have committed, He/She/It makes good things happen for you. Is that religious? Fine. Then I am out-and-out pious!

**From Danny's "Rookie Retreats" Seminar**

. . .

The regular parishioners of St. Mary's 7:30 a.m. Mass never knew what to make of me. When I first started coming, I hadn't been to church in so long that I didn't know business casual had infiltrated even the house of God. I wore the same suit I would wear for a keynote, and people stared at me. Who was the new guy? Who dresses like that? Then I had my injury and stopped going to Mass. I'm sure they wrote me off as a guy in crisis, needing a quick fix of atonement. Then my back improved to the point where I could endure Mass, but only by kneeling the entire time. In a Catholic Mass, you only kneel near the end when you celebrate the "mystery of faith." The rest of the time, just as you settle in your seat, everyone rises, and then, for reasons I could never figure out, you sat back down again. This gets alternated several times in a highly arbitrary manner. So now I had returned, and even though I had dialed down the clothing, I was still getting stares. "He's back. And kneeling the whole time! Imagine how bad his sins must be this time! This guy is a player!"

I liked church. I always felt cleaner when I left. It was one of the few times in my day when I didn't feel like I should be somewhere else. I had read enough Christopher Hitchens to have my doubts about organized religion, but I was always attracted to what Jesus advocated, even if I felt the Church was often hypocritical and behind the times. It irritated me that there were no female priests, the Roman Catholic Church's stance on gay marriage appalled me, and the fundamental notion that our club was the only club (if you don't believe, you're damned) never made sense to me. But I tried to separate my relationship with God from the dogma, and for the most part I had pulled it off. Until today.

It was time for the homily, and I always felt bad for our priest. He wanted desperately to be funny, as most speakers do, and he always tried to open with a joke, as most speakers do, and he always bombed. Crickets. He would wait an excruciatingly long moment for laughs that weren't coming. Then he started the sermon, and the day's subject was the anniversary of *Roe v. Wade*. "As Catholics, it is our duty to resist the fourth decade of the senseless murder of millions of babies!" I felt the blood rush to my head. This is suburban Connecticut, the most azure of blue states. I looked around me at the women in the audience and saw many from my generation. We were teenagers when the legislation was passed, even younger when the Pill was introduced. When a female got pregnant in our time, the two questions everyone asked were how could she let that happen and where is she getting the money to take care of it? Taking a guess, I estimated the odds that twenty to thirty women in these pews were being accused of murder. They would be expected to put money in the collection box and on their way out shake the hand of the priest who was accusing them.

I was so enraged that my back no longer hurt. I got off my knees and waited for Mass to end and the priest's receiving line to start. I normally left early, so the priest was surprised when I told him I had a problem with the Mass today. I told him if I wanted to listen to Fox News I could stay at home. I said that I thought love was so rare that I didn't care what form it came in, gay or otherwise; that I was more concerned about the insidious nature of priest pedophilia, which never seems to make it into the sermons; and that I sure as hell didn't think life started at conception—it started at birth. "So you tell me, Father—maybe I just shouldn't be a Catholic? Maybe I don't belong here." He told me, in the most annoyingly unperturbed voice, that I just needed to ask for God's forgiveness for being completely wrong. The people in line behind me were looking down at the ground. They weren't used to conflict here. I knew I should have walked away, but I have always had this thing about getting in the last word.

"Let me ask you something, Father. If a pregnant Catholic woman gets killed in a car crash, how many funerals do you hold?"

"Uh . . . one."

"Exactly."

I don't know what I was expecting. Applause? To be excommunicated? For the father to rip off his collar and admit his life was meaningless and the entire religion a scam? Yes, any of those would have been nice. Instead he smiled and said that obviously this was a personal matter for me, that he was sorry for the pain I have caused or been part of, and that he was available for confession or to talk in his rectory at any time. He told me to go in peace, which was a really lovely way of saying that the people in line behind me were getting restless.

. . .

It was raining so hard that I could barely see the clinic's front door through the windshield. Another ten minutes would mark an hour, and I would have to put more change in the meter. Kelsey told me she would text me when she was on her way out. She told me in no uncertain terms that I was to wait in the car.

A month after our meeting, it was clear that Syd and I would not be getting back together. I would not be going home. I had sat down with Kelsey to let her know about my decision, to ask for her understanding. I thought it could go one of two ways. She could obviously be angry and bitter that I was choosing not to give us a chance, or she could take the high road, be like ice, and tell me she had known it all along. But we'll never know. Kelsey, it turned out, had news of her own.

"Let me guess. She's pregnant."

I gave Syd the look I see on politicians' faces when they can neither confirm nor deny something that is clearly true. I told Syd I needed more time. That I couldn't come home right now. I told her that, because Kelsey would not give me an answer on what she was going to do about being pregnant. Kelsey told me she wanted nothing from me, but she knew I couldn't live with that. She tried to reassure me that it was no trap, that she taken all the precautions she normally did. She said the same thing happened with Desiree. "I'm just freaky fertile!" was her clinical opinion. She said she was torn, that she didn't want me to hate her for the timing, and yet she wasn't going to apologize for wanting to have a child with me. I told her I would respect and honor any choice she made. And I meant it. Choices have consequences.

"Here's what is important to me," Syd said, in a voice more exhausted than angry. "I want to be the one who files the divorce papers. I want to be the one on record as having ended this. Do you understand?"

Kelsey texted me that she would be out shortly. It wasn't raining when she went in, so I replied that I could come in with an umbrella, and she texted back that I was to stay in the car. Much later, when word of all of this got out to the staff at the office, the reaction was split according to gender. The men sighed and said life is all about timing and luck, and the women all accused Kelsey of having created her pregnancy out of thin air. Women can be so cruel to each other.

"So all you know, really, is that she came out of the clinic?"

"You never went in with her?"

"You never saw any documentation?"

But I knew things as I watched Kelsey make her way from the clinic front door to my car. I knew lying about being pregnant and faking an abortion was a move Kelsey was absolutely capable of conceiving and carrying out, but I knew she wasn't lying. I knew by her dead eyes that looked straight ahead. I knew because she made no jokes, which was her fundamental way of dealing with pain. I knew because when we got to my condo, she collapsed on the couch, her soaking wet jacket still on, and asked me to leave the television off so she could sleep. When I tried to take her jacket off so she wouldn't catch cold, she viciously pushed my hand away. She saw the helpless look on my face and said she wasn't mad at me, and I wanted to ask her how she could not be. I had dreaded having to tell Sydney that Kelsey was pregnant and hated myself for knowing I would now cause her even more terrible pain, but I never had to do it. Kelsey called me and told me she was getting an abortion that Friday. If we were to have a future, it should come because we want to be together, not because circumstance made us be together. She said she didn't want me hating her, but as I sat across from her in the silent living room and listened to the heavy breathing of her sleep, I worried that she would always hate me.

And as I quietly made a meal, watching the microwave countdown carefully so I could stop it before it buzzed and woke her, I worried that I might hate her too. For so long fatherhood had been the thing I wanted to avoid the most, and then it became the thing I wanted the most, and now that it had become a measurable outcome, it somehow still seemed right to pass on it. It was her call, of course, but I never fought her. And what did that mean? Did I want children? Or only Sydney's children? And as I watched Kelsey sleep, I wondered if we could possibly get past this. Could we someday say with a straight face that it just wasn't the right time? Were we being wise or foolish? Would we someday have a chance to make a different choice, or was that just what we would tell each other whenever regret made a run at us?

## CHAPTER 20

# Collaboration

Interviewing is a performance art far more critical than your work habits. Right now I have a mask on, my "speaker mask." This is not who I really am. And you have an audience mask on. You're not normally this engaged and respectful. We teach our candidates how to create the right mask for themselves and custom fit it for their interview. Does this help them get the job? Yes! Is it right? Is it fair to the person interviewing them? Hell, yes, they're wearing a mask too! They're not the boss you will come to know any more than you are the employee you are pretending to be. You can fight the system and lose, or learn to play it better and win.

**From Danny's "The Performance Art of Interviewing" Seminar**

. . .

Sydney stared at me from across the long mahogany table. Our lawyers were chatting each other up in the hall.

"Okay, I can't figure it out. I know it's pretty standard for people getting divorced to change their look, but those frames are way too big for your eyes and head, you need a haircut in the worst way, and the George Clooney three-day stubble is just not working."

She playfully rubbed my cheek and said she was sure glad she wasn't kissing me anymore—that must hurt!

And hurt it did! I did everything I could do to hide the pain reverberating through my head. She withdrew her hand because the lawyers were entering the conference room. My doctor had told me that since I was stubborn about not taking narcotics, I would have a tremendous amount of pain in the near term. He said I had great elasticity in my skin, and being a nonsmoker would greatly reduce my swelling, but at the end of the day, face-lifts were a fairly brutal operation. "We cut you, yank up the loose skin, and tie it up. You can't expect that not to hurt!" Sydney kept staring at me. It had been five weeks since the operation, and while keeping my hair long covered the incisions in my temples, and the close-cropped beard and thick-framed glasses hid most of the swelling, she knew something was different. Luckily, she was distracted by the minor matter of divvying up all our assets and the real-world concerns of alimony, taxes, real estate, and the great unsaid—the future. She was a tenured professor with a good salary, a beautiful woman barely forty who attracted men with ease. It was absurd to think she'd end up alone, and yet her lawyer, her divorced friends, and the human part of her that wanted me to suffer for choosing Kelsey, all told her to negotiate as if she would end up a bag lady. "Get what you can from him now; he won't take care of you once those papers are signed. He certainly has proven he is two-faced." And I had. And now, I actually was.

Kelsey's sister had visited. We hadn't met before. Kelsey didn't talk much about her family, and I wanted to get the download on their early years. Her sister polished off a twelve-pack of beer and late that night, her buzz lowering her defenses, looked me up and down and said, "So Kelsey was right, from the neck down you look like you're in your twenties! Damn! Good for you!" A week later I was trying to teach Kelsey how to play tennis. She was a natural, and we had a blast. When our hour was up, two women about my age came on court, and one of them, dressed in expensive Fila gear and carrying a bag with three racquets, a serious country club mom, glared at Kelsey and said to me, "I think it's wonderful you are teaching your daughter to play." I smiled and walked away. Kelsey was furious at the woman for making the comment and angrier with me for not telling her that Kelsey was my girlfriend. For my part, I was angry with the woman, Kelsey, and above all, time itself. When I showed Kelsey the website of the cosmetic surgeon the next day, she melted down.

"She didn't think you were my father, Dan. She was interested in you and angry that you're with a younger woman, so she said that to shame you. How can you not see that? You don't need a fucking face-lift!!"

I had asked the doctor how soon I could work out after the rhytidectomy. He said he was concerned about me lifting weights for at least two months because he imagined I would hold my breath or make facial expressions when exerting myself and that could affect the desired results of the face-lift. When I made it clear to him that I had to return to the gym as soon as possible or muscle atrophy would sink in and I would lose a year (and all the steroid benefits) of hard training, he sighed.

"I don't know . . . because you are a forty-seven-year-old man. Most of the face-lifts I do are on woman within a few months of their fiftieth birthday. I'm not even sure you need to do this. I know you have deep labial lines, but there's no fat in your face. You could gain weight and look much younger. After forty, you have a choice: be lean and look old, or be fat and have a crummy body. Why not try fillers first before we cut you up?"

"No. No fillers, no creams, no retinoids, no glycolic acids, Botox, Dysport, thermage systems, or laser peels." They had minor effect, were unpredictable result-wise, and had to be done every few months forever. If I was going to do it, I was going big or going home. I had to give him credit when he suggested, given the fact that I was in the throes of divorce, that I wait a year since he was risking a $20,000 fee that was not covered by insurance and therefore a cash deal. I shook my head and declared that if I were not a professional speaker, a man whom audiences expect to look the same as the guy on the videos they download, I would not be here. "This isn't about a personal crisis or vanity. This is purely a professional decision based on the unfair necessity of maintaining a public persona." He shrugged, and we scheduled the surgery, but he was the only person I managed to fool.

A couple of weeks later, I woke up in the condo, and a thousand knives seemed to be stabbing me in the face. Every plastic surgeon's website tells you to expect moderate but tolerable pain when you get a face-lift. That is a joke. Face-lifts hurt like hell. I wanted to go through the first horrible week alone, but they wrap the bandage around your head so tightly that there is a real risk of choking the first two nights. Kelsey asked her ex to take Dez for a few days and stayed with me. On the third day the bandage comes off, and then the swelling starts in earnest. As I tried to emerge from the foggy haze of the narcotic, I heard Kelsey on the phone talking to a friend.

"Oh my God, he looks like the Elephant Man. You can't believe it!! His face is as big as a pizza—only it's all purple!! I'm serious! It is everything I can do not to dry heave in front of him! I traded in a per-fectly good-looking husband for a circus freak. Wait until he goes under and I'll send you a pic! So trippy!!"

When she came in the room, I told her I'd heard her, and she froze. Then I started to laugh, which made her start to laugh, and she hugged me gingerly. I pulled her to me and tried to kiss her, which made her laugh harder and roll away, but she rolled on top of me. I gave her a look that assured her it was okay, and I pulled down my pants, and she undressed beside the bed and then left the room. She came back in with a paper bag and handed it to me and said, "You think only guys get away with this move? Wear this, you are fugly, but I still want sex."

. . .

Now that I can look back and concede what I couldn't then—that I got a face-lift to appear a more viable partner for a beautiful young woman seventeen years my junior—I would still recommend it. If you have the discipline to resist the doctor trying to upsell you. I didn't want "no wrinkles", I wanted to be able to express myself; if you have the dis-cipline not to get carried away—the doctor wanted to "pull up" five to seven centimeters, which would have completely changed my appear-ance, but I vetoed that and settled for three; and if you have the patience to wait five months for the tissues to settle; you will find, as I did, that you look refreshed. Less tired. A few years younger, but nothing overt or crazy. The test was not the people I saw every day, but the audiences who would see me once a year at their annual conventions. No one ever mentioned anything about my face, because I didn't seem to look any different from the way I did in the videos they saw, which ranged in age from as recent as a few months to as many as five years ago. The only comments I got were, "You never seem to age; it's very annoying." Only one woman said to me flatly, "Your surgeon, by the way, is excellent." Since I had the lift way before most people do, I now have friends who are considering it and asking my advice. I tell them what my surgeon told me: "Every single person you see on TV over forty has had work done. Every single one." I just wish the websites and consults were more honest. They should say, "It will hurt more than we admit, it will take longer than we claim, and it will do absolutely nothing to quell the deep-seated fears that brought you in here." But other than that—yeah, it works great.

"She hasn't called me since that night," Sydney offered during a break. "As long as you keep her in check, we can keep our court date. Okay?"

"It was alcohol-fueled, Syd, which I'm sure you can appreciate. It clearly was not in my interest for her to call you, and it just as clearly, given the financial ramifications, was not part of my 'collaborative' strategy."

Sydney had suggested we do a "collaborative divorce." We each would have a lawyer to sit in meetings and guide us, but there would be no trial, no points of evidence, no discovery, or depositions. No playing gotcha. Either of us could withdraw and go to trial if an agreement could not be reached. It was supposed to be the way civil, reasonable people got divorced.

And it was. Until one night when I was on the road and Kelsey went out after work with friends. At 1:00 a.m., once she got home, she decided it would be a good idea to weigh in on the divorce proceedings. She drunk-dialed Sydney, waking her out of a sound sleep, and told her,

"Stop being a bitch and just let him go. He doesn't love you. He loves me and my daughter." In her morning stupor, Kelsey hadn't remembered making the call, so I knew nothing about it until I landed at the airport and returned to the Warrens' condo. There was a red light signifying a voice mail, but voice mails were usually friends of the Warrens who didn't know they had a tenant. Then the phone rang, and it was Mr. Warren. He said he hoped I didn't mind, but he had been in town yesterday, and stopped by to check on the condo, and since I wasn't home, he had retrieved his voice mail messages.

"I hope I'm not overstepping, but your lady friend seems quite upset. I've been married fifty-one years, and I think I know a little something about how to fix situations like this. If you'd like to hear it, that is."

I had no idea what he was talking about. I asked him if I could check the message and call him back.

"Danny, if that fucking cunt *ever* calls me again, it will cost you more than it already is going to cost you, and it is going to cost you fucking big! I'm calling Natalie in the morning and telling her to tear up the agreement and start over."

Within a few minutes, I was brought up to speed. Sydney walked me verbatim through Kelsey's call, informed me that a forensic accountant was being hired to establish the value of my business. Sydney said, "If I get half the business, the first thing I will do is fire that little bitch." I was shaking when I called Kelsey, who checked her phone and admitted there was a call to Sydney at that time, but she had no recollection of making it. She was begging me for forgiveness when I hung up. I sat on the ottoman in front of the recliner and felt numb. We had agreed the business was off-limits, which had allowed me to be more than generous with our other assets. I figured I could always make more money. Now

Sydney was threatening to take half. And I couldn't blame her one bit. After a few minutes of staring into space, I went to the phone, deleted the voice mail, and called Mr. Warren. I apologized sheepishly for the language he'd heard, and then I got to the real purpose of the call. *Who was I, with the mess I had made, not to accept advice from someone who had managed to stay married for five decades?* I asked him what I should do.

"Two words, son. Whitman's Sampler . . . hasn't failed me yet."

Sydney's lawyer, Natalie, was much sharper than my lawyer. She had originated the collaborative concept in Connecticut. She was pleasant and empathic, extremely deferential to my lawyer, made it clear she was only here to answer questions and guide the process to mutual resolution, and was an absolute assassin. She handed out the latest iteration of our agreement and left us alone to read through it.

"So, are you two living together? I ask fully aware that you don't have to answer."

I wasn't sure I knew the answer. The truth would be as maddening for Syd as it was for me. Most nights I stayed at my condo, but Kelsey and Desiree and I were together on weekends. There were amazing days, where I would spend mornings with Dez, sitting on the couch with her while she drank juice boxes and I read *The New York Times* and sipped coffee. I would rant that it was perfectly obvious that Iraq not only had no weapons of mass destruction but that this war was starting to seem to be more about Halliburton profits than it was about avenging 9/11, and Dez would nod and say, "For real!" Kelsey would make her way downstairs in sweatpants and a wifebeater left over from her ex, looking ridiculously sexy, offering a "What's up, Pooh Bear?" to Dez and twirling her around. I would hand her a cup of coffee as she made breakfast, and we'd talk about the day. Maybe a trip to the Lake Compounce amusement park. Maybe a drive to the shore. For the first time, I understood that parents weren't necessarily negligent or crazy when they lose track of their kid or their kid drowns at a crowded beach. I would watch Dez like a hawk, but she was so small and there were so many kids that every few minutes I'd lose sight of her and panic. "Stay where I can see you!" I'd say too loudly, and she'd look scared.

Kelsey would squeeze my arm and say, "Easy." Maybe we'd grab a basketball and I'd lower the basket on the hoop in the yard and teach her foul shots. Or maybe we'd go to the movies, and I'd be surprised to learn some of the big studio animated movies included jokes and cultural references designed for the parents, and after, we'd sit in Ruby Tuesday's and discuss Dez's friends in school. She had boyfriends (plural, mind you), and she talked about them like a coed out to lunch with the girls. "I like Ben, but he just stands there all during recess, and when you ask him what he wants to do, he doesn't say anything. So lame." I knew she was simply a mimic, stealing phrases and even eye and hand motions from her mom, but it slayed me. There were many nights like this, and on these nights I had a feeling that was foreign to me: I felt like I was where I belonged.

"You know what? Never mind. I don't want to know. Not healthy. Just a reflex."

The maddening truth was Kelsey and I broke up twenty times during the time I went through the collaborative divorce process. That's the actual number. Every time I would wrap my head around my new reality—*yeah, it was messy, and I would have preferred a different path, but in the end, I was meant to be here, and I'm going to stop controlling and just let it happen*—then Kelsey's dark side emerged, and I got scared to death. This led to the pattern we repeated twenty times: dark, usually humiliating event, confrontation, breakup—period of time to get over it—miss each other, reach out abjectly via email or phone—but not at the office, remain cool and detached there—reunite and commit to never engaging again in such nonsense—repeat.

Professional speakers live for aphorisms and quotes. I took pride when something I said was repeated by other speakers, printed on flyers and brochures, and became part of the lexicon of the average recruiter. Words I still believed in. And for Kelsey and me, our destructive pattern came down to a debate about the following famous phrase: A drunken man's words are a sober man's thoughts.

Kelsey thought this phrase was ridiculous and written by a person who had never gotten really wasted. Kelsey's position was as simple as it was self-serving. She was a blackout drunk; she remembered nothing about what she said or did when she was under the influence of alcohol or drugs. Once she was told what she'd said or done, she acted shocked and asserted the words and deeds were without meaning.

I believed the phrase completely. I thought alcohol lowered your inhibitions and revealed character and true feelings. It was partly my fear of this kind of surrender that kept me from ever getting too drunk. It turned out this fear was unfounded, since on the few occasions when I would over indulge, I was the quintessential sentimental, happy drunk. I would tell you I loved you over and over ad nauseam. But since I couldn't say those words very easily while sober, it still reinforced the phrase's dead-on truth.

I was a "sucker setup" for an addict. First, I was a control freak. I could never imagine relinquishing myself to a drug that might harm me. Second, I was a fitness freak. Once I had a few hangovers and found myself unable to work out the next day, it was game over. Add in all the extra sugars in alcohol and a beer belly, and it was easy for me to give it up. And third, like any kid who came of age in the late 1970s I had been exposed to pot and cocaine and I had chased the euphoric sensation of a buzz, but I didn't have the addiction gene. One drink, a couple of hits off a joint, a line or two of coke, and I would spend the rest of the night saying, "I'm good, thanks." When a friend, already wired out of his mind, would sit and pour the entire vial he had on the table and snort until it was gone, I would ask him why he wouldn't save some for later or, God forbid, next weekend, and he would look at me like I was crazy. "Stop? But there's some left!"

I never understood why Sydney, and later Kelsey to a far greater degree, wouldn't stop something they knew to be harming them. Later I would learn about "enabling" and "codependence" and how addicts instinctively saw me coming. A natural caretaker and strong presence who would not only be there for them but also stupidly think he could change their behavior through logic and love. But as a guy so damaged by the insecurities his shame-based life had instilled, he would always see the behavior stemming from addiction as a judgment on his own love and worthiness. So he would never demand change. His demons would harbor their demons.

*. . . are a sober man's thoughts . . .*

"Dan, please don't look at me that way. I'm sure it's horrible, but I don't remember . . . "

And I would fill Kelsey in on her latest drunken gaffe. Numbly, head down, I would recount:

" . . . We were dancing, you saw a guy, you forgot I was there and you went over to him and started dancing with him, right in front of me . . . "

" . . . I went to the restroom, came back, and you weren't at the dinner table. You were at the bar, chatting up a guy, a younger guy. Tell me again how you're only attracted to older guys . . . "

" . . . We were moving from foreplay to the main event, and you were so drunk you fell asleep. I had my mouth on you and heard you snore. That's very empowering for a guy, Kel . . . "

" . . . It was 4:00 p.m. when I called from my hotel. You were clearly altered. I told you not to go pick up Dez from day care, and you told me to 'man the fuck up.' What does that even mean?"

I asked Sydney, on our way out to the parking lot after our lawyers had walked us through the timeline of our dissolution, if I could ask her something without her thinking I was taking a cheap shot or talking about us. I knew by this time that she had been attending meetings and simply knew more than I did about the subject. This woman, who had breached my trust, still commanded it in certain matters.

"Do you think there's such a thing as a blackout drunk?"

"No," she said, shaking her head sadly. "I think that's what we say to cover up our horrible choices."

On behalf of all the weak-ass couples the reader might have known who do what we did—break up; tell everyone we are broken up; recite the latest outrage; elicit sympathy from friends who know full well they are wasting their breath while they are telling you it is for the best; sheepishly admit later we are giving it another go; over and over—you should know that *every* time couples like us act out our charade, we are utterly convinced this is it. No way back. Until we find one.

But I had no right asking Syd. I should have pleaded the Fifth when she asked about my situation with Kelsey or told her it was not her concern. But I was still so in need of her approbation, still so unsure of letting us go, that I used telling Sydney as a way of burning the ships once the troops had landed. If I told Sydney that I was done with Kelsey, I would have no choice but to stay the course.

Instead I went back to Kelsey *again* but didn't have the decency to update Sydney. Inevitably, friends of hers would see Kelsey and me at a restaurant or a movie and report back to Sydney, who would be furious with me for not telling her. She no doubt assumed I had never broken up with her, but the truth was worse: I did it so often that it seemed crazy even to me.

Near the end of the divorce process, during final negotiations, I got what I deserved for sharing selectively with Sydney. Kelsey and I were in one of our "off" periods, and when one of those got prolonged, Kelsey often played the financial card, insinuating that she didn't realize how hard it was being a single mom in a commission job, conveniently leaving out her $200K W2 and her penchant for spending wildly, but saying since we were "broken up," she couldn't afford the paint job her house sorely needed. Beset by guilt and trying no doubt at some level to work my way back into her good graces, I hired a painter and wrote a check. But I forgot that the canceled checks went to my former home address. Sydney saw the notation, "paint for Kel's house" and lost her mind.

Sydney called me at the office and asked if I were going to be home after work. She had a matter to "dispose of." The legalese construction matched her tone. Clipped. Formal. But even though I was uneasy, I wasn't ducking her when I told her she'd caught me on a night when we were doing an awards banquet for a record quarter. We had rented a bus from a limo service, and I wouldn't be getting back to my car until at least 9:00 p.m. I asked if we could do it in the morning. She said that was perfect. Then she repeated the word "perfect" slowly and told me to have a good night. So I knew something was coming but managed to put it out of my mind while I handed out awards, pumped up the egos of the top partners, and challenged the junior people to work harder and join their ranks. I am constantly asked at seminars about how to motivate salespeople, and I tell managers to stay away from long-term goals, a trip to the Bahamas, or a year-end bonus. Salespeople aren't sure they will be alive in an hour, let alone in the Bahamas a year from now. They want short-term goals. "What do I get if I have a good month, week, day?" And they want recognition. So we gave them both. A banquet, a trophy, a check, all based on recent successes. As I looked around the bus, I took great solace in the fact that while my personal life was a mess, these people didn't know that. They were a happy, productive team. And they trusted my leadership. Then the bus pulled into the parking lot, and one of my partners looked out the window and said, "Uh-oh." And then I heard what came next. Whoever said it was drunk, but everyone laughed, and their illusion of my sagacious stewardship was shattered.

"Saint Sydney's Revenge!!"

My car was no longer visible. She had piled every piece of clothing I had on the roof and then created a border around the car with Hefty bags of more clothes and items like plaques and trophies and pictures. Anything associated with me or our life was paraphernalia to her now.

To Kelsey's credit, she went immediately to her car and left. She knew I needed to be alone with this public humiliation. A couple of the guys asked me if I wanted help, and I waved them away. I spent the next hour walking from my car to the dumpster at the far end of the parking lot.

When I was done, I called Sydney and rather than confront me, she let it go to voice mail. But I wasn't angry. I told her that I had the wonderfully weird desire all people who divorce someone they truly love are familiar with: I wanted to tell my old best friend, Sydney, about this crazy thing that had happened to me; only the crazy thing itself had been perpetrated by my new best enemy, Sydney. I told her that it was indeed "perfect" and that keying my car would have been far less effective and was beneath her. I didn't ruin her big night by trying to explain the check or telling her it didn't mean what she thought it meant. I told her I was sorry and hung up.

On the day of our final collaborative divorce hearing, I woke up completely convinced I had everything figured out. I wasn't in a midlife crisis. I was simply exhausted. I had a lifelong habit, taught to me by my first creative writing teacher, of keeping a notebook by my nightstand in case the muse visited during the night. I often went to bed, with no idea how to present an idea in a seminar or resolve a scene in a play, and woke to find the answer in barely legible notes. I also often woke to find no notes or notes that made absolutely no sense to me, but the point is, I trusted the method. That morning, my notes were—

- *Not happy alone, but not sad either.*

Some people can't be alone for five minutes. The idea of bringing a book into a restaurant and eating alone mortifies them. Some people can't leave a relationship without having one to go to. Despite what had happened, I knew this wasn't me. I liked my own company, and I was never bored if I had something to read. My curiosity exceeded my need for company many times over.

- *Introverts are not losers.*

I was, at my core, an introvert. Yes, I spoke in front of large crowds for a living, so I know it sounds incongruent to claim to be an introvert.

But I had simply figured out early on that extroverts win, and I dialed up that part of my personality to give the world what it wanted so that it would reward me in return. Sydney used to say I cried more on stage and was more emotionally available to my audiences than I was to family, but she didn't understand that being on stage created the separation I needed in order to be open. The audiences were close enough to hear me, but not close enough to touch me. I controlled the intimacy.

• *Genetics rule.*

My dad died at sixty-seven of a stroke. Everyone in my family but me had blood pressure and weight issues. I believed I had only twenty years left. There were things I wanted to write and philanthropic goals I wanted to fulfill. I wanted to die penniless, having given everything away to worthy causes. I wanted to have mattered. I fully believed I could ride out the last two decades alone, and that without the drain on my energies that women like Kelsey and Sydney required, I could get more done.

I folded up my notes and was going to put them in my burgeoning ideas folder. But instead—as a way to prove to myself they were indelibly etched into my brain—I threw them away.

. . .

Natalie started the hearing off with fireworks. She said Sydney had agreed to not pursue her right to half of my businesses as long she got the previously agreed upon terms, and, "Oh yes, one more thing—she should get half of your 401(k) plan. If that is okay, we can get this done immediately."

For the first time in the months-long proceedings in which he was steamrolled by Natalie, my lawyer got angry. He said that was crazy. "She has her own 401(k) at the college! She's forty! They're not retiring tomorrow!"

I waved him off and smiled. *Now you're in my house*, I thought. I launched a spontaneous and eloquent defense. I made it clear: "We all knew this was coming, due to my relationship with a younger woman, so this is at once very human of Sydney and very wrong. I believe she will regret it. I had both my businesses before I ever met her, and the notion that she supported home and hearth while I went out and made money is quaint, but completely baseless. We both have careers. She is as good at hers, if not better than I am at mine. And we are still early in those careers. To split retirement monies is simply a punitive measure designed to hurt me for my choices. Coming from a woman who left the marriage first takes . . . well . . . let's use a different word than the one I was thinking . . . nerves."

Natalie smiled and took a moment to use a tissue to wipe down her glasses.

"Are you through? You sure? Because I really like to listen to you talk. It's pretty clear after all these meetings, Danny, that you are the smartest person in this room. You're probably the smartest person in most rooms you're in, but whenever you are done talking, I'm getting half of that 401(k) for Sydney."

My lawyer, seeing me about to redline, suggested a cooling-off period of a day or two. He wanted to debrief, but I summarily dismissed him, looked at Natalie and Sydney with professional disgust, and told them I'd get back to them. The reality was I didn't even know what half of my 401(k) plan meant to me in real dollars—this was all about my lifelong loathing of finishing second.

. . .

It was still late morning when I got back to the office, and Leah told me Kelsey had "emailed in sick," and she gave me that look. We both knew that was often code for too hungover after a Thursday night out to make it in on Friday. I'm sure I was inverting my anger from the hearing, but instead of going to the gym at lunch, I drove to Kelsey's house. It was the usual scene. The bedroom was dark. She was practically comatose. Her party clothes from the night before were on the floor in the adjacent bathroom. No amount of drinking could ever make her forget to apply her "zit cream," and it was smeared across her face, giving her an apparitional glow. When I leaned in to wake her up, I could smell the alcohol on her breath and coming from her pores. I was leaving her a text telling her to call me if she needed me to pick Dez up from day care when my phone rang. It was Sydney. I closed the bedroom door and took the call at the top of the stairs. Sydney let me have it: "Don't storm out of meetings like you're too good for everyone else and we're all wasting your time. Don't act like I am asking for a house in the fucking Hamptons when I ask for half of an established asset which Natalie says is due me, and by the way, fuck you. I could take so much more and you know it . . . "

And then, gearing up to swing low and retort savagely, I saw myself in the hall mirror. Or did I? *Could that be me?* The guy with the practically purple vein sticking out of my forehead, the guy whose face was so contorted with rage and misplaced frustration that he could feel his fore-arms and hands shake? Was this who I was? *No. No!! This ends now.*

"Danny? Are you still there? I swear to Christ if you hang up on me . . ."

"I'm here, Syd. You're right. You're completely right. And I'm sorry. I was being reactive. Shadowboxing. You and Natalie write up whatever you think is fair. The 401(k), whatever else you want—write it up, and I will sign it. And I will execute whatever is in it. We good?"

"I don't understand. What just happened?"

. . .

Desiree was a creature of habit. She liked the fries at Ruby Tuesday's. We were halfway through when I saw Kelsey at the hostess stand. She had dark circles under her eyes and had her hair back in the ponytail that said she couldn't bring herself to shower. She made her way over, slid in beside Dez, and started eating her fries. She knew coming here would deflect any conversation we might have about her breaking her latest not-drinking promise. Three fries in, she had to practically sprint to the bathroom.

I was thinking things worked out for a reason. I would extricate myself from both this dysfunctional situation, and my marriage, and start the monastic life I at some level always thought I was meant to live. My energy and sense of peace would be restored. Then Desiree said she was wondering if she could ask me something but please don't get mad.

"Are you going to be my Daddy now?"

"Do you want me to be?"

"Yes, please."

"Dez, you have a Daddy. He loves you very much."

"I know . . . but like, my Dan-Daddy. Like, take care of us."

I guess the monastery will have to wait.

## CHAPTER 21

# Texting

**Moderator:** We have a question—ironically, from Twitter. Jeff wants to know why people text him back when he calls them. He preferred the days when he could talk to them live.

**Danny:** Jeff has to get over it. Nostalgia is the call-in-case-of-emergency number for people who are afraid of change. People tell you they text because it is faster, or easier. That's crap. They do it because they get to do the important part—say what they have to say, without the part they don't care about—hearing what you have to say. And they get to be mean and say things they would never have the guts to say to your face. The problem is, it backfires, because now there is a record of their meanness, and the person who received it looks at it over and over again, making forgiveness hard and trust impossible.

**From "A Live Webchat with Danny"**

. . .

The doctor on call in the emergency room said it would be a few hours before they would know anything, so I sat in the waiting room lounge and scrolled through my texts from Kelsey. I told myself I was looking for clues for when the period she would later call "Crazytown" started, but I think it actually was my way of staying connected to her while she was in the ICU fighting for her life. A form of praying. The first text I saw was, of course, the last one she'd sent, the one I'd gotten while wandering to the bathroom at the Bellagio in the middle of the night. God, was that last night? How long have I been awake?

**If you ever talk to Desiree again, tell her I loved her.**
**I'm so sorry. I just took 37 Tylenol pm.**

I didn't take it seriously at first. She was simply upping the ante. I hadn't responded when she sent me the text I retrieved when I landed in Vegas:

**I quit my job. I'm serious. I want my partner equity money. I'm**
**moving back to California and you will never see me or Dez again.**

And I didn't respond when she sent me two more texts disavowing the first and begging me to call her. Then came two more where she promised me I had misunderstood the situation with her ex. Then, finally, throwing the Hail Mary, she sent a text admitting that what I assumed happened had in fact happened and that she had lied when she denied it and that she certainly couldn't blame me for walking away. Not after all she had put me through during (ah . . . this was the first time she used the phrase — see how texts document things and can come back to haunt you?) her "Crazytown" phase. When I finished my speech and turned my phone on, there were two more texts. One told me if I gave her another chance she would go to rehab, and the other, sent an hour later, told me she didn't need rehab and to fuck myself.

But there was something about the suicide message I couldn't ignore.

Not the message itself—she was absolutely capable of lying to that extreme—it was the specific number: "37 Tylenol pm." When Kelsey lied, she tried to talk in generalities so she had room to maneuver; when she told the truth, she backed it up with detail. I still assumed it was an act, but some instinct told me to play it safe. I called her next-door neighbors, lovely people who had heard our epic fights on many a night, and told Ben I'd gotten a scary message from Kelsey and asked could he please check on her? It was already 6:00 a.m. in Connecticut, and I knew he was up because I saw him many a morning when I went to the gym.

While I waited for him to call me back, I realized I would never get back to sleep and, this being Vegas, there was twenty-four-hour room service, and I could order breakfast. I was on the phone with the bright young lady in guest services when my cell buzzed. Ben was freaking out. Kelsey was unconscious. Vomit everywhere. The Tylenol bottle empty on her nightstand. An ambulance was on the way. They were going to take care of Desiree. Ben sheepishly asked me if he should call Kelsey's ex, which told me he knew what had happened the previous week. "Of course," I told him. I raced to the airport and sat there for two hours before it opened. I knew that made no sense, but I had to feel like I was doing something to get to her. Now I was the one texting. Ben. Kelsey's ex. Her parents. No one got back to me. This was long before Wi-Fi on airplanes. I got off the plane in Hartford six hours later, and there were a handful of texts and voice mails. I was used to getting off planes and being deluged by a combination of vitriolic and lovesick calls and texts from Kelsey, but instead of hearing her voice, there were a series of grave sounding proclamations. "She's in critical condition." "It doesn't look good." And from her ex, "Well, she's fucked up good this time. Stupid bitch."

Every other time I had been in waiting rooms at hospitals, I'd felt annoyed by the number of people ahead of me and I would do an inventory assessment. Who was worse off than my torn Achilles or strep throat and would be taken first? How long was I going to have to wait? (That guy is bleeding; he's in for sure. That woman's ankle is not broken; she can stand it on for God's sake, but she's crying so hard I'm sure they'll take her next.) But this time I was alone, and I missed all of them. I wanted someone to commiserate with, someone to save me from the only tape that was playing in my head over and over—*I used to break their hearts. Now I'm killing them.*

The doctor on call came in, asked if I was there for Kelsey, sat down next to me, put his hand on my knee, and leaned in, like a basketball coach explaining why he took me out of the game. His fatigue and heavy-eyed dolefulness scared the hell out of me. He asked if Kelsey was a heavy drinker. I first shrugged and then said yes. He said he assumed she's been that way for a long time. Probably since her early teens. "Here's the thing. If you or I took thirty-seven Tylenol PMs, we'd wake up with one helluva headache and we'd feel like shit, but we'd get through it. But when you are a heavy drinker, and your liver is at all compromised, and then you add in thirty-seven Tylenol PMs, you're in real trouble. We're trying to get the poison out, but there's a danger her organs will shut down before we turn the corner. Right now, I'd say it's very possible we'll lose her. I'm sorry."

I nodded stoically. As if I knew this already and had made all the necessary moves to carry on. No biggie. But my face betrayed me. He patted my knee, and his eyes welled a little.

"You the reason she did this?"

I nodded, which dried his eyes instantly. He told me he'd let me know and walked out, leaving me with nothing to do but scroll through the texts of my past few months. When had this all unraveled? It seemed to happen the moment I was legally free and we were making a go of it. I stopped scrolling when I saw

**Hi Babe. I'm home, just crashing on the couch.**
**Where are you? You coming over?**

. . .

I was filling my tank in a gas station a few miles from her house, and I looked up absentmindedly and saw her silver Volvo parked in the middle of a strip mall across the street. There was a Planet Fitness she didn't belong to, a medical supplies store she was too young to frequent, and a grocery store I knew she didn't favor. She was not alone in the car. She and whoever was in the passenger seat were doubled over, not in a romantic way, but as if they were trying to get at something in the center console or playing cards on the dashboard. So I sent a text asking what she was doing, and when I got the "crashing on the couch" mendacious reply, I waited. A large man—no wait—a boy really, maybe early twenties, in the requisite sweat suit and baseball cap, with long hair spilling out underneath, got out of the car. He leaned over, rested his forearms on the driver-side door, and I held my breath to see if he was going to kiss her. They both laughed for a bit, and he waved and walked down the mall sidewalk, and Kelsey drove off. My heart sank. No, it wasn't a tryst; it was a business transaction. I didn't know if that made it worse or not.

For weeks, I had been defending Kelsey to people in the office. We were now public about our relationship, and people took sides. The senior people, still in shock over Sydney and I ever breaking up, thought I had lost my mind. Then there were the people loyal to Kelsey who thought it was fantastic. And a few women in the office, long my "work wives," thought they owed it to me to snap me out of what to them was insanity. Kelsey painted them as threatened by her potentially becoming my wife and, by extension, their boss. So my default setting was to defend Kelsey whenever I was told by a self-appointed committee that they were sure Kelsey was doing cocaine when I traveled and drinking and going out more often when I was gone than I knew. I told them I knew the signs and if she was doing cocaine, I would know. She'd be up until all hours; she'd be wired, hiding in bathrooms every ten minutes. I'm not a fool.

What I didn't tell them was that I did know she was using cocaine. I knew because she told me. She was smart enough to know if she hid it, she'd eventually be caught. So she played the card that worked best: My fear of being uncool. My shame of being too old for her. One weekend when her sister Elsie was visiting, she said Elsie had scored some coke. It had been ages since Kelsey had tried it, and she knew it was eons since what she called my "Michael Milken days," and she asked if I wanted to go for it, "just once, let go a little." So I did. And it was wonderful. When I hear friends talk about how they can't believe some celebrity or even some coworker or neighbor ended up in rehab after nearly losing everything they owned to a cocaine habit, I ask them if they had ever tried it. And if they say no, I tell them not to judge. It is an amazing drug. Until you have felt the astonishing euphoria, the sudden vibrancy with which you experience everything from conversations to sex, you don't know. We made a fire that night. Elsie drank beer, and

Kelsey and I shared wine, and we all did lines. We laughed most of the night, they told incredibly intimate stories of their childhoods, and Kelsey and I made love until Dez knocked on our door. It was light outside. When she mentioned a week later, "Elsie donated another gram to the cause," I told her I was worried about her sister and her, especially given her alcohol issues. She suggested a pact. She never buys it; she never does it, unless she is with me. If Elsie scores any coke, Kelsey hands it over to me and I divvy it up as I see fit. When I say enough, we stop. No questions asked. We use it for fun on special occasions. She asked, "Is that '1985-enough' for you?"

When I got to her house, she was crashed on the couch, as her cover story required. I made a beeline upstairs and, knowing she wouldn't have stashed it in the bathroom (Dez often went through her medicine cabinet and pretended to be "getting ready" by putting on Mom's makeup), I started going through the drawers in her dresser. Bam. Three little bags. I put them in my jacket pocket and said nothing until later the next night when I was outside in the yard hitting lob wedges. She came out and looked behind her to make sure Dez was nowhere in sight.

"You want to talk about this?"

"I suppose you want credit for not having him come to the house?"

"He did come to the house once, but he brought friends and it scared me. I thought this was safer."

"A drug dealer came to your house?! Where your six-year-old lives. Fantastic. Do you get it?! Cops follow these guys. If you're buying on a day they're busting, it's over for you. They make no distinction between user and dealer when they hand out prison sentences. You lose Dez, your life. Jesus Christ!!"

"I get it. It was dumb. I'll stop. It was just a goof. It's not that I can't stop. It's not like it's my thing! Okay?! So, just out of curiosity, what did you do with it? That was like three grams! Do you still have it?"

. . .

A nurse who looked like she was high school age told me Kelsey was now in a private room where I could sit with her. She told me to follow her. I made small talk by asking if she was doing an internship, and she smiled and said she had graduated nursing college four years ago. I could tell I had vaguely annoyed her, and I weighed the merits of telling her that in what seems like an instant, a man assuming she is much younger will be the highlight of her day.

Her room was freezing, and yet Kelsey's hospital gown was covered in sweat. I asked for a cold compress and wiped the part of her face not dwarfed by the respirator hose. Heaving up and down, it seemed impossibly large for her mouth. There it was. This was real. It seemed to me I should be angry. I should be thinking of Desiree at home, about to become one of those kids fucked up forever because they grew up without a mom. I should be cursing Kelsey for her appalling lack of impulse control. But I couldn't feel anger. The room was peaceful. The syncopation of the respirator and the rhythmic beeps of the monitors reminded me of Kelsey humming tunes while she stacked groceries in the fridge. When I tried to summon anger, all I could conjure up was our first day on the beach together as a family and my toenails. I inherited my dad's toenail fungus, and my nails were yellow and brittle and gross. I never wore flip-flops, and I put socks on at the gym quickly to avoid detection. Sydney dubbed them "dino toes" and would often point them out to friends, deeply shaming me. By the time I was at the beach with Kelsey and Dez, I knew the drill. Little kids would always see my toes, get grossed out, and ask me what was wrong with my feet. I took off my shoes and socks and waited. Dez saw my toes, glanced over at Kelsey, who gave her a stern look, and then Dez turned away. She had been prepped to ignore my feet and say nothing. Kelsey, without me ever talking about it, could sense my shame and sought to spare me. I wanted to curse her for wanting to leave us, yet all I could think was how kindhearted she was.

I had scrolled over the "day after Rhode Island" text, felt the sting all over again, and then scrolled back and read it. Did she know by telling me to leave her that it would make me want to stay, or was she really trying to save me from her?

**Dan, you should leave me. I'm trying to be kind to you and we both know when it comes to you, that is not my default setting. Leave me.**

Some friends of ours were getting married and we decided to throw them a party and use the occasion to showcase our new transparent relationship. ("Don't judge us for leaving marriages and blowing up everyone's world until you see us together!" was a banner ad we wanted to attach to those prop planes that fly over the state beach.) I rented a huge house in Westerly, in Rhode Island, and we did it up big time. I hired a guitar player Kelsey and I had seen in a Newport club. We had caterers and a wait staff and tents and yard games and enough booze and food to serve twice the number of anticipated guests. I was working hard to be the uberhost, filling glasses, setting up croquet and volleyball courts, and making runs to the store for ice.

It was a hot and humid day, and I never noticed how much Kelsey was drinking. I never saw the idiot who slipped her the ecstasy, not that it would have mattered—ecstasy (now known as "Molly") was well after my time as a partier, and I had no idea what it was. I knew vaguely that it was the "date rape" drug on college campuses and that it was proffered or slipped to women in nightclubs to lower their inhibitions, but I had no experiential knowledge. The party was a huge success; even the work folks who had deep reservations about us as a couple had no issues with how I was with Desiree, and I could sense their surprise at my ease with stepdad status. They all came from Connecticut and had long drives home. The sun and partying wore folks down, and when they started to leave, I was grateful for an end to the long, stressful day. But Kelsey had crossed over. She was begging everyone to stay, calling them pussies and old geezers. She was slurring her words, but she wasn't just drunk. She was touchy and intense. Not the fidgety "cocaine-wired" glow I had seen before. Different. About to burst.

I began to clean up while the hard core lingered and opened beers. I went outside and started filling garbage bags with paper plates and beer cans. By the time I came back, only our guests of honor and a few of their friends were left. It was 1:00 a.m.—to them it was prime time. I wanted them gone. Not so subtly, I started putting the booze in boxes and washing dishes. Finally they got the message and announced they were leaving. This freaked Kelsey out. She suggested they all go out to a dance club. When they declined, she went over to the groom's buddy— a handsome kid who could have passed as a marine cadet, rugged and jacked—and planted a long kiss on him and asked him why he would leave a hot girl like her. It got deadly quiet.

Later I would empathize with the kid, who gave me a "hey, I didn't do anything, but your girl wants me, dude" look, but at the time I was enraged. The guests of honor had seen Kelsey's act before, pitied my plight, and tried to move things along. But as we said good-bye at the door and they thanked us for the party, Kelsey took the cadet's hand, stuck it inside her shorts, guided him down between her legs, and started grinding against him. Even the kid was mortified.

An hour later, she was passed out on the overstuffed club chair in the living room. She was still there when she woke in the morning and saw my packed bags in the foyer. The plan was to have the party and then stay at the beach for the week. She saw the look on my face and asked me what she'd done. I told her the truth, blow by blow. When I got to the last part, where she had placed his hand inside her shorts in front of me, she inhaled sharply, as if a long needle had been plunged into her belly. I was in the car halfway home when she sent her text telling me to leave her.

I'd spent a career telling candidates who were staying at bad jobs too long that to ignore their experience was truly pathetic, and yet the last thing I wanted to do after reading her text was to leave her. I wanted to save her.

. . .

**Did you go to your actual physical mailbox and receive my proposal? Do we have a deal? Come on, you *have* to be impressed with someone my age going to the post office and buying a stamp (especially when I could have left it on your desk, which I kinda wish I did, cause the post office rivals the DMV for timesuck)! Dan, I'm serious.**

**Do this, and we'll live erratically happy ever after.**

The nurses were changing her clothes and bedding when the doctor ducked his head in and said we should probably talk in the hall. I knew this had to be a bad sign. Good news in public, bad news in private was a code I lived by at work.

"Here's the deal. The liver is unresponsive. If the levels don't turn soon, and the liver goes, the other organs follow suit. Not much we could do. We'll know by morning. But be prepared. Do you have power of attorney?"

I said her parents were on the way. I had no actual standing. I asked about a liver transplant, and he informed me that it was not allowed for suicide attempts. Liver donations were not to be wasted on someone who could attempt it again. I told him I didn't think she meant to kill herself. We had broken up. I wasn't communicating. She was just trying to get my attention.

"If she pulls through, you should stick with that story. Otherwise, they'll take her kid."

Kelsey's proposal had three components. Two were serious, one was a spurious offer meant to show gravitas:

- She would no longer socialize with her ex-husband on weekends when I traveled to speak. She would adopt a more conventional and appropriate approach to their co- parenting, and she understood it was strictly forbidden for her to allow him to stay over.

- She would stop drinking and the use of any recreational drugs. She felt cold turkey was the only way for her. All in. When I broached a twelve-step program, she bristled and said she was a young woman used to partying, not an addict. This was simply about maturation.

- She offered to give me the password to her phone and said I could spot-check it any time. She knew I would find such an arrangement preposterous and sad and would reject it outright. I read my reply and shook my head. She had trained me to make life-sized decisions via text, and she played me like a virtuoso.

**Yep, you have a deal. (Although forget the third one. I don't want to read your phone. I want to believe there is no reason to want to read your phone. Why can't you get that?)**

I went back inside Kelsey's room and now the anger flowed freely. I paced in circles around her bed. Is it ever okay to be in an ICU unit and want to shake the hell out of the patient and scream at her? "Kel, no one is worth this! Least of all me! What about Desiree? How could you do this to her? What do I tell her?" I had often heard parents, even my own, say that they would die for their kids. I always thought at some level it was easy to say, since the likelihood was that you would never be tested. Parents die before their kids. Still, at that moment, it was not a hollow bromide, but a simple truth. To give Desiree back her mom, I would have taken Kelsey's place in a second.

"And were you trying to die?" I asked her out loud. "Or was this just another test for me to pass? Take enough pills to get sick and get me running home to take care of you? Did you just overestimate the number? You didn't have to test me. You just needed to keep me safe. All you had to say was that you couldn't keep up the deal. I would have wished you well and said good-bye. Instead you had to make it impossible for me to live with myself if I ignored this latest humiliation. You didn't need to test me. I wanted to stay."

**Hey, Superstar! How'd the keynote go? Did you get a standing O?**
**(If I remember correctly, I gave you one of those before you left!)**
**I'm going to Katie's bachelorette party for an hour after work.**
**Be home early. Club soda per our deal!! Who knew I could still**
**be so funny sober?! Love you. Travel safe home to me.**

I looked out the window and saw cars dropping off visitors. Everyone had the same grim countenance, but they would shake it off the moment they walked into their friend's or family member's room and replace it with a strained enthusiasm. Boredom was the best deal they could cut at a hospital, and they feared much worse. Kelsey and I shared an unbreakable bond: We thought the biggest sin was to bore another person. You knew she was drunk when she would interrupt you and say, "You are boring me!" I sat back down on her bed and watched her breathe and told her she was boring me. "Do you really want to go out being boring?" And in a memory jump cut I remembered resigning from my volunteer job at the suicide line a few years earlier. I was telling Traci, the program manager and a true pro, that I was bored silly. I had pictured myself talking jumpers down from ledges with unassailable logic, while I traced calls for the police; or soothing young lovers' anguish and convincing them not to go to the garage, but to face the fact that there are multiple soul mates in a long life. (Were there?) Instead, we had two lists at the center. One was the "lethals," the people who had called before, had a plan, and were judged to be dangerous. If a lethal called, we were to let a supervisor know and not take the call ourselves. The other list was the "chronics." Mostly elderly or shut-ins. People who had outlived their people.

They wanted to complain. About their pain, about Congress, or about some minor slight they had suffered at the hands of a retail worker or customer service representative. They either had no one they could talk to or the people they did know would no longer listen to their nonsense. They knew if they called the suicide line, we had to listen.

We learned in training that there is no universal understanding of why people attempt suicide. Rich people do it. Healthy people do it. Young people do it. People with loved ones do it. We learned that suicide rates are high among blind people who have their vision restored. (What a cheery thought. "Now that I can see the world for what it is, check please!") The one thing you learn if you spend any time in a suicide prevention center is that loneliness is the law of the land. It is the great killer, surpassing all the wars and diseases put together.

I didn't have the energy or the makeup for the work. I still thought everything was a matter of will and effort. I wanted to tell the chronics to do something about their problems or stop calling, and I never got a lethal call in any of my evening shifts. Type A to the max, I only half jokingly suggested to Traci one night when we got no calls in the first four hours that we make things happen by cold calling. "Hi, this is the suicide hotline, just reaching out. Anyone there depressed?"

This was when Traci suggested I find some other volunteer work. I had a mad crush on her because I generally fell in love with anyone doing what they were destined to do with passion. Traci belonged right where she was. When a lethal call came in, it was transferred to Traci, and we would all gather around her desk and listen to her talk the person through his/her moment of doubt. Like a good public speaker, I noticed she knew how to build to a memorable close, and as I leaned over and kissed the tip of Kelsey's nose, I found myself borrowing Traci's line, as all speakers are apt to do: "Tomorrow will come. Tomorrow will come."

## CHAPTER 22

# *Prayer*

We ring a bell in my office when we close a deal. It makes me really nervous when a recruiter rings the bell softly. It means that while the candidate accepted the job, at some gut level you know the deal is going to fall apart. You heard something in their voice; your gut knows. So you try to appease the gods. You ring the bell softly and pray you're wrong.

**From Danny's "Intuitive Closing" Seminar**

. . .

A week before Kelsey's suicide attempt, I took the 6:00 a.m. to Hartford from US Airway's Charlotte hub. Conferences had figured out that if the speakers were scheduled first thing in the morning, the attendees would follow them right to the airport, and consequently, vendors—who had paid big money for their booths and expected business from conference customers—would face disastrous afternoons in terms of reduced revenues. So they started to book my session at the day's end, which was not optimal energy-wise for me, but I had to admit it worked. People would stay to hear me. But it meant I couldn't fly home at night, and I was determined not to repeat my mistakes. Sydney once told me our marriage had no chance up against my ambition, so I no longer would speak two days in a row and miss whole weekends. Family first. I landed at 8:00 a.m., and when there was no text from Kelsey, my gut started to churn. Our deal was less than a month old.

The first sign of trouble was Desiree playing in the living room by herself. She told me her mom was sleeping. That normally meant a hangover. I saw the pizza box on the counter and asked her jokingly if she had pizza for breakfast or if she wanted me to make her some eggs. She told me her daddy had made her breakfast, but she would eat the leftover pizza for lunch. Rookie recruiters always start to speak too quickly when they realize their deal is going south, and I often tell them to breathe and speak super slowly. I tried to be nonchalant with Dez, and even though I felt horrible exploiting her innocence, it was go time.

"Daddy made breakfast? Super cool. Is he still here?"

"He left for work. He says he hates working Saturdays."

"I know the feeling. So did he get the pizza last night too?! Awesome! I'm going to go wake up your sleepy mom. You stay down here, and I'll come back down to make her coffee and we can go walk, okay? Hey, Dez, was your daddy already making breakfast when you woke up?"

"No, I woke them up, but mom went back to sleep."

Kelsey either thought she would be up before I got home or was so wasted she was oblivious, but there were beer bottles piled high in the recycling bin. On the railing of the deck, there were more bottles. Upstairs, I sat by her for a moment, watched her sleep, and assessed the bed. Kelsey was a thrasher when she slept, so there was no way to tell if she had slept alone, and really—why was I bothering? I knew. As I watched her, something essential in me shifted. Did she love me? In her way, I'm sure. But there was some void in her I couldn't fill. No one could. Her eyes opened, and when she saw me, her instinctive response was to smile wide and hug me. She was as genuinely glad to see me as she must have been to hear I had missed the evening connection and wouldn't be back until today. I abbreviated the hug and told her what I knew. The deal was broken. We were broken. Enough. She was now wide awake and wheeling and dealing.

"He didn't stay here, Dan. He did bring her a pizza last night while I was at the bachelorette party. She had to eat dinner. He's her father. I came home. Bonnie was with me. We exchanged pleasantries. He left. He didn't make her breakfast. He lives an hour away. He didn't drive here this morning. Don't be silly."

"Why would Dez say that he did, Kel?"

"Because she's a kid! She wants her mommy and daddy together. Listen, you want to get her up here and scare her by interrogating her, bring it. Listen to me. I fucking know what is at stake here. I know what it would mean if I were lying to you. My hand to God, he didn't stay here. Bonnie came over after her party, she got high, she was drinking— it was her bachelorette party for Christ's sake—and he drank some beers here, yes. I don't control his drinking. But I didn't drink, and then he left, and Bonnie and I hung out. You have to believe me."

Recruiting is a high turnover industry. Straight commission. Highly competitive, and you are at the mercy of candidates and clients that are either lying outright or unable to access their own fear of change. But for me, it was always easy. I was the youngest Rookie of the Year ever, the youngest Recruiter of the Year ever, the youngest manager ever, and it was all because I could read people's true intentions. I was born with this gift. My records stood until I hired then-twenty-one-year-old Kelsey—who shattered them all because she had the same gift.

I looked into her eyes; we were two titans of guile and manipulation standing face-to-face, and I knew she was lying. And it suddenly occurred to me that I could prove it.

I waited until I was at my condo to call Bonnie.

"Hey Bonnie, thanks for calling back. I get that this is weird, and I hate to put you in this position . . . Yeah, I figured you figured it was about last night."

Ten minutes later I was off the phone. Yes, Kelsey had been drinking at the bachelorette party—doing shots with a random guy who was hitting on her, in fact. Yes, Bonnie had come home with Kelsey, but mostly because Kelsey insisted on getting high. Yes, the ex-husband was there. Yes, they drank together. Yes, it got weird and inappropriate, and they were groping each other on the couch. Bonnie at that point decided to leave. It was around 2:00 a.m. Yes, if she were me, she would find it impossible to believe he ever left. Yes, she would be shocked if they hadn't slept together. And yes, she was sorry for me. I told her I had no choice but to use the information and disclose the source. She said that was fine. She had had half a mind to call me anyway.

After the call it was my intention to simply write Kelsey a long email sharing what I knew and ending our relationship. But I didn't even open my laptop. I picked up the phone and called her and quickly found myself screaming at the top of my lungs. Even with her long history of deception, Kelsey had never been absolutely busted. There was never a scenario that she couldn't plausibly lie her way out of, and when this reality was coupled with never having heard rage from me at this level before, she didn't know what to do. She just kept murmuring, "No, no."

But they were no longer denials of fact, just the protests of a child who didn't want to lose what they were clearly about to lose.

I had lost nearly everything I had and violated every value I thought I lived by. But now I was going to lose Desiree. I would never help raise her. I would never matter to her. She would forget me. It had taken awhile, and I had fought a good fight. But shame won, because just before asking Kelsey one last absurd question, I thought, *I'm just not good enough. I haven't done enough to deserve love.*

"Why do you have to be like this?!"

I had taught Kelsey that when a candidate got over the top emotionally, and by now I was wailing, you have to get quiet. Be dispassionate. Take it down. Her voice was clear and calm.

"There is no me, Dan. There is only whatever 'me' anyone else needs to see in the moment. I figure it out, I give it to them, and then they don't hurt me. There never was a me."

. . .

I held Kelsey's hand and then rubbed it on my face and felt the bristles of a two-day beard. I had now been awake since getting the text in Vegas, nearly thirty hours ago. Kelsey's parents, no doubt knowing only that I broke up with her and, with no idea why, wanted nothing to do with me. We took turns alternating between the waiting room lounge and her room. I was in the lounge restroom when my phone rang and Kelsey's name flashed on my screen. For an odd second, I thought she was calling me from her room. She was okay! But wait, how did she get the respirator out, how . . . and then I realized Desiree had found her mom's phone, probably still on the nightstand.

"Can I talk to Mommy?"

"No, Dez, she's in with the doctors, and they're giving her medicine right now."

"I want my Mommy!!"

"Dez, listen to me. Dezzie, calm down. Listen to me. We can't bring her home until she gets all her medicine. Don't you want her to come home? Then we have to wait and let her get better, right?"

"Yes. Okay. But you need to promise me. Mommy always says if Dan promises you something, it always happens. Promise me she's going to come home."

Once I got inside her room, I waited until Kelsey's mom closed the door behind her, and I locked it. I pulled the chairs away from the bed and cleared some space. Go big or go home. I got on my knees. I wasn't a holiday Catholic. I wasn't even a lapsed Catholic. I was raised Catholic by parents who didn't make us attend church—more from lack of money for the right clothes than lack of conviction—and after my first communion, I never went back. I didn't walk into a church again until my college friends started to get married. I did believe in God in general and Jesus in particular, but I also was attracted to the purity of atheism. We Catholics tried to lead good lives to win the prize of eternal life; atheists tried to lead good lives because it was its own reward. But I still felt, marrow deep, that there was *something*. Something that didn't determine your fate, but was pulling for you. Let's call it God, and let's make a play for his grace, just in case I haven't worn out my welcome.

"Okay, I know this is cheesy. But I got nothing. I know how much I have fucked up, and I know you can make a really good case that this is what I deserve. But how about Dez? She had no part of this. And she's a really good kid. You gotta give me that, right? Look, I hate negotiating with a weak hand. That's not what I teach. But cards on the table. Bring her back. Give her a chance. She's got such a good heart. Do it, and I will go to church every week for the rest of my life. And, bonus—you know I'm good at recruiting, and I will sell this. I will bring people in. I will pack that church! I know your numbers have been down. Look, we'll figure it out. But do this, and I won't ever ask for anything again. Never. Please. I'm going to cross myself and say 'Amen' now, because I never memorized any of the actual prayers. But I will remedy that too! So. Okay. Amen."

Don't you hate it when you get called on your own crap? Even if it's God?!

An hour later I got an email from my marketing assistant wondering if I needed any edits to my PowerPoints for tomorrow's seminar. Wait, what day is this? And I realized that I had a two-day "Retreat with Danny" at my office starting in a few hours. Two full days of mentoring, role-playing, and lectures. It was too late to cancel. People had already flown in. These were subscribers to my website who had planned this trip for months, people investing in me, people who believed I could change the course of their lives. Yeah, that's me, all right. I change the course of lives. I was trying to figure out what to do, since I wasn't about to leave Kelsey's side, when the doctor came in. I knew from the way he opened the door. Kelsey's parents didn't have our gift. They were fooled by his face, which was clearly trying not to smile until he broke the news. But I knew. Sometimes the gift is a curse. The world just doesn't have as much to show you.

"Well, it's nice to be young and strong. Once we got the poison out, the blood levels reversed almost immediately. Everything's fine. We're going to take out the respirator, and she'll have a very sore throat, but otherwise she'll just feel like she took a long nap."

. . .

They never told us about this part in suicide-hotline training: If they survive, they have no idea what they put people through. We were in Kelsey's room an hour later, and she was in full performance mode. Chastened enough to not piss us off, but also trying to show she was in high spirits and not at risk. Blow job jokes about the respirator. How flat her stomach was and her plans to write a suicide diet book. Her elderly parents, anxious to make the long trip home, bought into it all. Just another impulsive move by our jocund adopted child, the same girl who stole their car at twelve and went for a joyride. They started talking about staying at Kelsey's for a couple of days until she got home, but as long as she was okay, they really had to get back.

But I wasn't buying. Nothing had changed. She hadn't spent the past two days reading texts that documented our long siege. While she called this time-out, I had relived the stalking. Showing up at my gym at 5:00 a.m. in a party dress, still drunk, wanting to talk. Calling me at 2:00 a.m. and telling me she had "just run into Mariah," and she wanted me to know Mariah said that Danny had to buy people's love because he couldn't earn it any other way. When I wouldn't respond to anything else, she sent me a text at 3:00 a.m. one night that said, "I just got fucked by a young dude I picked up. How does that feel?" This was followed by a text at 8:00 a.m. saying she had just read the text and of course it wasn't true and she was sorry for her monstrous assertion.

I watched her sipping ice chips in her bed and realized that in her mind this had worked out well. After all, here I was. Kelsey was still in danger, and I was a big part of the problem. Suddenly I could see it was in my power to help, to break the pattern. I had the power to change things. She kept staring at me, measuring, waiting for me to say something. But I took out my phone, scrolled to her number, punched the green icon, handed the phone to Kelsey, and before Desiree could pick up, I went out in the hall, locked myself in the restroom, and tried to summon up The Lord's Prayer from forty years earlier. When I got to St. Mary's the following week, I discovered that what I had actually prayed consisted of a mix-and-match medley of The Lord's Prayer, the Hail Mary prayer, and the Now I Lay Me Down to Sleep prayer, but I had been a professional speaker long enough to know that while people forget what you said, they remember how you made them feel. I knew God got the gist. I was grateful.

## CHAPTER 23

# Surrender

"I don't know why people say, 'I hate to say I told you so.' I love saying I told you so. I live to say I told you so, and brother, I fucking told you so!!"

Rummy was in rare form. I had invited him to my office to do a "Q&A with a Million-Dollar Producer" for a group of rookies. I moderated the discussion, setting him up for his favorite stories and teeing up his best comebacks. (I got the very best people to appear on my website in no small part because I was an excellent wingman.) Now, we were in my private office, and flush from the energy that comes from killing it in front of an audience, he wanted the details nobody on my staff knew. Headhunting is in some ways sanctioned rumor-spreading, and it didn't take long for people to hear about Kelsey's suicide attempt and the penultimate circumstances of the night of Bonnie's bachelorette party. In the weeks that followed, I wouldn't comment when people asked me about her, and most could sense my pain and respected my self-imposed gag order. Rummy was having none of that.

"So you tore up her non-compete and let her go to work for a competitor? I get it. She's a single mom and has to make a living. Fair enough."

The reference call with her potential new employer was unbearable. Kelsey and I agreed there was no coming back to the office, but I had no idea until he called how difficult it would be for me to formally, finally part with her. Her new boss-to-be was understandably wary. "Why was she available if she was the top producer? Why would you let someone with so dazzling a future leave? Did she do something unethical or illegal? Did she have some personal problems?" He said he wasn't going to hire her unless I got real.

"You want real? You got it. She fucked up all right. You know what she did? She got involved romantically with the boss. That would be me. Now I'll let your imagination take it from there, but let's just say it wasn't an easy dynamic. But it is a windfall for you, my friend. This is your lucky day. She is a supremely talented recruiter."

Rummy said he would bet anything I paid out Kelsey's entire equity monies to make sure she was okay. I nodded, and he shook his head and laughed. What I didn't tell him was that I also paid her mortgage months in advance and started a college fund for Desiree.

"Here's what I don't get: She gets released from the hospital; she gets the kid back; her parents don't live around here. She's out of a job and an addict if ever there was one. Who took care of her?"

I shrugged like I had no idea and it wasn't my problem. But for weeks I made meals, washed clothes, took Desiree to day care and picked her up, and sat with them both in the evening. I wasn't about to abandon her. I knew how easily she could pick up her phone and text her cocaine dealer and make the pain go away. I had to be sure she was okay before I let go. And I knew if I told others about any of it, they would remind me that I was simply falling victim to her manipulation. But they weren't in that hospital room, and they didn't see her in the days that followed. Numb. Fragile. So scared. People throw around facile terms like "enabling" and tell you that you have to let addicts bottom out in order for them to get ahold of their lives, and while I knew it to be true, I didn't have the heart for it. I don't know if I fooled my colleagues and partners at the office, but Rummy saw right through me.

"All right. Look. I'm not going to bust your balls for getting her through the crisis. I'd have probably done the same thing. But now you know the recidivism rate is sky-high in cases like hers—for a reason. She's not ready. Take it from an old coke head, you're going to get another call, and it's going to be the same thing all over again."

"I don't know, Rummy. I mean I hear what you're saying but . . ."

"I know you don't know. I *do* know. That's what's so great about me. Unfortunately, I had to get really fucking old to get all this knowledge, but I know! Here's something else I know: Addicts don't have soul mates. She figures out you're no longer going to give her what she needs, and she will find another chump. So get over yourself and let go! For her sake!"

And I did let go. But Rummy was right.

We needed an encore. A few months later, in the middle of the day, Kelsey's sister called. She said she knew it might be adding insult to injury, but she couldn't leave work and didn't know who else to call. Kelsey had called her, clearly out of her mind drunk or drugged or both. It was a Tuesday morning. She didn't know if she was home, but she couldn't imagine she would be in any condition to pick Desiree up from day care in a couple of hours. Could I check on her?

Kelsey was lying on her bathroom floor. She was groggy, but not unconscious, vomit all down her dress. She had been getting ready to drive to work. Jesus. I cleaned her up, led her back to bed, and went downstairs. It was the first time since I'd known her that I couldn't bear to look at her. I went downstairs, made coffee, and stared into space. I didn't know what to do or how to help her.

But Kelsey did. She came downstairs a few minutes later with the overnight bag we often used on long weekends to Naples or Vegas. "I know it's a workday, and I don't mean to trouble you, but could you give me a ride? I called a rehab center, an hour from here, and got all the necessary intel. They have a bed available right now. I should plan on at least thirty days. They don't take insurance."

I nodded. "Are you really ready?" Maybe she was being reactive. Maybe she should sleep on it? But I could see she was ready. I was the one who suddenly wanted her to think it over. I knew there would be no turning back. I wanted rehab to work, and I knew she wanted rehab to work. But what if it worked? It meant the end of us, and as much as I knew that was probably for the best, it scared the hell out of me. She was about to take on rehab, and I was the one facing demons. She smiled and told me what I had taught her to say to candidates when they got an offer and wanted to think about it until morning.

"What am I going to know tomorrow that I don't know today?"

Once she had her first cup of coffee, she was in high gear. All in! First she called her boss, who by now knew her potential and eagerly granted the respite. She called her ex, and to his credit he stepped up, gave her props for the move, and said he'd take Desiree until she got home. He was now with a new woman he would later marry, and his anger was giving way to sympathy. The rehab center was in the toney hills of Litchfield County. When we pulled up to it, it looked seedier than either of us had imagined. Men were smoking on the front porch as we walked up, and they stared at Kelsey in a licentious way that made me want to reverse course. How could I leave her with them? For thirty days?! But how could I not? I suddenly remembered my father, he of the third-grade education who gets smarter every year he is dead. When I had asked him how I would know if something was the right thing to do, he'd said, "You'll know because it will feel like it's not."

While I paid them and gave them contact information, Kelsey was subjected to a frisk and briefed on the detox she was about to endure. The only fight she put up was when they confiscated her cell phone. She explained she had a daughter who would freak out if she didn't talk to her daily. Unimpressed, they told her Desiree could call or visit on Saturdays. They gave me my receipt and started to show Kelsey to her room. When I went to follow, they told me, "You can leave. We'll take it from here." I don't know what I expected. How about a chance to sit in a private room, to explain how I would worry, how much I hoped I was doing the right thing, how much I loved her. Just more time.

"You want me to get you out of here, kiddo? Say the word and we leave. We'll figure out some other way."

"Nope, I am bought in, Boss. I'm going to kick some rehab ass. Don't give up on me, okay?"

I don't know if I ever loved her more. And I never did give up on her, only on us.

## CHAPTER 24

# Early Morning Phone Calls

The hardest part? There is no hard part. Being a speaker is a rush like no other. The travel? Nah. I hate when people bitch about the travel. I always keep in mind two things: Any one of you would take my speaking gig in a heartbeat, so if I don't want to go, there's always another speaker who will; and I try never to take for granted the miracle of travel. I wake up in Hartford and go to bed in San Fran. Really? And in between I can nap, or eat, or read? Poor me. But . . . I guess the hardest part for me is between 4:00 and 6:00 p.m. on a Saturday. The witching hours. The conference ends at three, and during the afternoon sessions, the vendors strike their sets, the audience wheels in their luggage, and by 4:00 p.m. the hotel is completely empty. Like a neutron bomb landed. It's too early for the bar or dinner crowd, too early to get room service and rent a movie in bed, or fire up the Kindle. So I walk. The same halls that for two days were electric with energy and ambition and concupiscence cloaked as networking are now utterly silent and as wide as an interstate. I feel like a ghost. It makes me wonder if the conference ever happened. It is early, and it is Saturday and I'm in this amazing city and I could do anything I wanted. But I don't know what that is. Anyway, is it fair to call this "hard"? Come on. Speakers are spoiled brats. It's awesome.

**From Danny's "How to Be a Speaker" Seminar**

. . .

"Hi Russ. It's Danny Cahill. A blast from your past. So . . . question. If I wanted to see you as my therapist, even though you were my marriage counselor, would that be weird, unprecedented?"

"Danny—are you okay?"

"So you know I travel a lot, but actually I'm home this weekend. And I have some time. Let's see. Oh, I could actually do now if you could squeeze me in. If it's not unprecedented. Or weird."

"Danny, do you know it's six-thirty in the morning?"

"For the record, I've been holding off calling you for like two hours."

"Understood. Meet me at my office at eight."

Russ had never seen me scared and that scared him. He just sat back and motioned for me to begin the download. What a great job therapists have. No prepared script or "relationship-building questions" culled from an online profile. No chitchat, no ice-breaking. Go.

"I'm going to tell you what happened, but I want you to know I didn't just fold. I tried. For months. I even got cats. Two Maine Coon kittens. Stella and Gabby."

"Cats. You're saying, instead of socializing or dating."

"Dating. Jesus. I don't understand rebounds. How do people do it? The last thing in the world I want to do is date. I wouldn't wish me on anyone. I've been reading about *nibbana*. You know about that?"

"Sure. The Buddhist belief that if you let go of sexual desire you reach the far shore of enlightenment. Doesn't sound like your speed to me."

"Okay that hurts. It's true, but it hurts. Yeah, it was crap. But it gave me something to hold on to for a little while, you know?"

"That's what a rebound does too. So you got two cats, the same breed as you had with Sydney. Did they help?"

"They were perfect. And no, they didn't help. I wanted to take care of something, I wanted to love something, and I missed Hadley and Gatsby so much, it seemed like a great idea. But I couldn't play with them. It just made me sadder. I got a pet-sitting service to come over while I was at work and when I traveled. And it didn't matter! They started pissing everywhere! Like in a crystal bowl on the top level of my bookshelf! I took them to the vet, and she said they were lonely. I said, 'I got two of them so they'd have each other to play with,' and I told her about the pet-sitting service, but she shook her head and said, 'They want you. We call it "protest pees".'

"So I sat them down and said, 'Look, I was a kid during Vietnam, I understand protest. Get a sign, fucking march, but don't piss on my floor.' Anyway it got worse. I realized I didn't want them—I wanted Hadley and Gatsby—and I didn't miss loving them so much as I missed watching Sydney love them. I heard about a woman at the gym who was devastated because her fourteen-year-old cat had died. I took them to her that night. So that worked out."

"Yeah, more loss, that worked out great. This was a couple of months ago? What happened then?"

"Solitary confinement. I'd get through work, and all I wanted was the cessation of noise. An error message came up on my cable system and instead of calling tech support, I unplugged the television. I stopped playing music at home or in my car. On weekends, I played a game with myself. Could I get through the entire weekend without using my voice or talking to a human? No one called me, so that was easy. Everyone texts now. At the gym, I caught on to the trick hot women use, and I put on headphones even though I wasn't playing any music. At church I would recite the prayers and responses in my head and just nod when it was time to say 'peace be with you' to my pew mates. I went to a movie, and when the ticket taker asked me what movie I wanted to see, I tried pointing to the title posted above his head, but when he asked which one I was pointing to, I left and went home. Like a crazy person. I remember being angry when Leah called me after *60 Minutes* one Sunday to discuss a deal we had going down Monday morning. I had a new personal record going for radio silence."

"Okay, I get it. If you can't have peace, you can create quiet. How are you passing the time before bed?"

"Reading, mostly. I started *Infinite Jest* again. I might not be smart enough or white enough for that book."

"Any change in your personal habits? Hygiene?"

"Look at you all zeroing in. Not so much hygiene. I'd be mortified not to be clean, even if sitting home alone. But I did one day look at my bathroom sink countertop, and the lineup of products dedicated to elongating my life's status quo:

- Rogaine to prevent baldness

- the first of ten daily bottles of Glacéau smartwater

- a multivitamin

- CoQ10

- fish oil for the heart

- a low dose of aspirin to avoid strokes

- DHEA to naturally raise testosterone levels (candy compared to the by now long-defunct synthetic steroid days)

- Vitamin D. Necessary because we can only get Vitamin D from the sun, and since I slather myself with sunscreen lotion to avoid wrinkles and melanoma, in that order, I need 5,000 IUs.

- alfuzosin to be able to get through a day without having to pee every five minutes

- saw palmetto for prostate health

- branched chain amino acids for protein synthesis and bigger muscles

- nitric oxide mixed with creatine to increase vascularity

"I stopped taking them. All of them. Do I look balder, more wrinkly, wimpier?"

"I hardly recognized you. And no contact from Kelsey since you broke it off?"

"I get texts when she gets her latest chip from AA. Pictures of Desiree. It's her way of letting me know she's okay. I don't sense any agenda beyond that. I'm proud of her. She's getting healthy. I miss them."

"You know that people can get through these things. Trust can be restored."

"You tried to sell that to Sydney and me. 'Truth over time equals trust.' I think that's crap. I think people stay together once trust is breached because they're weak, or scared, or dependent on the other person for money or some form of support. I think it's lazy. Look, I didn't call you at an embarrassing hour to get you to give me a blueprint for swallowing my pride and finding a way back to Kelsey. Something has happened."

Russ sat back. Did he know? No, I could tell he didn't know. What is amazing is that I didn't know *even as it was happening*. I would act and find a way to ignore the clear explanation for my actions. It was as if I were sleepwalking. It started Friday night at the gym. I had no idea what to do with myself, and the entire weekend loomed. My friends, especially those from work, were still giving me space from the Kelsey crisis, and the friends I had spent a decade with during my marriage were avoiding taking sides by having no contact with me. I had friends from the speaking business who were also clients, but I needed desperately to keep the construct I had created in place. *Danny saw this coming. Danny created this. Danny is always okay. Danny has it all figured out. Danny has a plan!* I was on a stationary bike when I saw people pouring out of a Body Pump class, their skin glistening and pink, the women wrapping the pullovers they wore into the class around their butts and heading up the stairs to their cars. I jumped off the bike and hustled to the exit just so I could walk upstairs with them. I had a deep need to draft off their chatter, their groupthink, their energy. I never said a word to them, but I drank in their aura. I got to my car and realized I had become this creepy version of a vampire.

The next morning a Paul Bunyanesque guy, cheery and happy, knocked on my door and said he was wondering if I had any odd jobs he could do around the place. He had electrical skills, some plumbing aptitude, was happy to move furniture, and wasn't above cleaning. He had been laid off after six years at an automotive aftermarket distributor and had four kids to feed. At first I said I was sorry but would take his business card, and then, I told him to follow me to the garage. I had twenty years of trophies and plaques, either earned in sports or given to me as a speaker. I had all the photos of my early family life and all the years with Sydney. I had all the manuscripts of plays I had produced and all the DVDs and CDs I had sold over the years to the recruiting industry. And I had all my books and all the books I had insisted Sydney let me take when I moved out for good. The detoured detritus of a life. I asked Paul Bunyan what he would charge me to empty the garage. Put it all in his truck and take it somewhere far away. He said it would take him three hours and $300. I told him he could take all day and handed him $500. He came to me several times over the next couple of hours. "This looks expensive. You sure? Some of these books look like first editions—aren't they valuable?"

"Keep them for yourself or get rid of them. Your call. I just want it all gone."

Upstairs I think I told myself I could help Paul Bunyan by cleaning out drawers and closets. But I only went to one drawer. I pulled out my last will and testament. I read through it. My business was left to my partners; my money to my family and to Kelsey and Desiree. I had a 1.6-million-dollar life insurance policy that still had Sydney as the beneficiary. It wasn't an oversight. I changed the will when I got divorced, but I never took her off the policy. I had never really been happy before her. I wanted it commemorated in some real, measurable way. I knew she didn't need or want the money. I wanted her to know what she meant to me. I remember thinking it was all so clean. It had all worked out. It was Saturday. My housekeepers would be here Monday. It wouldn't be pleasant, but it would just be a few hours. How bad could it smell?

"How were you going to get a gun?"

"How'd you know I was going to get a gun?"

"You're a guy. Guys use guns. Usually pointed at their head. Where all the trouble is."

"I wasn't sure how I'd get him to do it, but Victor in my office sold me the gun Syd made me get rid of. I was going to tell him I had an issue with a break-in and wanted to buy another one. I left him a voice mail, but he hasn't called me back. That was last night."

Russ was trying to figure out his next move. I had been through the suicide training. I knew having a plan was a really bad sign. If I were still at the center, I'd be yelling for Traci, and she'd be tracing the call and sending the cops. Russ took a deep breath and then surprised me.

I was prepared for the standard suicide protocol:

- In two consecutive years, I had lost my mom, my wife, my house, and all the accoutrements of homeostasis, and then before taking a breath, I had fallen for Kelsey. It was predictable. Kelsey tried to commit suicide to get attention; I want to die to end the attention I'd worked so hard to get. And I thought Russ would remind me of my sibilant, seething tones in Kelsey's hospital room, where I told her, "This is on you! No one did this to you! This is on you!" Wasn't that true for me? Wasn't this just proof that I never thought the rules applied to me?

- This was depression, pure and simple, triggered by loss. It was okay for motivational speakers to be depressed. In time and with treatment, I'll feel different. But what if I wasn't depressed? What if this was the very essence of clarity? What if I now saw that I had exhausted the way I was taught I should live, and it was now perfectly appropriate for me to control the endgame? What if it were just as simple as my pitch count was high and it was time to go to the bullpen? Every time I went with my father to pick up my mother in the nursing home where she worked, I saw what that kind of place looked and felt and smelled like. Why should I have to justify to anyone that I didn't want to end up there?

- There is so much more for me to do. I became successful so young. I have no blueprint for what to do next. I've only thought of business as a way to secure my life after so much childhood uncertainty. I've only thought of women in terms of desire or family or caretaking. Now I can redefine success and what it means to be intimate with a partner in a broader context. I wasn't going to buy this. It always gutted me when I saw aging athletes clinging to shadows of themselves: a paunchy Michael Jordon missing dunks in the open floor for the Washington Wizards; Jimmy Connors stalling for time because he couldn't catch his breath after a grueling point against the enfant terrible Agassi; Peyton Manning's sad excuse for a spiral, thrown short to hide his lack of arm strength. No one goes out on top, because you don't know you've passed it until you're past it. Why not take a stand? Why not say it was a good ride, but now the ride was over? Why not do things on my terms? Why not just admit something had been extinguished and simply get out of the way?

But I got no such protocol. Russ rubbed his eyes and leaned back. He still hadn't had his morning caffeine. I had messed with his biorhythms.

"I hope you don't."

"You hope I don't. That's all you got? So, four years of med school, and you come up with 'I hope you don't'?"

"Yep, that's it. You've been nothing in your life if not resourceful. If you want to do it, you'll figure out a way to do it. So all I can say is, I hope you don't. I think it would be a shame."

"Isn't that horrible though? I've reached an age where it wouldn't be shocking, or beyond comprehension, or tragic in any meaningful way. All it is, in its best light, the most it can be, is a shame. God, I hate that word."

"Okay. Sure. I have one other thing. Then I'm going back to bed. I hope you don't, because I would miss you. I'm quite sure I'm not the only one."

"You're not saying that because you're out of network and I pay cash?"

"It's a factor. What do you say we go after this for a while? See what happens? How about Tuesday nights at 6:00 p.m.?"

"That's a pretty good closing question there, Russ. Somebody has been paying attention in here. All right. I'll be here at six on Tuesday. And if I'm not here . . . "

"You killed yourself. I understand."

"I was going to say the traffic is bad that time of day and I might be late. You really should reconsider taking appointments this early."

## CHAPTER 25

# Big and Little

When I first started working with Nina, the doctor had to give me lidocaine shots in my back the day before therapy for me to be able to endure the treatment. I thought she was called "Nina, the Form Nazi" behind her back, but it turns out she gave herself that nickname. She made you hate her. And she made you better. For the entire hour you were in physical therapy, you were simultaneously trying not to cry, begging Nina to have mercy, and wondering (if you're me), what sick childhood atrocities forged her need for vocational sadism forty hours a week. Only in a sports medicine clinic or at a porn shoot could you walk by a room where a woman is yelling, "Deeper, I need it deeper! Yeah, that's the spot! Hit that again!" and not even be curious enough to look in. Business as usual.

When I was introduced to Nina, I was ashamed of my atrophy since the accident, and I told her she had to help me get back to the point where I could squat again. She asked me what I did for a living. When I told her, she shrugged and said, "So what do you need big legs for?" I loved that Nina was humorless and all about business, and she loved that I was willing to work hard. When she asked for fifteen reps, I gave her twenty-five. When she told me to go home and ice and stretch three times a day, I did—five times a day. We never discussed the fact that she gave no props for you doing what was best for your body, but she could tell by my increasing range of motion and the give she felt in the muscle tissue that I had done my homework, and she would nod and grunt. When she dug her elbow into my fragile IT band to break up the scar tissue and I had to hold my breath not to cry, we had our only friendly exchange.

"You have a very high pain tolerance."

"Well, I'm divorced. This is nothing."

She barked an abrupt laugh and got back to the business of beating me to a pulp.

. . .

Today, though, Nina seemed to be taking it easy on me. Or so I thought.

"Does this hurt? No? How about this? Hmmm. Good. Okay, we're done. You don't need any more sessions."

"No more sessions? Like, ever? Really? No more lidocaine?"

"You have no pain. You have complete range of motion. What do you want from me? You're healed."

"I can squat? Deadlift?"

"Sure. Just not heavy. Do higher reps."

"That's so cool. What do I need big legs for, right? Is that a smile, Nina, the Nazi?"

"I would tell you to go home and ice and use the foam roller, but you have the look you get when you have a plane to catch or a speech to give, so I'll hold my breath. Do it as soon as you can."

I didn't have a plane to catch, but I was amped up and anxious about a meeting in Hartford—way outside of my comfort zone. Nina walked me to the checkout station, and I thought of how odd it would be to have her job. If I do my job right, my clients give me more jobs to fill, and our relationship deepens; if she does hers right, we never see each other again. Sensing this, she gave me our first and only hug, and I told her I was apprehensive about not seeing her or the doctor again. It was hard to trust the thought of my back staying pain-free. Nina nodded. She had heard it before.

"A lot of people don't know what to do without pain in their lives."

. . .

I sat in the sad excuse for a waiting room. What did I expect—the whole operation was donation funded. Of course it would be a vinyl, stain-ridden grey couch and black folding chairs. I pretended to read the brochures, but it was just a way of getting rid of nervous energy. I had done my homework. Big Brothers—which became Big Brothers Big Sisters of America in 1977—was just over one hundred years old, and the largest donor-based volunteer mentoring program in the country. Ernest Coulter, a New York City court clerk, and a guy I would have loved to meet, saw too many kids losing their way and ending up in trouble. He could plainly see that not having a paternal presence was the cause (in those days fathers died, now they far more often pick up and leave the family), and he decided to do something about it. He started Big Brothers in 1904. His legacy? Kids in Big Brothers Big Sisters are forty-six percent less likely to use drugs, twenty-seven percent less likely to drink, fifty-two percent less likely to skip school, and thirty-three percent less likely to hit someone than kids who are not in the program. *God*, I remember wondering as the lady assigned to my case shook my hand and led me into her office for my interview, *if they don't drink, do drugs, skip school, or hit someone, what are they going to regret?* I was pretty sure I knew the answer for the kid who got me as a Big Brother.

"So tell me, Mr. Cahill, are you sexually attracted to young boys?"

This came at the end of the interview, and I didn't see it coming. Up until then, it was strictly basic background stuff. What did I do? Did I have the time to devote one night a week to meeting with my "Little"? (I would be his "Big." I kind of loved this vernacular.) Did I understand that I was not to give any money to my "Little," or to his parents if they asked, and I shouldn't spend much on the appointed night? A meal or a movie was fine, but no gifts, no lavish outings. She told me I had to understand, "There is no need to buy affection. We find that doesn't work." I fought the urge to tell her it not only worked but was also kind of a lifelong operating principle of mine. Since I taught interviewing for a living, I had anticipated all of these questions and felt I was killing the interview. But back to the bombshell. Was I sexually attracted to boys? On one level, I got it. Of course she was going to ask this! For a pedophile, the Big Brothers Big Sisters program was a candy store. So what is the right response? If I act outraged (that after already doing the background check they could ask me such an appalling question), then is *that* how pedophiles act? Are they skilled at acting outraged? Or do I just try to stay calm and smile and simply say no—or is *that* what pedophiles do, because they absolutely know the question is coming? It didn't matter, because I could feel my face heat up, and that meant I was beet red. How much more guilty could I seem? Just put an ankle monitor on me and put me on the list where I can't live within a hundred miles of a school.

"Relax, Mr. Cahill, we have to ask. Your response is exactly what I needed to see. Gideon and his mom are down the hall. You ready to meet your Little? Let me give you some background."

Okay. Let me just say this and be done with it: I assumed I was going to get a kid from the projects, and despite my arch-liberal political bent and my thirty years of fighting employment discrimination and employing a diverse staff, I thought my Little would be non-Caucasian. But Big Brothers Big Sisters serves all communities, and they try to make your get-togethers convenient by having the Littles and the Bigs come from as close to each other's towns as possible. Gideon was a Jewish kid who lived in Canton, the next town over from me in the suburbs. Until he was thirteen, life was pretty conventional, middle-class fare. Dad was a fireman, Mom was raising Gideon and his younger sister, Beth, while she went to school part-time. Two years ago Dad quit the department and got a job driving eighteen-wheelers, so he was gone during the week and home on weekends. This caused stressors in the marriage, and then one day Dad announced that he was leaving in the morning on his normal run but was not coming back. Ever. Mom and Dad divorced. There were disagreements about money; things got more brittle. Dad cut off communication. Gideon thought of his dad, especially the fireman he had grown up with, as a hero. He blamed his mom for driving him away. He was mean to her and Beth and was struggling at school. His mom, trying to hold the world together, deeply resented Gideon for hating her when she was the one who stayed. After a year of daily battles, someone suggested Gideon needed the Big Brothers program.

The lady assigned to my case closed the file folder on her desk and told me now would be a good time to decide whether I wanted to continue.

"So, let's be real here. This is his mom's idea and Gideon doesn't really want to do this."

"That's very common. More common than not. Would you rather pass?"

"Hell, no. Let's do this."

His mom told me she thought I would be younger. Okay, that's not a good start. Then she asked me if the Porsche 911 in the parking lot was mine. When I said yes, Gideon made a fist and pumped it in the air. His mom said she would not allow her son to be in that car. She wasn't provided my DMV history, and while she wasn't casting aspersions, fast cars with the top down are dangerous, and she couldn't live with herself if her son had brain trauma from an accident. If I didn't have another vehicle, this probably wasn't going to work out.

"Mom, don't be a dork. I want to ride in that car."

"I understand, ma'am. I have another car, a four-door sedan. I'll drive it whenever we see each other. And I haven't had a moving violation since I was eighteen. For the record."

The counselor suggested that Gideon and I share some private time. We sat and stared at each other for what seemed like hours, but there was an oversized analog clock on the wall directly above Gideon's head, so I could see that it actually took less than thirty seconds for him to break the silence.

"I thought you'd be younger too. I don't know why. It's fine."

"I thought you'd be black. It's also fine."

"It sucks about your car."

"Dude, give me three weeks to work on her. My charm is irresistible. You'll end up driving the damn thing."

"You don't know my mom. She's kind of insane."

"All mothers are insane at some level. So, since you're so concerned about my age, and believe it or not, there are people in the world older than forty-seven, I've sort of been in training for you. I had a back accident at a gym awhile back, but I've been cleared. So you name it— paintball, go-carts, batting cages—I'm good to go."

"Yeah . . . so . . . I'm not into any of that. I don't do sports. I think jocks are idiots. Do you have an Xbox at your place I can play?"

"I don't even know what that is."

"What do you think the most delicious menu item at Taco Bell is?"

"I've never been in one."

"Never? In your life?"

"I've managed to survive. Do you like movies?"

"Sure. Horror movies. I think Wes Craven is a genius. His gore is real—you know? When arms get blown off, it is supposed to hurt, blood should spurt! What was the last horror movie you saw?"

"*The Omen*. 1974. I hid under my bed for a week. I'm just about over it."

We were at an impasse when our counselor and his mother came in. I understood the deal. She had a quota. There were tons more boys than there were volunteers. She needed to make things happen, but she also knew she couldn't force it, and I could tell she was concerned about how I would react to his mom's slightly hostile energy.

"So," she asked timidly, "what are we thinking?"

"Well I can't speak for Gideon, but it's pretty obvious we have zero in common. We wouldn't know what to do with each other. So, in other words, we are all in. I'm going to learn the intricacies of Xbox, whatever that is, and go to horror movies, and eat Taco Bell, and you, young man, are going to do some exercise and learn to respect your body. I figure one week we do something you're good at and the next we do something I'm good at. Deal?"

Gideon smiled and nodded. I raised my hand to fist bump him, and he told me fist bumps were "so last year" and that he had a lot to teach me about not embarrassing myself. We agreed to make Fridays our nights.

Before I left, the counselor asked to see me for a debrief. She said there was one more piece of business. The attrition rate is especially high among volunteers. People like me get into the program and then business conflicts or family issues or the realization of the emotional commitment sets in, and they terminate the program after a few visits. This has a devastating effect on the young boy, who in most cases has already lost a dad. Gideon was especially vulnerable given his fragile relationship with his mother and the way his father had left.

"So you're saying, 'Don't do this if you're going to bail'?"

"I'm asking you this, Danny. Why do you want to do this? Why are you really here?"

I knew what I was supposed to say: "I'm a middle-aged guy with resources and time and I just want to give back to the community," or "I'm a professional mentor who has become wealthy due to the quality of my advice and wisdom, and now I want to expand my range to young people," or even the simplest explanation of all, "I never had kids and this is sort of the next best thing."

But none of those were the truth. So I went with the truth. For a change.

"I need a friend."

My counselor sat back in her chair and took a deep breath. She said that was the real answer for most people who come into the program.

And most admit it a year or two later, but she had never heard anyone admit it before starting the program. Most were too ashamed.

And then I said one last thing. Something you hear all the time but that is hardly ever true. And now, somehow, it had become true for me.

"There's nothing to be ashamed of."

# About the Author

Danny Cahill started his career at the headhunting firm Hobson Associates right out of college. He was its rookie of the year and subsequently its youngest top producer and its youngest manager. At twenty-seven, he bought the company and built it into one of the country's largest privately held search firms. His success led to a speaking career that culminated in being awarded the recruiting industry's first (Knutson)"Lifetime Achievement Award."

In his other life as a playwright, his works have been produced off-Broadway and he has won the Maxwell Anderson, Emerging Playwright, and CAB theatre awards. His first book, *Harper's Rules*, won an Axiom award.